SERMON ANALYSIS

A Preacher's Personal Improvement Textbook and Workbook

JAY E. ADAMS

ACCENT BOOKS
Denver, Colorado

A division of Accent Publications, Inc.
12100 West Sixth Avenue
P.O. Box 15337
Denver, Colorado 80215

Library of Congress Catalog Card Number 85-73072

ISBN 0-89636-193-4

To
All those preachers who love their Lord
and their people
well enough
to
continually improve
their preaching of the
Word

Contents

Part One:
Sermon Analysis
Textbook

Introduction

Why study other men's sermons? A legitimate, important and timely question. Homiletics professors rightly decry the tendency to copy the exegesis and thrust of others. However, every pastor or pastoral student can gain great profit from the study of other men's sermons if the goal of that study is personal improvement not plagiarism.

The purpose of SERMON ANALYSIS is just that: growth and learning—for increased pulpit power. By focusing on the style and methods of others, your own unique style of preaching will be strengthened. Oliver Wendell Holmes once said, "I have milked many cows, but I have made my own butter." The goal of this book is to help you become a better dairyman.

The techniques of sermon analysis gleaned by precept, example and practice are critical. Seminary professors individualize and personalize theory and critical thought, pointing out areas in which you might improve and showing you how to make the necessary changes. But once out in the pastorate, that honing ceases. Personal improvement may suffer. But that long, dry period of wandering in the homiletic wilderness is not necessary. SERMON ANALYSIS is a means whereby every minister of the Word can begin and continue a lifelong process of personal improvement—from seminary until the Lord retires him.

In the privacy of your study, you may work steadily on the improvement of your preaching. Seasoned pastors may find that they can best study the principles of this volume in the more disciplined structure of a small group of peers gathered for that purpose. Such group study may provide additional encouragement, insight, and that quickened response to growth.

But whether alone, in a classroom or a group study, the important thing to keep in mind is the preservation of the individualized nature of the work so that each participant focuses on that area which is of the greatest value to his own preaching. The sermons provided here will give you the basic keys. Each exhibits different qualities. The individual student of SERMON ANALYSIS is encouraged to find additional sermons and apply the principles here to each for an ongoing personal course of improvement. It teaches methods for reaching solutions.

So what must you do?

In undertaking a personal study of growth and improvement of your preaching ability, one *primary principle* must guide everything you do. This principle must be learned, adopted and closely followed. Without it there is danger of going astray and injuring rather than strengthening your preaching.

Whenever change is considered and made, there is the risk of going the wrong way. But standing still and doing nothing will cause your preaching to atrophy. Remember the axim, "if you don't use it, you lose it"? It is also accurate to say, "what you don't improve, you lose."

It is only through profitable, conscious effort that you retain the skills you now have. A lack of growth will lead to sameness, sameness to empty forms and spiritless ritual; and vitality sapped leads to boredom and staleness. The skills and abilities of a preacher stagnate only briefly. Then they move either forward or backward.

So what is the *primary principle* that will help you meet this ongoing challenge? Simply, but profoundly: *All principles, practices and procedures discovered in sermon analysis must be tested by the Scriptures.*

Nothing from the sermons of others must be adopted which is not taught, demonstrated by apostolic example, or shown to grow out of Biblical principle. The sermons of others must never become the standard for your preaching practices. The Scriptures alone must be the cornerstone for this.

So why study the sermons of others? Why not simply study the example of preaching in the Bible? These reasonable questions deserve a satisfying answer.

Studying the preaching in the Bible is essential, but there is also value in studying the sermons of others to discover what they have learned as they have searched the Scriptures. The study of sermons is as vital as the study of commentaries. Studying the sermons of others may make you aware of Biblical principles and practices that previously escaped you. Moreover, from the wider spectrum of sermons, you can study the ways and means by which others have worked out Biblical principles and practices in a contemporary setting that may be similar to yours.

In this study you can learn ways of bridging time and culture gaps. You can discover ways of preaching Christ from Old Testament narratives, from poetry, from apocalyptic materials and from books such as Proverbs. A careful study of sermons will enable you to benefit from others' study as well as avoiding dead-end streets they have traveled before. You can avoid many stumblingblocks and save valuable time.

Truly the study of preaching in the Bible has also been neglected. Much work in the analysis of the preaching of Jesus and the apostles needs to be done. But by looking for (and using) good examples of Biblical preaching in a more modern context, you can apply these principles in a personal study of Biblical sermons. This volume will involve you in a case study of applied Biblical theory, equipping you for continued personal, spiritual and professional growth.

But before you accept or adopt anything, be absolutely sure that there is a Biblical warrant for doing so.

Another vital principle is that you do not try to learn everything from one or two preachers. They have their own imbalances and have developed strengths in some areas more than others. Therefore, the second principle in SERMON ANALYSIS is: *Discover each man's area or areas of strength and focus only on these.*

Take time to discern both the strengths and the weaknesses lest you imitate both. A balanced growth in preaching will only result if you search out those who are best in each area of preaching and study them for their strengths alone. When you learn the best from the best about illustrating, outlining, introductions, conclusions, et cetera, you will improve in a balanced way. The sermons in this book were selected for the strengths they portray. The introduction to each man's preaching will present at least one feature that is worth studying. However, in most cases, you will discover that the preacher has several areas of strength from which you may wish to select one or more features for study.

A third principle: *Confine your study largely (though not exclusively) to the great preachers who preached weekly to a local congregation.* The traveling preacher can develop a repertoire of a few dozen sermons and use them again and again, polishing them until they really shine.

You must prepare and deliver two brand new sermons each week, plus prayer meeting talks/devotionals, wedding and funeral messages, and who knows what else! The traveling preacher can preach globally, more generally, covering wide expanses. You must speak more narrowly, specifically and to the particulars of your individual congregation.

While there may be much you can learn from the traveling preachers (e.g., how to use an illustration effectively), it is primarily from the preachers who preach weekly that you will learn the most in such areas as the selection of preaching portions, exegesis, and application.

One
SELECTING THE SERMON

The following method for analyzing sermons provides a basic, proven, easily learned and satisfactory way to acquire and develop the art. But only persistent, regular effort in following the principles and procedures suggested in this book will build the skills and patterns needed. There is no substitute for consistent effort. In a six week period of such effort, you should begin to gain some noticeable proficiency in sermon analysis and should have garnered some valuable firstfruits from your study. After a six month period, you should be able to use the tools of analysis expertly and with an abundant harvest. Inconsistent results ordinarily will be due to the neglect or faulty use of one or more of the steps in the process, to irregular and undisciplined habits, or both.

Step One

A. Play the tape, watch the video recording or read the sermon.

There are, of course, different ways to study sermons and there are real differences between listening to, viewing and reading a sermon. The most obvious is that in reading, neither voice nor bodily action is discernible. You must work with words on paper alone. The audio tape adds another dimension, and video one more. But in adding there is also subtraction. You will find it possible to concentrate on a written sermon in a way different from how you hear or see a sermon preached. Eliminating voice and/or bodily action enables you to focus on other aspects of a sermon with less distraction. But, naturally, if you are studying some aspect of voice or delivery, you will need more than the printed page.

Similarly, video allows for the direct study of bodily action in a unique way: by turning off the sound, you can more readily focus your attention on how the speaker uses his body when speaking. Notice, for instance, the important place facial expressions, posture and gestures play in communicating meaning and, especially, tone to what one is saying. Because many of the best examples of bodily action and use of the voice are found on radio and television, not in recorded sermons, spend time studying these very important elements in those media.

The vast majority of matters having to do with preaching—and, in particular, with the sermon—usually can best be studied in written form. The very best arrangement for studying preaching (which, admittedly, is not available in many instances) is to obtain copies of the sermon in written, audio and video form. Then, each area of preaching can be studied separately from its peculiar vantage point.

This course will concentrate on written materials alone. Fortunately, the bulk of the great preaching heritage we possess, because it comes from an era in which audio and video recording was unknown, has been preserved in writing. And this is the form that is indispensible to us. That means that, largely, you will be working with the sermons of men who are now dead. One reason for using sermons from the past is that we are too close to today's preachers to make valid judgments as to whom, in our own time, history will judge to be the greats. I have, therefore, included contemporary preachers only when there was something special that they had to offer which could not be found in sermons of the past.

B. Read, listen or view the sermon (either one in this book or one found elsewhere).

But do not attempt to analyze the sermon. Think about it generally. Read, listen or view it simply for your own spiritual profit. If you begin with analysis, you will never know which sermons you want to analyze. Determine first, in a more general way, what sort of preaching you want to study. Usually, this cannot be determined by looking first at parts; so begin with the whole, not as a critic, but as a hungry sheep who needs to be fed.

C. Ask yourself questions about the sermon.

Was I helped by it? If so, in what ways?
Was I challenged? How?
Am I likely to be different in some way for having received this preacher's message?
Did I like the sermon?
Did I learn anything about God, the Bible, myself?
Was it likely to help the people to whom I preach?

Consideration of these types of questions will help you to determine if you want to spend time analyzing the sermon. There is no sense analyzing sermons that you think are worthless, mediocre or even only fair. Be sure that, according to your overall impression, every sermon you choose for analysis is, in your estimation, very good or exceptional.

There are, of course, exceptions to this rule. You may not be blessed by a sermon of Norman Vincent Peale or Harry Emerson Fosdick, for example. Yet, while rejecting content, you may wish to study the sermon to learn how to tell stories effectively or ways to implement a sermon by the use of "how-to" materials. Similarly, you may profit from a study of the person's clarity of language or from his concern for life-situation preaching.

However, in assessing the overall worth of a sermon, you would be wise to consider the opinion of other people as well as your own. If half a dozen others, whose judgment you respect, say that they were greatly helped by a particular sermon, you should study it. It is possible that what you think is good preaching, and actually is not, may be a part of the problem!

The evaluation of editors of sermon anthologies whose judgment you respect should also carry some weight with you when making your selections. They may know something that you don't. Teachers may also be able to give you some good advice along these lines, and you ought to ask effective preachers whose sermons they find helpful. But, in the final analysis, you and you alone must be the judge in selecting the sermons that you want to study.

Two
SINGLING OUT ONE FEATURE FOR STUDY

Step Two

A. Reread, re-listen to or re-view the sermon and identify the element(s) and aspect(s) to be studied.

Having selected a sermon, actual analysis may begin. You want to discover what it was that struck you about the sermon. Was it something about the content or about the form or both? That is the first and broadest decision to make. This judgment may not be easy because the two are not totally separable. Yet, in most instances, you will be able to place the feature to be isolated roughly in one or the other of these two areas.

If you think that the feature you want to study is an element of content, ask, "What is it about the content that impressed me?" Was it the exegesis? Was it the newness of the truth, or the precision with which it was presented? Was it the illustrative materials? What? Clearly, the minute that you isolate the feature, you will also want to ask questions about the form. Was the precision merely a matter of sharp and accurate thinking or did it include a very precise vocabulary as well?

Again, if you think that the feature to be studied lies in the area of form, try to determine just what it is about the form that is exceptional. Was it the outline, the introduction or the conclusion? Was it the language—its vivacity, concreteness, beauty, vividness, strength, boldness, clarity? Or what?

B. Single out at least one feature and consider it.

If there is more than one feature you want to study in the sermon, make a note of it and study it later. You do not want to confuse yourself by attempting to handle more than one thing at a time. If you push too hard at first, trying to learn all that you can, you will learn less. Don't look for the esoteric; at first, work with the obvious.

This will take some detective work. Do not put down the sermon until you have located at least one outstanding feature—a principle or practice—that you think would be worthy of study, even if you have to wrestle with the sermon six or eight times! Only after you have attempted the following procedure with no success should you drop that sermon for the time being and move on to another that you find easier to analyze.

The detective work is aimed at uncovering exactly what it was that made the sermon seem exceptional during your original appraisal. This work can be greatly facilitated by using a systematic approach to find the feature that you think is most important to you for now.

But let's change our figure of speech from a "detective" to an auto mechanic.

When a skilled auto mechanic looks under the hood of your car, he instantly understands what may appear to you to be a confused mess. Why? Because he has been trained, and has had experience in locating problems. He knows how a car works and what usually goes wrong. Sometimes he can go straight to one particular element on the basis of the overall symptoms and quickly remedy your problem. At other times, he follows a familiar, prescribed routine, moving from item to item until he finds the source of your difficulty. It is something similar to this which must be done in sermon analysis.

The mechanic may analyze separate systems such as the fuel system or the electrical system, in order to trace different problems.

Let's say that your engine will not start. In such cases, the mechanic may decide the problem is most likely in the electrical system. Yet, he may not have any idea which part of this system is the cause of the problem. Among the various elements is the battery, the starter and the switch into which you insert your key. He may, therefore, move from one element in the system to the next, examining each, until he locates the problem. Because he knows the system, he can move systematically. When he finds where the problem is located—let's say there is no current flowing from the battery—he must then determine what aspect of the battery is causing the problem. Is there a corroded connection? Is a post loose? Does the battery need recharging? Is it hopelessly dead? Each of these aspects calls for a specific remedy. It is not enough to say, "The problem is the battery."

Now, you may view sermon analysis in a similar way. Here, too, though you are not looking for weaknesses but for strengths, you will examine *systems*, *elements* and *aspects* of sermons. You also need to move systematically.

There are four systems operative in a sermon: (1) the content system; (2) the organization system; (3) the language system; and (4) the delivery system. And each of these systems is comprised of various elements which, in turn, may be examined from numerous aspects.

Please notice, though, that the spiritual dynamic in preaching is separate. The Holy Spirit is not a system, but a Person who is operative in the preacher and in the congregation. These systems outlined here do not operate mechanically, like an automotive system, but within a personal context. The relationships of these persons to one another and to the sermon can make all the difference. In speaking of these systems, I shall assume a proper relationship between the preacher and the Holy Spirit.

Now, let's say that you think a sermon is strong in content. But, you are not sure what it is in the content system that is especially significant. You begin, therefore, to focus attention on each element. Two of these elements, as I noted at the beginning of Step Two, are exegesis and examples (or illustrations).

As you eliminate from your consideration the other three systems with all of their elements, as well as the other elements in the content system, you find it easy to concentrate on exegesis separately. But suppose a study of the exegetical methods and results yields little? Exegesis proves average or mediocre. So you move on to the next element in the content system: the use of examples. By focusing on examples alone, you quickly discover that here, at last, is something truly exceptional. Eliminating all else, you now study these examples intensively.

But what is an intensive study of an element? It is a study of it in all of its pertinent aspects. You now begin to examine each aspect of the examples. You ask, what are their sources? In what places are examples used in the sermon? Are their tones and colors appropriate to the discussion at each point? Do they contribute to the mood of the sermon? For what purpose(s) are they used? Do they clarify? Do they concretize truth? Do they make it memorable? More interesting? How? How does the preacher introduce his examples? Are they short and pithy, long and detailed, or is there a variety? Do they contain dialogue and direct address? Do they have to do with things, persons in action, animals? In which aspects of the use of examples does he excel? Eliminate the rest.

In this manner you can analyze and locate the operative factor or factors that you wish to study in a sermon.

C. Check up once again on the importance of the study to you.

As you study this way, you will conclude that it was not the whole sermon that affected you as we have seen. Probably one or two elements made you single it out from other sermons as outstanding. But, now that you have located the operative element, or elements, that made it outstanding, ask yourself, "Is this element, or the particular aspects of it that I have isolated for study, really going to contribute enough to my preaching for me to spend the time necessary to assimilate them?" Is the feature one that you really need to study? Be honest. There is little profit in studying the thing(s) in which you already excel.

Three
ANALYSIS OF ELEMENTS AND THE PREACHER HIMSELF

Step Three

A. Having isolated an element, analyze all its aspects.

We have already spoken about this, but now we need to see it as a distinct step in the analytical process. And, I would like to give a few more examples in more concrete terms.

As I have already noted, when discussing the detective/auto mechanic and his work, you must first locate the outstanding element. Then, having determined what it is and that it is worth your study, you need to analyze the element itself by considering each pertinent aspect of it.

State, in one sentence, on paper, exactly what you have concluded about the element. For example, "Barnhouse is a master of illustration." Then, after examining that from all angles, add to your statement all the illuminating, explanatory and qualifying comments you think are valid and helpful: "He is best at description; he can make a truth live. He does not always use his illustrations as well as he might. Sometimes he uses too many. Sometimes he uses them when they are not needed. His illustrations are always clear, always appropriate, to the point and usually interesting. He uses illustrations that come from his own experience and they are quite varied."

With these additional statements you begin to see a deeper conception of Barnhouse's use of illustrations. You can apply this. Now you can determine which kinds of things you wish to emulate. Perhaps what strikes you most about Barnhouse's illustrative method is the prime source of his illustrations—his own experience. You may have difficulty using personal experiences as illustrative materials. So, now, you want to learn just how to do it. That means in your analysis of this single aspect, you will look at it from every aspect you think of (aspects of aspects!). You will ask such things as, "How does he keep from sounding self-centered? In what ways does he avoid bragging? From what areas of his experience, if any, do these illustrations principally come? How personal does he get? Does he let us feel what he experienced? How much detail does he use? Of what sort?"

All of this is an effort to . . .

B. Determine just how he achieves the effect that has impressed you.

In reaching such a conclusion, you note, for instance, that Lloyd-Jones not only "freckles his sermons with question marks," and "often uses question clusters in emotionally charged passages" (as most great preachers do), but he also "frequently moves thought forward by means of questions." You may jot down the additional observation that "he bridges transitional gaps between points and sub-points with questions." And, you write, "A favorite question of his is 'What does that mean?' " Finally, you end with this note: "Sometimes he uses one word questions like 'What?' and 'How?' effectively. This use seems to give 'punch' to the sermon and adds clarity to the thought through sheer simplicity." When you begin to make observations like these, you have arrived at the place where the study you are doing has become useful.

The sermons of Norman Vincent Peale may be profitably studied if you forget everything else and concentrate on his use of how-to implementation and his story-telling techniques. In any such study, you will focus entirely on technique, and be careful to eliminate all that cannot be squared with Biblical principles and practices.

Step Four

A. Study the preacher's biography in relationship to the feature you singled out.

When you do this, you will often discover clues and a rationale for why he preaches as he does and why he developed the feature that you are studying. Perhaps you have been struck by the frequency with which Phillips Brooks preaches about the incarnation, and especially about the Trinity. You may have even determined to study this feature of the content system. But, in conjunction with your study of the sermons, you also read Brooks's biography as collateral reading.

In your reading you discover that he was preaching in Boston which, at that time, was the seat of Unitarianism. Moreover, you read that in his childhood the family withdrew from a Congregational church that had become Unitarian and joined the Episcopal church. So here was Brooks, back home as an Episcopal minister to confront the Unitarian error. Brooks, however, was loved by the city, which even erected a monument to his memory; and, he was the most popular chapel speaker at Unitarian Harvard. He was even invited to become the school's chaplain. In all of this you discover something else. Brooks not only preached the Trinity with clarity in the seat of Unitarianism, but he did it winsomely.

After realizing this, you may wish to change your study from "How to preach the doctrine of the Trinity" to "How to preach winsomely in a hostile setting."

B. Look for a wide variety of factors in the biography.

Details of the preacher's life, the turning points and crises in his ministry, should be noted for their effect on his preaching. Problems that he faced, the work that he did other than preaching, comments of others about him and his preaching, items about his hobbies and special interests can all be of value. An example of this is Edward's interest in spiders and Spurgeon's study of bees. Other items worthy of note are what he said about his preaching and what others said. Sometimes important insights into the feature under study can be found in his theological and other writings. This is true, for instance, of Calvin who makes many valuable comments about preaching in his commentaries.

C. Count the cost before you undertake any study.

Whenever you determine to study some element in a man's preaching, recognize the fact that you may be taking on a fairly large study of the man as a whole. Be selective. Realize that you will be spending a long time with him—perhaps six months or more.

Of course, you may simply study his sermons, concentrating specifically on the element singled out and do nothing more. While this may be helpful, your understanding of the whole can be more greatly enhanced if you do a full study. For instance, ask yourself the biographical question, "How did F.W. Robertson and Phillips Brooks develop the keen insights into sinful human character that made their sermons so penetrating?" The answer to that question requires study that is worth all the time required to find the answer.

So, let me reiterate. If you set out to study an element, and to study it thoroughly, in some instances you may be taking on a formidable task. Yet, the growth and satisfaction gained will be worth every minute you spend on it.

One final word: in and of itself, the careful, analytical study of sermons encourages growth as a preacher. You will acquire a heightened awareness and consciousness of what is involved in good preaching simply by your intensive study of sermons and the preachers who preach them. This growth cannot be so well-defined or precisely stated as can the more technical elements or aspects of elements that we have been considering. But it is every bit as real. Indeed, it may be the principal gain.

Four
WHAT'S NEXT?

Step Five

A. Consider other sermons by the same preacher.

Any careful, adequate study of a featured element in someone's preaching will eventuate in a study of as many sermons by that individual as is feasible. It is true that, in some cases, there are hundreds—even thousands—of sermons extant. Unless the feature is of such great importance that you are going to write a book about it, I do not suggest a comprehensive study of any preacher. But, in most cases, there is a reasonable number of sermons available, most or all of which would be adequate for a study of the sort that I am advocating.

"But," you ask, "what is a reasonable number? Suppose I want to study Spurgeon? You wouldn't suggest that I study every sermon in the Metropolitan Tabernacle series, would you? What about Chrysostom or Luther or Calvin?"

That is a fair question. What you are asking, in effect, is how much is "enough"? The answer to that is not precise. All I can say is to keep studying the sermons until you are satisfied. Although *satisifed* may not be the right word because some get satisfied too quickly while others seem never to be satisfied at all. But study until you reach a satisfying understanding of the feature you are studying. Satisfaction also means that you have begun to incorporate the feature into your preaching with obvious success. (See the next chapter.) And, that you understand it adequately enough not only to explain it to anyone who might ask, but also to reproduce it in other contexts and passages with alacrity.

When you read other sermons by the same preacher ask the following questions: "Do these sermons make a similar impact on me? Is the feature in the first sermon an exception or is it typical? Does the same element that struck me in the first sermon stand out as an operative feature in the rest? Are there other features that did not appear in the first sermon that might also be worthwhile studying?"

Don't get sidetracked here. If you have determined to study one feature as worthwhile, stay with it. Simply jot down everything that occurs to you about the second, intriguing feature and leave that for a later study at another time.

These, and other questions of the same order, should lead to much helpful material that will enhance your understanding of the element being considered.

Let me also encourage you to recognize that while the study of an element occurring in one sermon alone may be profitable, studying the elements that you find to be a preacher's strong points in all or many of his sermons will be even more profitable. So, when you discover your element occurring regularly, rejoice; you are probably on to something big!

Let's be concrete. A thorough study of the use of oral English in the sermons of Peter Eldersvelde or Joel Nederhood is one of the best ways to learn the values, methods and techniques of writing and speaking in this style. Because they produced their sermons for radio, they wrote them out in full. Yet, they wanted to be conversational, and sound spontaneous rather than written. Therefore, they cultivated a style of written English that approximated the best oral English spoken.

One of the problems with other published sermons is this: While preaching from notes, the sermon was taped or taken down in shorthand. Because extemporaneous speaking, on the whole, does not look good in print—and it shouldn't—(see my comparison of written and oral English in *Pulpit Speech*), the preacher revised the sermon before giving it to the publisher. So in many cases what you have is the sermon, not as it really was preached, but as it has been doctored to make it sound better in print. As a result, since no one is ever taught to write oral English, this revised version often sounds too bookish.

In contrast, Eldersvelde and Nederhood have cultivated a written/oral style. There is no revision. Paradoxically, therefore, one of the best ways to study the qualities of good oral English is to study it in written form. What you have in the doctored form is usually more stilted.

To return to the point of studying more than one sermon, let me suggest that if you were analyzing the use of contrast and antithesis in Brooks's sermons, you would definitely learn a great deal more from studying a number of sermons rather than one. Chrysostom's amazing ability to respond to congregational feedback or his ability to preach to a special occasion is best studied, not by analyzing the sermons on the statues alone, but also by considering the sermons on Eutropius and others as well.

B. In studying additional sermons, try to determine more about how the preacher achieves the effect through the element that you are studying.

Ask, "What commonalities are to be found in the various sermons?" Also ask, "What are the variables?" If the same effect can be achieved with some of the variable aspects of that element missing, then it seems evident that those variables are not essential to the feature and may be eliminated from your consideration. Or, you may discover that the variables are present to make the element acceptable in the particular context in which it is used in a sermon. Either way, the study of commonalities and variables in multiple sermons enables you to make sure that you have isolated the essential aspects of the element that you are studying and not incidental ones. The study of a single sermon does not provide that safeguard.

Step Six

A. Keep a growing notebook of your studies.

Write out, in a paragraph or two, all that you learn about the element you have studied. Describe it in detail. Photocopy excerpts from sermons in which it appears and paste or staple these alongside what you have written. Specify all that you know about it: What the element is and what effect it achieves. Why the preacher developed it as he did and how he used it. When he used it and when he did not. What forms he gave to it under what conditions. What it takes step by step, aspect by aspect, to achieve the full effect and how he refined it over the years.

If you are diligent in recording these facts, you will preserve material that otherwise might be lost. And, this book will become a valuable volume to which you will find yourself turning again and again while preparing sermons. I urge you to keep full notes on the results of your studies.

Five
USING WHAT YOU HAVE LEARNED

Step Seven

A. Add your own twist(s).

Think carefully and deeply about the element that you have studied and its use. As you do, bring any of your own ideas to bear upon it. How would you use it differently? For what purposes? In what ways? Ask yourself, "Must there always be the same aspects? Must they always be used in the same order?" and similar questions. In succeeding paragraphs, clearly marked as your own contribution to the study, allow your creativity to add other angles or aspects to the element under consideration. On the whole subject of creativity, see my book *Insight and Creativity in Christian Counseling.*

However, do not begin to make these sorts of alterations until you have successfully used the feature as the preacher did. Then you will be in a position to know whether or not your new angle is an improvement. After you have tried out your twist(s), you should note what they are and how well they worked. If they do not improve the sermon, you will probably want to scratch them out.

B. Improve sermons where you can.

Certainly it is possible to improve even the sermons of great preachers. As we have seen, they are not equally strong in every area. For instance, you may practice turning a lecture outline into a preaching outline if an otherwise strong message fails in that respect. (For details on this and other such matters, see my book, *Preaching with Purpose.*) Indeed, many of the sermons in the workbook section of this book could be improved by doing just that.

In a number of other sermons, discover the great difference it makes when you turn all of the first and third person language in a particular section into second person terminology. Try it on one of Calvin's sermons reproduced in this book; then read the sermon both ways out loud, noting the improvement.

Perhaps surprisingly, reading aloud is an essential part of analysis. From this practice you can learn much about cadence and sound combinations, about sentence length and variety, about rhetorical devices such as periodic sentences, question and exclamation clusters, and about many other stylistic matters. Make it a regular practice to read every sermon that you analyze out loud at least once.

Also, try increasing the strength of a sermon that is already strong in one or two elements by adding the strong elements of another preacher. You will be amazed at how greatly changes like this immediately improve a message, turning an already good sermon into a very powerful one.

After you have become adept at making such improvements, take some of your own previously constructed sermons and do the same thing to them. But always *begin* with others' sermons; it will be easier to apply the principles more objectively there. Then, once having learned how to use the principles, techniques and skills to improve the existing sermons of others, you will be better prepared to remold your own.

In this process, you should discover that working at the improvement of sermons will create an attitude that will carry over into your own sermon construction. Increasingly, you will find yourself more and more critical of what you have done. You will be less satisfied with the sort of preparation that you have settled for in the past. You will find yourself constantly changing and refining to get a sermon just right. This mindset could be the most vital asset you acquire from your study of sermons.

Step Eight

A. Determine to use the feature you have studied in sermons you are currently developing.

Decide how to use the feature in your sermons. Determine which sermons call for the use of this element, and actually knead it into the dough of them.

Clearly, the methods of analysis proposed do not include copying. They present ways of utilizing a principle or practice that you, by hard labor, mine from the sermons of others and make your own. You do not copy; you learn how to do what someone else did. This is the difference between tracing an artist's drawing, and learning, through the study of paintings, to become a competent artist oneself.

As a matter of fact, the preacher whose methods you study may not have been able to articulate as clearly what he was doing as you can. You may have studied the process and practice more thoroughly than he. Usually, you will not adopt the element without putting your own twist on it. Indeed, if you have noticed a common feature in several preachers, you may have studied them all and, together with your own angles, end up with a composite that isn't exactly like that which any one of them used. It will have become distinctly your own.

The important thing is to begin to employ what you have learned.

B. Tape your sermons and listen critically to them for the impact of the new element.

Honestly determine whether you think the inclusion of the new element made a significant difference. If not, try to determine whether you used it skillfully enough or whether there were aspects that were awkwardly handled. If there was awkwardness, determine if it stemmed from the neglect of some aspect(s) of the element that you previously overlooked. Restudy the element for such missing aspects. Then, having taken all possible measures to improve upon your development and use of the new feature, use it again, and again and again, all the while improving on what you are doing, until it has become an effective and integral part of your preaching repertoire.

Conclusion

Sermon analysis—the process of breaking sermons into their constituent parts—will not do everything for you. But it is important to learn because, like automobiles, sermons come as wholes. Most people cannot analyze preaching adequately because they listen to the whole and ignore the individual parts that make up the whole. That is well and fine for the average listener, and even for you initially (see step number one), but you must soon become expert in sermon analysis if you would improve your own preaching by the study of sermons.

There are other ways to improve preaching, but few as good as this one. The model sermons that you study when doing sermon analysis provide greater stimulation to thought about your own preaching methods and practices than any other comparable activity I know. You will be challenged, informed, rebuked and inspired—all in the course of study. Few other approaches to preaching improvement are as productive. I therefore urge you, even though sermon analysis done well takes time and effort, to make the attempt. If you do so properly, you—and your congregation—will be delighted with the results.

The sermons included in this book are good ones with which to work because each affords at least one (most afford more than one) helpful element that you may use in your preaching. There is a large variety of elements in the corpus of the sermons, but, of course, they do not contain all that you might learn. So, if there are other sermons that you would prefer to analyze, go ahead and use them. But, be sure to use some of those in the book, too, following the process of sermon analysis through step by step.

The blank column next to each sermon is for your initial rough notes. But what you write there should be considered preliminary to the permanent entries that you put into your own sermon analysis notebook.

Now that you know what to do, start immediately, allowing at least one hour a day to the project, five days a week. If you do, you will be amazed at how much you will learn quickly and how greatly it will affect your regular preaching. Best wishes!

SUGGESTED SERMON ANALYSIS LIST

Obviously, to analyze sermons, you will have to select those preachers whose sermons contain useful material. Opinions differ about such matters, but there is general agreement among homileticians about the value of the preaching of the men on the following list. You will want to add others; perhaps you will even wish to eliminate some. But, at least as a starting point, consider those on the list.

Not all of those listed are valuable in the same way or for the same reasons. Some men listed cannot be trusted for their exegesis, their theology, or their content. But, they may be useful for studying illustrative or other narrowly technical aspects of preaching.

At any rate, here is the list. The twenty-two sermons included in this textbook have been selected from the preaching of some of these men.

Old Testament Preachers

The Prophets
John the Baptist

New Testament Preachers

Christ
Peter
Stephen
Paul

Patristic Period (200-400)

Origen (180-253)
Chrysostom (347-407)
Augustine (354-397)

Scholastic Period (400-1500)

Bernard of Clairvaux (1091-1153)
Francis of Assisi (1182-1226)
Thomas Aquinas (1225-1274)
John Wycliff (1320-1384)
Giralamo Savanarola (1452-1498)

Reformation Period (1500s)

Martin Luther (1483-1546)
Ulrich Zwingli (1484-1531)
Hugh Latimer (1490-1555)
John Knox (1505-1572)
John Calvin (1509-1554)

Puritan Period (1600s)

William Perkins (1558-1602)
William Ames (1576-1633)
John Cotton (1585-1652)
John Owen (1616-1683)
Cotton Mather (1663-1728)

Revival Period (1700s)

John Wesley (1703-1791)
Jonathan Edwards (1703-1758)
George Whitefield (1714-1770)

Victorian Period (1800s)

Thomas Chalmers (1780-1847)
Horace Bushnell (1802-1876)
Horatius Bonar (1808-1889)
Henry Ward Beecher (1813-1887)
T. DeWitt Talmage (1832-1901)
Charles Haddon Spurgeon (1834-1892)
Phillips Brooks (1835-1892)
Dwight L. Moody (1837-1899)
Alexander Maclaren (1826-1910)

Modern Period (1900s)

Arthur John Gossip (1873-1954)
James S. Stewart (1896-   )
Harry Emerson Fosdick (1878-1969)
Norman Vincent Peale (1898-   )
Martin Lloyd-Jones (1899-1981)
Peter Eldersvelde (1911-1965)
Billy Graham (1918-   )
Joel Nederhood (1930-   )

Space has been provided with each period for the inclusion of names you may wish to add.

Part Two:
Sermon Analysis
Workbook

ORIGEN
(180/5 - 253/4)

Life

Origen grew up in a Christian home in Alexandria, Egypt. From his father he learned grammar, mathematics, logic and rhetoric. His father also taught the Bible to Origen, and required him to learn a passage a day.

Origen was sent to Clement's catachical school in Alexandria. In 202, during a wave of anti-Christian persecution, his father was beheaded for his faith. Origen's mother kept him from being martyred with his father only by hiding his clothes.

As a teenager, Origen began to teach informally and was immediately popular. When he was only eighteen, he filled the post that Clement vacated because of persecution. Soon he gathered a substantial following. He studied Greek and Hebrew, becoming proficient in both. He also knew Greek philosophy quite well. Provided with a generous grant, Origen was able to devote full time to his expositions on the Bible. Ambrosius, a grateful convert, provided shorthand writers to take them down.

Origen was an ascetic. He fasted constantly, wore no shoes, slept on the ground, and, according to legend, was castrated. His asceticism injured his health.

In 215 he was forced to flee Alexandria under persecution. He went to Caesarea in Palestine where he was asked to teach publicly. Demetrius, bishop of Alexandria, was angry with him for doing so because he was a layman, not an ordained minister. He ordered Origen back to Alexandria.

However, in 228 Origen was ordained a presbyter in Caesarea and then returned to Alexandria. Demetrius, angered at this, persecuted him and drove him from Alexandria. Demetrius finally had him excommunicated at a synod of bishops that he called for that purpose. Generally, this action was ignored.

Afterwards, Origen spent about twenty years in Palestine where he continued to teach and write. But once again persecution forced him to leave and for a time he traveled widely. Eventually, he was arrested, imprisoned and tortured in Tyre. As the result of this experience, he lost whatever health remained and died in Tyre at the age of sixty-nine, probably in the year 254.

Work as a Teacher and Preacher

Origen, the most important preacher of the third century, had a hard time in his own day and has a very bad press in our times. That he earned it by his teaching on allegorizing the Scriptures is true, but the fact that he also did expository work of a high quality is usually unknown. F.W. Farrar says, "He was by general admission the greatest, in almost every respect, of all the great Christian teachers of the first three Christian centuries" (*Lives of the Fathers*, pp. 291,292).

To Origen we owe three common preaching practices, other than allegorizing, that have strongly affected preaching ever since.

Origen established the practice of preaching on a text. If II Clement, the earliest extant post-apostolic sermon, is characteristic of preaching prior to Origen, then the value of this contribution can hardly be stressed enough. II Clement is a rambling, disunified address that says so much about so many things that it says too little about any one thing. Origen stressed exegesis and exposition. He has been called the "father of exposition," and he is frequently quoted by later commentators. The allegorical emphasis usually comes toward the end of the sermon. His commentaries, especially those on John, are the result of his preaching.

Seven shorthand writers took down exactly what Origen preached, which, at first, he revised prior to publication. Later, when he became more secure in his preaching, he simply published his material unrevised. Many of his sermons show penetrating insight into the meaning of passages. In one of his messages he says, "There is not one jot or tittle written in Scripture which, for those who know how to use the power of the Scriptures, does not effect its proper work ... blame yourself rather than the sacred Scriptures, when you fail to discover the meaning of what is written" (Petry, *No Uncertain Sound*, pp. 47,48).

Secondly, Origen established the form of the simple homily. The Greek word *homilia*—our English transliteration is homily—means "a talk or conversation with someone." *Sermo*, its Latin equivalent, from which our word sermon comes, also meant "talk or conversation." Both words indicate something of the informal character of early preaching.

In its simple form, the homily had little unity because no one telic or purpose unit was singled out (for more on telic preaching, see my *Preaching with Purpose*). He would make simple comments on a passage, stopping whenever he reached an appropriate point. Much of the preaching currently called "expository preaching" is little more than the simple homily. We see this style strongly exhibited in Sunday School and Bible class teaching.

Thirdly, Origen established the practice of preaching through the books of the Bible. Obviously, this practice is still widely followed and highly recommended.

Origen also produced the first critical work in church history. It is called the *Hexapala.*

The allegorical method, for which Origen was scourged, was not his brainchild. It was developed by Philo who applied it to the Old Testament. Clement adopted and adapted it to the New Testament; Origen picked it up from Clement.

The method originated with the Greeks who applied it to their religious poetry. By allegorizing the grosser passages concerning the Greek gods, they could explain away objectionable material. Philo, who was a hellenizer, used it for the same purpose when he applied it to the passages in the Old Testament that offended him. Origen's close association with the method comes from the fact that he adopted and popularized it. His popularity and influence, probably more than any other factor, caused him to become the model for much of the preaching that followed during the next one thousand years. (Indeed, allegorical preaching has never wholly ceased; it is still with us today.)

Origen's allegorical method consisted of three levels of interpretation:

1. The grammatical/historical (supposedly corresponding to the body)
2. The moral and doctrinal (corresponding to the soul)
3. The spiritual (corresponding to the spirit)

This third sense was the allegorical, in which there was a free use of the imagination.

Calvin's comments on Origen's allegorizing are instructive. In his commentary on II Corinthians 3:6 he writes:

> *The exposition [of the passage] contrived by Origen has got into general circulation that the letter means the grammatical and genuine meaning of the Scripture, or the literal sense (as they call it) and that "spirit" means "the allegorical or spiritual meaning" . . . during several centuries, nothing was more commonly said, or more generally received than this—that Paul here furnishes us with a key for expounding Scripture by allegories . . . This is a very pernicious error . . . imagining that the perusal of Scripture would be not merely useless, but even injurious unless it were drawn out into allegories. This error was the source of many evils. It not only opened the door to adulterating the genuine meaning of Scripture, but the more of audacity anyone had in this manner of acting, so much the more eminent an interpreter was he accounted . . . Thus many . . . recklessly played with the sacred Word of God, as if it had been a ball to be tossed to and fro. You could make any passage . . . mean anything.*

Elsewhere, under his exposition of I Corinthians 9:8 Calvin wrote:

> *Nor is it as if he meant to expound that precept allegorically, as some hair-brained spirits take occasion from this to turn everything into allegories. They turn dogs into men, trees into angels, and turn all Scripture into a laughing-stock.*

Origen was clearly a mixed bag. His impact on the church has been large and lasting. Whether the good outweighs the evil he has done to preaching, it is difficult to say.

Because of his great importance in the history of preaching, I have made these comments on Origen. However, because his preaching is not very useful for sermon analysis, none of his sermons are included in the preaching anthology.

CHRYSOSTOM
(347 - 407)

Life and Training

John Chrysostom was born in Syrian Antioch which, at that time, was the third city of the Roman empire. It was eclipsed only by the rise of Constantinople. The name Chrysostom, meaning the "golden-mouthed one," was later appended because of his outstanding preaching. He was a short, thin man with pale, hollow cheeks, a large, bald head (he said "like Elisha"), bright, deeply sunken eyes, a very wrinkled forehead and a straggly grey beard. He compared himself to a spider. So there is hope for the rest of us!

John was not converted during his youth. However, his mother, Anathusa, was a Christian. Like Monica, Augustine's mother, she prayed for her son's conversion.

At the age of twenty, he began to study for law under a famous rhetorician, Libanius. Libanius was probably the best known sophist of his day. He had been offered (but rejected) the chair of rhetoric at Athens. Libanius praised John highly. On his deathbed he was asked who was capable of succeeding him. He replied, "It would have been John, had not the Christians stolen him from us."

John actually began to practice law. He seemed to have a brilliant career before him, but his mother and a friend, Basil (who later entered a monastery), led him away from law. John got to know Meletius, bishop of Antioch, and, at length, was converted and baptized by him.

Ministry

ANTIOCH

John's own ministry began in Antioch, where he was ordained a deacon in 386 at the age of thirty-seven. On the occasion, he preached his first sermon. For the next twelve years he held a preaching position at Antioch and preached two or more times each week (Homily XI, Acts). Chrysostom had to warn the tightly packed crowds who stood to hear his preaching to leave their money and jewelry at home because the pickpockets were so active.

He was well known for his preaching and became more famous than Augustine. Not later than 381 he wrote *On the Priesthood*, Books 4 and 5 of which contain comments on preaching. Some excerpts follow:

1. "The good preacher is his own critic and indifferent to praise and dispraise." (Here is a principle worth thought and discussion.)

2. "Preaching is a work for God and its object must never be forgotten."

3. "There is no use to speak plainly and honestly if clumsy and halting... the beauty of the speech must always be at the service of what one has to say."

4. "The experienced preacher must constantly try to improve his art... [this is] even more indispensible for an eloquent than an ordinary preacher; he will decline unless he constantly studies."

5. "Speaking is an acquired art."

6. "Woe to the man who is detected in plagiarisms; he is regarded no higher than a common thief."

This was an age in which the audience applauded. In one sermon he declared, "You praise my words, and greet my exhortations with loud applause. But show your approval by obedience—that is the praise I want, the applause of your good deeds." This rebuke itself was loudly applauded!

Chrysostom often responded to feedback, using the occasion to more strongly emphasize his point. For instance, in the Fourth Homily on Genesis he says, "Please listen to me—you are not paying attention. I am talking to you about the holy Scriptures, and you are looking at the lamps and the people lighting them. It is very frivolous to be more interested in what the lamplighters are doing.... After all, I am lighting a lamp too—the lamp of God's Word."

He once expressed a sentiment with which every minister can readily identify: "My work is like that of a man who is trying to clean a piece of ground into which a muddy stream is constantly flowing."

The famous series of sermons on the statues is worth special comment. In 387 Theodosius I, Emperor at Constantinople, was faced with heavy military and domestic needs. Because of this he placed a special tax on all the wealthy centers in the eastern part of his empire. In Antioch, this caused great discontent. Chrysostom warned the people to avoid being stirred up by foreign agitators.

On February 26, when the edict was read, the crowd became deathly silent. Then, a mob broke loose, smashing everything in sight. They headed for the governor's palace. He fled. A boy threw a stone at one of the statues and the mob rushed upon all of the statues smashing them to pieces and throwing them into the street. Among others, were statues of Theodosius and his dead wife. It took the imperial troops three hours to restore order. By afternoon, everyone was afraid. Word of the event was sent to the emperor.

Aged archbishop Flavian went to Constantinople, a trip of five hundred miles, to plead for clemency. During the interim, Chrysostom preached these sermons. They were designed to bring repentance and to encourage the people to place their trust in God. He also reminded them of his warning.

Soon the soldiers arrived, and heavy restrictions were imposed. An army had been dispatched to punish the citizens before Flavian reached Constantinople. But when the soldiers arrived in Antioch, the monks persuaded them to withhold any actions until they learned of the results of Flavian's visit. They offered to forfeit their own lives if necessary. Chrysostom contrasted the monks with the city's pagan philosophers in one of his sermons: "The monks, who habitually live in the caves, came into the city, while the philosophers ran away from the city and hid in the caves."

Flavian got the pardon he sought, declaring, "I will not go back without one." The city rejoiced. This was a crucial part of Chrysostom's ministry. The city had been spared; he had been proven right, and he and his people had gone through the crisis together. After that, he was a power in his own right.

CONSTANTINOPLE

In 397 Nectarius, archbishop of Constantinople, died. He had been a loafer, living in luxury. Theophilus, archbishop of Alexandria, wanted his candidate, Isidore, to fill the vacant post. (Isidore was blackmailing him.) But Chrysostom was selected instead, and Theophilus became a bitter enemy.

However, Chrysostom was so well loved by the church at Antioch, the question was how to remove him from Antioch without inciting a riot. Asked to leave the city on a ruse, he was kidnapped and taken to Constantinople. He became archbishop of Constantinople, February 26, 398. In his first sermon he promised not to trust in the weapons of human dialectic, but in the spiritual armor of the Scriptures (Homily XI). Chrysostom immediately set himself to the task of reforming a corrupt city. He began with the clergy, many of whom were quite displeased with his appointment and became his bitter enemies.

Then, an interesting event occurred. In the year 399 Eutropius, the imperial minister, fell. Soldiers came to get him, but he fled into Chrysostom's church for refuge, clinging to a column that supported the altar. Ironically, while in power, he had forbidden the church to give refuge to anyone fleeing the government. Nevertheless, disregarding the law, Chrysostom received him. When the soldiers appeared, Chrysostom met them at the door with the words, "You come into this sanctuary only over my body." He then preached two great sermons on the fall of Eutropius, the first of which is included in this book. (Note how powerful it is and then reflect upon the fact that he had less than a day to prepare it!) At the appropriate moment, a curtain was drawn and there, clinging to the altar, was Eutropius. Chrysostom preached to him and then to the congregation in one of the most dramatic sermons of all time.

In the end, Theophilus got Chrysostom on trumped up charges and in 404 had him deposed and exiled. He died in exile.

His Preaching

There are over seven hundred sermons by Chrysostom extant, although many cannot be placed or dated.

In content, his preaching was exegetical, solid, practical and consisted of expositions of entire books of the Bible. (Genesis, Psalms, Matthew, John, and Paul's letters are all extant.) The material was not allegorical, but grammatical-historical in nature. He was opposed to the allegorizing of the Alexandrine school. Though Chrysostom was always in the thick of things, he was not radical. His ideas were moderate, though his language was often strong. He studied much and did solid preparation for his messages. If Augustine's great emphasis was grace, Chrysostom's was holiness. He attacked many of the social evils of his day.

The plan he followed was to preach either the *logos*, an address (cf. the sermon on Eutropius), or the *homilia*, a simple discourse. He often worked with a running commentary that was not as closely devoted to one purpose as was the homily of Augustine. He once said, "I treat so many things in each of my sermons and make them so varied because I want everybody to find something special for himself in them and not go home empty handed." Many of his sermons are in two parts: *exposition* followed by a *moral.*

By no means was he bound to his notes. He did not hesitate to digress when he thought it useful and even responded to feedback from the congregation mentioning their tears, applause, et cetera. This ability to respond is one of the factors to study in Chrysostom. The reformers, and even modern commentators, frequently refer to Chrysostom when discussing the meaning of a passage.

Evidences of Chrysostom's classical training, especially his training in rhetoric, are seen in his sermons, specifically in his use of language. He makes references to Greek authors, and his comments show that he studied their style. He speaks of the "smoothness of Socrates, the weight of Demosthenes, the dignity of Thucydides and the sublimity of Plato." His language was always lucid; sometimes also dramatic. He was quite strong on description, another element worth study. At times he could be florid.

His outstanding command of language led to his nickname, "The golden-mouthed one" (a title that probably was not used until the seventh century). He was also very good at the use of examples. These were chosen, usually, from ordinary, everyday life.

Chrysostom's preaching was extemporaneous, but not impromptu, though in later years some may have been. His sermons were taken down by shorthand, as delivered. He revised very little. He spoke from the ambo, the reader's desk, in order to get closer to the people.

He was always the master of the occasion. The full range of his abilities shows in his occasional sermons, especially in the *logoi.* This type of preaching was Chrysostom's forte, worthy of study by every student of preaching.

Chrysostom died September 14, 407 with these words on his lips: *doxa to theo panton heneka,* which means, "God be glorified for all things."

DISCOURSE
On Eutropius, the Eunuch, Patrician and Consul

"Vanity of vanities, all is vanity"— it is always seasonable to utter this but more especially at the present time. Where are now the brilliant surroundings of thy consulship? where are the gleaming torches? Where is the dancing, and the noise of dancers' feet, and the banquets and the festivals? where are the garlands and the curtains of the theatre? where is the applause which greeted thee in the city, where the acclamation in the hippodrome and the flatteries of spectators? They are gone—all gone: a wind has blown upon the tree shattering down all its leaves, and showing it to us quite bare, and shaken from its very root; for so great has been the violence of the blast, that it has given a shock to all these fibres of the tree and threatens to tear it up from the roots. Where now are your feigned friends? where are your drinking parties, and your suppers? where is the swarm of parasites, and the wine which used to be poured forth all day long, and the manifold dainties invented by your cooks? where are they who courted your power and did and said everything to win your favour? They were all mere visions of the night, and dreams which have vanished with the dawn of day: they were spring flowers, and when the spring was over they all withered: they were a shadow which has passed away—they were a smoke which has dispersed, bubbles which have burst, cobwebs which have been rent in pieces. Therefore we chant continually this spiritual song—"Vanity of vanities, all is vanity." For this saying ought to be continually written on our walls, and garments, in the market place, and in the house, on the streets, and on the doors and entrances, and above all on the conscience of each one, and to be a perpetual theme for meditation. And inasmuch as deceitful things, and maskings and pretense seem to many to be realities it behoves each one every day both at supper and at breakfast, and in social assemblies to say to his neighbour and to hear his neighbour say in return "vanity of vanities, all is vanity." Was I not continually telling thee that wealth was a runaway? But you would not heed me. Did I not tell thee that it was an unthankful servant? But you would not be persuaded. Behold actual experience has now proved that it is not only a runaway, and ungrateful servant, but also a murderous one, for it is this which has caused thee now to fear and tremble. Did I not say to thee when you continually rebuked me for speaking the truth, "I love thee better than they do who flatter thee?" "I who reprove thee care more for thee than they who pay thee court?" Did I not add to these words by saying that the wounds of friends were more to be relied upon than the voluntary kisses of enemies. If you had submitted to my wounds their kisses would not have wrought thee this destruction: for my wounds work health, but their kisses have produced an incurable disease. Where are now thy cup-bearers, where are they who cleared the way for thee in the market place, and sounded thy praises endlessly in the ears of all? They have fled, they have disowned thy friendship, they are providing for their own safety by means of thy distress. But I do not act thus, nay in thy misfortune I do not abandon thee, and now when thou art fallen I protect and tend thee. And the Church which you treated as an enemy has opened her bosom and received thee into it; whereas the theatres which you courted, and about which you were oftentimes indignant with me have betrayed and ruined thee. And yet I never ceased saying to thee "why doest thou these things?" "thou art exasperating the Church, and casting thyself down headlong," yet thou didst hurry away from all my warnings. And now the hippodromes, having exhausted thy wealth, have whetted the sword against thee, but the Church which experienced thy untimely wrath is hurrying in every direction, in her desire to pluck thee out of the net.

And I say these things now not as trampling upon one who is prostrate, but from a desire to make those who are still standing more secure; not by way of irritating the sores of one who has been wounded, but rather to preserve those who have not yet been wounded in sound health; not by way of sinking one who is tossed by the waves, but as instructing those who are sailing with a favourable breeze, so that they may not become overwhelmed. And how may this be effected? by observing the vicissitudes of human affairs. For even this man had he stood in fear of vicissitude would not have experienced it; but whereas neither his own conscience, nor the counsels of others wrought any improvement in him, do ye at least who plume yourselves on your riches profit by his calamity: for nothing is weaker than human affairs. Whatever term therefore one may employ to express their insignificance it will fall short of the reality; whether he calls them smoke, or grass, or a dream or spring flowers, or by any other name; so perishable are they, and more naught than nonentities; but that together with their nothingness they have also a very perilous element we have a proof before us. For who was more exalted than this man? Did he not surpass the whole world in wealth? had he not climbed to the very pinnacle of distinction? did not all tremble and fear before him? Yet lo! he has become more wretched than the prisoner, more pitiable than the menial slave, more indigent than the beggar wasting away with hunger, having every day a vision of sharpened swords and of the criminal's grave, and the public executioner leading him out to his death; and he does not even know if he once enjoyed past pleasure, nor is he sensible even of the sun's ray, but at mid day his sight is dimmed as if he were encompassed by the densest gloom. But even let me try my best I shall not be able to present to you in language the suffering which he must naturally undergo, in the hourly expectation of death. But indeed what need is there of any words from me, when he himself has clearly depicted this for us as in a visible image? For yesterday when they came to him from the royal court intending to drag him away by force, and he ran for refuge to the holy furniture, his face was then, as it is now, no better than the countenance of one dead: and the chattering of his teeth, and the quaking and quivering of his whole body, and his faltering voice, and stammering tongue, and in fact his whole general appearance were suggestive of one whose soul was petrified.

Now I say these things not by way of reproaching him, or insulting his misfortune, but from a desire to soften your minds towards him, and to induce you to compassion, and to persuade you to be contented with the punishment which has already been inflicted. For since there are many inhuman persons amongst us who are inclined, perhaps, to find fault with me for having admitted him to the sanctuary, I parade his sufferings from a desire to soften their hardheartedness by my narrative.

For tell me, beloved brother, wherefore art thou indignant with me? You say it is because he who continually made war upon the Church has taken refuge within it. Yet surely we ought in the highest degree to glorify God, for permitting him to be placed in such a great strait as to experience both the power and the lovingkindness of the Church:—her power in that he has suffered this great vicissitude in consequence of the attacks which he made upon her: her lovingkindness in that she whom he attacked now casts her shield in front of him and has received him under her wings, and placed him in all security not resenting any of her former injuries, but most lovingly opening her bosom to him. For this is more glorious than any kind of trophy, this is a brilliant victory, this puts both Gentiles and Jews to shame, this displays the bright aspect of the Church: in that having received her enemy as a captive, she spares him, and when all have despised him in his desolation, she alone like an affectionate mother has concealed him under her cloak, opposing both the wrath of the king, and the rage of the people, and their overwhelming hatred. This is an ornament for the altar. A strange kind of ornament, you say, when the accused sinner, the extortioner, the robber is permitted to lay hold of the altar. Nay! say not so: for even the harlot took hold of the feet of Jesus, she who was stained with the most accursed and unclean sin: yet her deed was no reproach to Jesus, but rather redounded to His admiration and praise: for the impure woman did no injury to Him who was pure, but rather was the vile harlot rendered pure by the touch of Him who was the pure and spotless one. Grudge not then, O man. We are the servants of the crucified one who said "Forgive them for they know not what they do." But, you say, he cut off the right of refuge here by his ordinances and divers kinds of laws. Yes! yet now he has learned by experience what it was he did, and he himself by his own deeds has been the first to break the law, and has become a spectacle to the whole world, and silent though he is, he utters from thence a warning voice to all, saying "do not such things as I have done, that ye suffer not such things as I suffer." He appears as a teacher by means of his calamity, and the altar emits great lustre, inspiring now the greatest awe from the fact that it holds the lion in bondage; for any figure of royalty might be very much set off if the king were not only to be seen seated on his throne arrayed in purple and wearing his crown, but if also prostrate at the feet of the king barbarians with their hands bound behind their backs were bending low their heads. And that no persuasive arguments have been used, ye yourselves are witnesses of the enthusiasm, and the concourse of the people. For brilliant indeed is the scene before us today, and magnificent the assembly, and I see as large a gathering here today as at the Holy Paschal Feast. Thus the man has summoned you here without speaking and yet uttering a voice through his actions clearer than the sound of a trumpet: and ye have all thronged hither today, maidens deserting their boudoirs, and matrons the women's chambers, and men the market place that ye may see human nature convicted, and the instability of worldly affairs exposed, and the harlot-face which a few days ago was radiant (such is the prosperity derived from extortion) looking uglier than any wrinkled old woman, this face I say you may see denuded of its enamel and pigments by the action of adversity as by a sponge.

Such is the force of this calamity: it has made one who was illustrious and conspicuous appear the most insignificant of men. And if a rich man should enter the assembly he derives much profit from the sight: for when he beholds the man who was shaking the whole world, now dragged down from so high a pinnacle of power, cowering with fright, more terrified than a hare or a frog, nailed fast to yonder pillar, without bonds, his fear serving instead of a chain, panic-stricken and trembling, he abates his haughtiness, he puts down his pride, and having acquired the kind of wisdom concerning human affairs which it concerns him to have he departs instructed by example in the lesson which Holy Scripture teaches by precept:—"All flesh is grass and all the glory of man as the flower of grass:

the grass withereth and the flower falleth" or "They shall wither away quickly as the grass, and as the green herb shall they quickly fail" or "like smoke are his days," and all passages of that kind. Again the poor man when he has entered and gazed at this spectacle does not think meanly of himself, nor bewail himself on account of his poverty, but feels grateful to his poverty, because it is a place of refuge to him, and a calm haven, and secure bulwark; and when he sees these things he would many times rather remain where he is, than enjoy the possession of all men for a little time and afterwards be in jeopardy of his own life. Seest thou how the rich and poor, high and low, bond and free have derived no small profit from this man's taking refuge here? Seest thou how each man will depart hence with a remedy, being cured merely by this sight? Well! have I softened your passion, and expelled your wrath? have I extinguished your cruelty? have I induced you to be pitiful? Indeed I think I have; and your countenances and the streams of tears you shed are proofs of it. Since then your hard rock has turned into deep and fertile soil let us hasten to produce some fruit of mercy, and to display a luxuriant crop of pity by falling down before the Emperor or rather by imploring the merciful God so to soften the rage of the Emperor, and make his heart tender that he may grant the whole of the favour which we ask. For indeed already since that day when this man fled here for refuge no slight change has taken place; for as soon as the Emperor knew that he had hurried to this asylum, although the army was present, and incensed on account of his misdeeds, and demanded him to be given up for execution, the Emperor made a long speech endeavouring to allay the rage of the soldiers, maintaining that not only his offences, but any good deed which he might have done ought to be taken into account, declaring that he felt gratitude for the latter, and was prepared to forgive him as a fellow creature for deeds which were otherwise. And when they again urged him to avenge the insult done to the imperial majesty, shouting, leaping, and brandishing their spears, he shed streams of tears from his gentle eyes, and having reminded them of the Holy Table to which the man had fled for refuge he succeeded at last in appeasing their wrath.

Moreover let me add some arguments which concern ourselves. For what pardon could you deserve, if the Emperor bears no resentment when he has been insulted, but ye who have experienced nothing of this kind display so much wrath? and how after this assembly has been dissolved will ye handle the holy mysteries, and repeat that prayer by which we are commanded to say "forgive us as we also forgive our debtors" when ye are demanding vengeance upon your debtor? Has he inflicted great wrongs and insults on you? I will not deny it. Yet this is the season not for judgment but for mercy; not for requiring an account, but for showing loving kindness: not for investigating claims but for conceding them; not for verdicts and vengeance, but for mercy and favour. Let no one then be irritated or vexed, but let us rather beseech the merciful God to grant him a respite from death, and to rescue him from this impending destruction, so that he may put off his transgression, and let us unite to approach the merciful Emperor beseeching him for the sake of the Church, for the sake of the altar, to concede the life of one man as an offering to the Holy Temple. If we do this the Emperor himself will accept us, and even before his praise we shall have the approval of God, who will bestow a large recompense upon us for our mercy. For as he rejects and hates the cruel and inhuman, so does He welcome and love the merciful and humane man; and if such a man be righteous, all the more glorious is the crown which is wreathed for him: and if he be a sinner, He passes over his sins granting this as the reward of compassion shown to his fellow-servant. "For" He saith "I will have mercy and not sacrifice," and throughout the Scriptures you find Him always enquiring after this, and declaring it to be the means of release from sin. Thus then we shall dispose Him to be propitious to us, thus we shall release ourselves from our sins, thus we shall adorn the Church, thus also our merciful Emperor, as I have already said, will commend us, and all the people will applaud us, and the ends of the earth will admire the humanity and gentleness of our city, and all who hear of these deeds throughout the world will extol us. That we then may enjoy these good things, let us fall down in prayer and supplication, let us rescue the captive, the fugitive, the suppliant from danger that we ourselves may obtain the future blessings by the favour and mercy of our Lord Jesus Christ, to whom be glory and power, now and for ever, world without end. Amen.

HOMILY
Concerning the Statues

An exhortation to virtue—and particularly upon the passage, "God was walking in Paradise in the cool of the day:"—and again on the subject of abstaining from oaths.

Ye have lately heard, how all Scripture bringeth consolation and comfort, although it be an historical narrative. For instance, "In the beginning, God created the heaven and the earth," was an historical declaration; but it was shewn in our discourse, that this sentence was one pregnant with comfort; as, for example, that God made us a twofold table, by spreading out the sea and the land at the same time; by kindling above the twofold lights, the sun and moon; by determining the twofold seasons of their course, the day and night, the one for labour, and the other for rest. For the night ministers to us no less benefit than the day. But as I said with reference to trees, those which are barren, rival in their utility those which bear fruit; since we are thus not necessitated to touch those trees which are pleasant for food, for the purposes of building. The wild and untamed animals are also subservient to our need, in no less a degree than the tame animals; by driving us together, through the fear of them, into cities; making us more cautious, and binding us to one another; and by exercising the strength of some, and freeing others from their sicknesses; for the physicians concoct many medicines out of these; and by reminding us of our ancient sin. For when I hear it said, "The fear of you, and the dread of you, shall be upon all the wild beasts of the earth:" and then observe, that this honour was afterwards curtailed, I am reminded of sin, which hath dissipated the fear of us, and undermined our authority. Thus I become a better and a wiser man, whilst I learn the harm that sin hath occasioned us. As then, what I said was, that the things alluded to, and others of a similar kind, which God, who is the Maker, knoweth of, contribute not a little to our present life; so now also I say, that the night no less than the day brings along with it its advantage, being a rest from labours, and a medicine for disease. Often, indeed, physicians, though exerting themselves in many ways, and preparing an endless variety of remedies, are not able to deliver the man who is labouring under infirmity. But sleep coming upon him of its own accord hath entirely removed the disease, and freed them from an infinite deal of trouble. Night, again, is not only a medicine for bodily labours, but also for mental diseases, in giving rest to anguished souls. Ofttimes it happeneth that some one hath lost a son; and comforters without number have been of no avail to withdraw him from tears and groans. But on the approach of night, conquered by the despotic power of sleep, he hath closed his eyelids in slumber, and received some small relief from the miseries of the day time.

And now, I pray you, let us proceed to the subject which hath given rise to these observations. For well I know, that ye are all eagerly awaiting this matter; and that each one of you is in pain till he learn on what account this Book was not given from the beginning. But even now I do not see that the time is fit for a discourse on this subject. And why so? Because the week hath nearly arrived at its close with us, and I fear to touch upon a subject, the exposition of which I should presently afterwards be obliged to cut short. For the subject requires of us several days in succession, and a continuous effort of memory: wherefore we must again defer it. But take it not amiss! we will assuredly pay you the debt with interest; for thus it is expedient both for you, and for us who are to discharge it. Meanwhile, however, let us now speak on that subject which we left out yesterday. And what was it we left out yesterday? "God was walking," it says, "in Paradise in the cool of the day." What is here meant, I ask? "God was walking!" God was not walking; for how should He do this who is everywhere present, and filleth all things? But He caused a perception of this sort in Adam, in order that he might collect himself; that he might not be careless; that in flying and in hiding himself, he might present beforehand some portion of the excuse, even before any words had passed. For even as those who are about to be led to the tribunal, to sustain the charges respecting the crimes they have committed, present themselves before those who are to try them with a squalid, begrimed, sad, and subdued visage, in order that from their appearance, they may incline them to lovingkindness, mercy, and forgiveness, so also did it happen in the case of Adam. For it was necessary that he should be led to this Tribunal in a subdued state. Therefore God took him beforehand, and humbled him. But that some one was walking there, he perceived; but whence came he to suppose that God was walking there? Such is the habitual custom of those who have committed sin. They are suspicious of all things; they tremble at shadows; they are in terror at every sound, and they imagine that every one is approaching them in a hostile manner. Often therefore the guilty, when they observe people running on another business, suppose that they are come against them; and when others are conversing one with another on quite a different subject, they that are conscious of sin suppose they are conversing about them.

For such is the nature of sin, that it betrays whilst no one finds fault; it condemns whilst no one accuses; it makes the sinner a timid being; one that trembles at a sound; even as righteousness has the contrary effect. Hear, at least, how the Scripture describes this cowardice of the former, and this boldness of the latter. "The wicked flee when no man pursueth." How doth he flee when no man pursueth? He hath that within which drives him on—an accuser in his conscience; and this he carries about everywhere; and just as it would be impossible to flee from himself, so neither can he escape the persecutor within; but wherever he goeth, he is scourged, and hath an incurable wound! But not such is the righteous man. Of what nature then is he? Hear: "The righteous is bold as a lion!" Such a man was Elias. He saw, for instance, the king coming towards him, and when he said, "Why is it that thou pervertest Israel?" he answered, "I pervert not Israel, but thou and thy father's house." Truly,the just man is bold as a lion; for he stood up against the king just as a lion doth against some vile cur. Although the one had the purple, the other had the sheepskin, which was the more venerable garment of the two; for that purple brought forth the grievous famine; but this sheepskin effected a liberation from that calamity! It divided the Jordan! It made Elisha a twofold Elias! O how great is the virtue of the Saints! Not only their words; not only their bodies, but even their very garments are always esteemed venerable by the whole creation. The sheepskin of this man divided the Jordan! The sandals of the Three Children trampled down the fire! The word of Elisha changed the waters, so that it made them to bear the iron on their surface! The rod of Moses divided the Red Sea and cleft the rock! The garments of Paul expelled diseases! The shadow of Peter put death to flight! The ashes of the holy Martyrs drive away demons! For this reason they do all things with authority, even as Elias did. For he looked not on the diadem, nor the outward pomp of the king, but he looked on the soul clad in rags, squalid, begrimed, and in a more wretched condition than that of any criminal; and seeing him the captive and slave of his passions, he despised his power. For he seemed to see a king but in a scene, and not a real one. For what was the advantage of outward abundance, when the poverty within was so great? And what harm could outward poverty do, when there was such a treasure of wealth within? Such a lion also was the blessed Paul; for when he had entered into the prison, and only raised his voice, he shook all the foundations; he gnawed in pieces the fetters, employing not his teeth, but words; on which account it were fitting to call such men not merely lions, but something more than lions; for a lion ofttimes, after he hath fallen into a net, is taken; but the Saints when they are bound, become still more powerful; just as this blessed man did then in the prison, having loosed the prisoners, shaken the walls, and bound the keeper, and overcome him by the word of godliness. The lion uttereth his voice, and putteth all the wild beasts to flight. The Saint uttereth his voice, and driveth away the demons on every side! The weapons of the lion are a hairy mane, pointed claws, and sharp teeth. The weapons of the righteous man are spiritual wisdom, temperance, patience, contempt of all present things. Whoever hath these weapons shall not only be able to deride wicked men, but even the adverse powers themselves.

Study then, O man, the life according to God, and no one shall conquer thee at any time; and although thou mayest be accounted the most insignificant of men, thou shalt be more powerful than all. On the other hand, if thou art indifferent about virtue of soul, though thou wert the most powerful of men, thou wilt easily be worsted by all that assail thee. And the examples already quoted proved this. But if thou art desirous, I will also endeavour to teach thee by actual facts the unconquerableness of the righteous, and the vulnerable condition of sinners. Hear then how the prophet intimates both these particulars. "The ungodly," saith he, "are not so, but are like the chaff which the wind scattereth away from the face of the earth." For even as chaff lies exposed to the gusts of wind, and is easily caught up and swept along, so is also the sinner driven about by every temptation; for whilst he is at war with himself, and bears the warfare about with him, what hope of safety does he possess; betrayed as he is at home, and carrying with him that conscience, which is a constant enemy? Such, however, is not the nature of the righteous man. But what manner of man is he? Hear the same prophet, saying, "They that trust in the Lord are as Mount Zion." What means then, "As Mount Zion?" "He shall not be shaken," saith he, "for ever." For whatever engines thou bringest up, whatever darts thou hurlest, desiring to overturn a mountain, thou wilt never be able to prevail; for how canst thou? Thou wilt break in pieces all thine engines, and exhaust thine own strength. Such also is the righteous man. Whatever blows he may receive, he suffereth no evil therefrom; but destroyeth the power of those who take counsel against him, and not of men only, but of demons. Thou has heard often what engines the Devil brought up against Job; but not only did he fail to overthrow that mountain, but drew back exhausted, his darts broken to pieces, and his engines rendered useless, by that assault!

Knowing these things, let us take heed to our life; and let us not be earnest as to the goods that perish; neither as to the glory that goeth out; nor as to that body which groweth old; nor as to that beauty which is fading; nor as to that pleasure which is fleeting; but let us expend all our care about the soul; and let us provide for the welfare of this in every way. For to cure the body, when diseased, is not an easy matter to every one; but to cure a sick soul is easy to all; and the sickness of the body requires medicines, as well as money, for its healing; but the healing of the soul is a thing that is easy to procure, and devoid of expense. And the nature of the flesh is with much labour delivered from those wounds which are troublesome; for very often the knife must be applied, and medicines that are bitter; but with respect to the soul there is nothing of this kind. It suffices only to exercise the will, and the desire, and all things are accomplished. And this hath been the work of God's providence. For inasmuch as from bodily sickness no great injury could arise, (for though we were not diseased, yet death would in any case come, and destroy and dissolve the body); but everything depends upon the health of our souls; this being by far the more precious and necessary, He hath made the medicining of it easy, and void of expense or pain. What excuse therefore, or what pardon shall we obtain, if when the body is sick, and money must be expended on its behalf, and physicians called in, and much anguish endured, we make this so much a matter of our care (though what might result from that sickness could be no great injury to us), and yet treat the soul with neglect? And this, when we are neither called upon to pay down money; nor to give others any trouble; nor to sustain any sufferings; but without any of all these things, by only choosing and willing, have it in our power to accomplish the entire amendment of it; and knowing assuredly that if we fail to do this, we shall sustain the extreme sentence, and punishments, and penalties, which are inexorable! For tell me, if any one promised to teach thee the healing art in a short space of time, without money or labour, wouldest thou not think him a benefactor? Wouldest thou not submit both to do and to suffer all things, whatsoever he who promised these things commanded? Behold, now, it is permitted thee without labour to find a medicine for wounds, not of the body, but of the soul, and to restore it to a state of health, without any suffering! Let us not be indifferent to the matter! For pray what is the pain of laying aside anger against one who hath aggrieved thee? It is a pain, indeed, to remember injuries, and not to be reconciled! What labour is it to pray, and to ask for a thousand good things from God, who is ready to give? What labour is it, not to speak evil of any one? What difficulty is there in being delivered from envy and ill-will? What trouble is it to love one's neighbour? What suffering is it not to utter shameful words, nor to revile, nor to insult another? What fatigue is it not to swear? for again I return to this same admonition. The labour of swearing is indeed exceedingly great. Oftentimes, whilst under the influence of anger or wrath, we have sworn, perhaps, that we would never be reconciled to those who have injured us. Yet afterwards, when our wrath was quenched, and our anger allayed, desiring to be reconciled, and restrained by the obligation of these oaths, we have suffered the same anguish, as if we were in a snare, and held fast by indissoluble bonds. Of which fact the Devil being aware, and understanding clearly that anger is a fire; that it is easily extinguished, and that when it is extinguished, then reconciliation and love follows; wishing this fire to remain unquenched, he often binds us by an oath; so that although the anger should cease, the obligation of the oath remaining may keep up the fire within us; and that one of these two things may take place, either that being reconciled we are forsworn, or that not being reconciled we subject ourselves to the penalties of cherishing malice.

Knowing these things then, let us avoid oaths; and let our mouth continually practise the saying, "Believe me;" and this will be to us a foundation for all pious behaviour; for the tongue, when it has been disciplined to use this one expression, is ashamed, and would blush to utter words that are disgraceful and ugly; and should it at anytime be drawn away by habit, it will be checked again, by having many accusers. For when any one observes him who is not a swearer giving utterance to foul words, he will take his advantage over him, and ridicule, and exclaim tauntingly, "Thou who sayest in all affairs, 'Believe me,' and venturest not to utter an oath, dost thou disgrace thy tongue with these shameful expressions?" So that being forcibly urged by those who are with us, even if unwilling, we shall return again to a pious behaviour. "But what," says one, "if it be necessary to take an oath?" Where there is a transgression of the law, there is no such thing as necessity. "Is it possible then," it is replied, "not to swear at all?" What sayest thou? Hath God commanded, and darest thou to ask if it be possible for His law to be kept? Why, truly it is a thing impossible that His law should not be kept; and I am desirous to persuade you from present circumstances of this; that so far from its being impossible not to swear, it is impossible to swear. For behold, the inhabitants of the city were commanded to bring in a payment of gold, such as it might have seemed beyond the power of many to do; yet the greater part of the sum has been collected; and you may hear the tax gatherers saying, "Why delay, man? Why put us off from day to day? It is not possible to avoid it. It is the law of the Emperor, which admits of no delay." What sayest thou, I ask? The Emperor hath commanded thee to bring in thy money and it is impossible not to bring it in! God hath commanded thee to avoid oaths! and how sayest thou, it is impossible to avoid them!

I am now for the sixth day admonishing you in respect of this precept. Henceforth, I am desirous to take leave of you, meaning to abstain from the subject, that ye may be on your guard. There will no longer be any excuse or allowance for you; for of right, indeed, if nothing had been said on this matter,

_____

_____

_____

_____

_____

_____

_____

_____

_____

_____

it ought to have been amended of yourselves, for it is not a thing of an intricate nature, or that requires great preparation. But since ye have enjoyed the advantage of so much admonition and counsel, what excuse will ye have to offer, when ye stand accused before that dread tribunal, and are required to give account of this transgression. It is impossible to invent any excuse; but of necessity you must either go hence amended, or, if you have not amended, be punished, and abide the extremest penalty! Thinking, therefore, upon all these things, and departing hence with much anxiety about them, exhort ye one another, that the things spoken of during so many days may be kept with all watchfulness in your minds, so that whilst we are silent, ye instructing, edifying, exhorting one another, may exhibit great improvement; and having fulfilled all the other precepts, may enjoy eternal crowns; which God grant we may all obtain, through the grace and lovingkindness of our Lord Jesus Christ, by whom and with whom be glory, to the Father, together with the Holy Ghost, for ever and ever. Amen.

AUGUSTINE
(354 - 430)

Aurelius Augustinus, known commonly as Augustine, was more than a three-letter man. At once, he was the greatest theologian of the ancient church (considered the founder of systematic theology), the greatest apologist, and the greatest Christian writer from Paul to the Reformation. In addition, he wrote the first systematic book on Preaching, *De Doctrina Christiana*. It is likely that Augustine would have approved of this book. In his homiletics textbook he said that in learning to preach the use of models is more fruitful than the learning of rules. He, himself, was a remarkable preacher whose influence continues today.

Sketch of His Life

A. Family

Augustine's mother, Monica, is one of the most famous mothers in history. A Christian, she prayed for her son's conversion for over thirty years. Augustine was converted at the age of 33, and she died the very year he was baptized. His father, Patricius, remained a pagan until near the end of his life in 372 when he finally became a Christian. He was a man of strong temper, and was ambitious for his son's success.

B. Birth and education

Augustine was born November 13, 354 in Tagaste, a small village of North Africa. His early studies in Tagaste and in Carthage consisted of grammar and rhetoric. At the age of twelve, he engaged in further studies of grammar at Madaura south of Tagaste, where he also received a traditional Roman education in literature and the classics. During this time, he mastered the study of Aristotle.

At this time, the best education in Africa was to be found at Carthage. So, five years later, steeped in Latin literature, he went to Carthage to study rhetoric. He was weak in Greek and strong in Latin. Like some other great preachers, he disliked mathematics. He learned Cicero fully and quotes him often about rhetorical matters. Part of his training consisted of declamation.

At Carthage he lived a rather wild life. He took up with a woman who became his concubine and at the age of 17 he had a son born out of wedlock by the name of Adeodatus.

While in Carthage he became a Manichaean. For nine years he was a "hearer" before being admitted to full membership in the sect. Manichaeans rejected the Old Testament, held to a dualism of matter and spirit, considered matter evil and sin an involuntary action that required no repentance. For Augustine's own description of Manichaeanism, see his *City of God*, pp. 446,447 (Modern Library edition).

C. Early Career

While at Carthage Augustine became a teacher of rhetoric and for ten years taught in his own school. During this time, he won a crown as a prize for the best poem of the year. At this period in his life, he believed in astrology and studied horoscopes. He was fast becoming Cicero's all-around man. At 26/27 he wrote his first book, *On the Fitting and the Beautiful* (no longer extant) and dedicated it to a Roman orator Hievius, whom he had never met but whose works he admired.

After a while, however, he began to have doubts about Manichaeanism. Then came the test: Faustus, the great apologist of the Manichaeans arrived in Carthage. Listening to him, Augustine found that he could refute every one of his arguments. Study of Faustus's book on the Old Testament led to the same conclusion: he could counter him point for point. He characterized Faustus as a "silvery" speaker, but with little or no content.

In 383 Augustine went to Rome. He had become disgusted with the wildness of students in Carthage who were so unruly that they broke up his lectures. But in Rome he discovered that teaching conditions were not much better, just different. There he ran into a new, but equally serious, student problem: students soaked up all they could from a teacher then left without paying their fees.

Disillusioned by such treatment, in 385 he took a publicly supported post as a teacher of rhetoric in Milan. Here, he became interested in neoplatonism. But of greater significance, he heard Ambrose preach. He was impressed with the eloquence of Ambrose's sermons, characterizing them as much better in thought and matter than those of Faustus. In 387, he was converted to Christianity and baptized. While praying in a garden he heard a child say *"tolle lege,"* "take up and read." He took up the New Testament and read Romans 13:13-14 and this led to his conversion. Soon he abandoned rhetoric, declaring that he would no longer be a "seller of words" and returned to Tagaste.

D. As a Christian

At the age of forty (391), Augustine went to Hippo, in North Africa, where he became bishop in 395. He established a theological seminary where he taught and wrote for all of Africa. He worked there for 35 years until his death in 430.

Augustine as a Preacher

There were few good preachers from Paul to the Reformation. These names stand out: Origen, Augustine, Chrysostom and Bernard.

A. Fame and effectiveness

As a priest Augustine preached; that, in itself, was exceptional. Before this, only bishops preached in Africa. He broke the precedent. While still a priest, his preaching was so highly acclaimed that he was invited to preach before the council of bishops in Hippo (390). Great crowds came to hear him. According to custom, the congregation stood while he preached. The preacher sat.

Augustine's sermons were taken down in shorthand. He used very simple language and said that he tried to preach to "poor artisans and fishermen." Although there was some allegorizing, which he learned from Ambrose, these sermons were exegetical, Biblical and theological. Some of his sermons were very brief. There is one that is only eleven lines in the original, but he preached morning and evening, nearly every day.

Augustine's preaching was effective. There was an annual festival at Hippo called the *Laetitia* ("joy") which was characterized by gluttony, drunkenness and wild reveling. Augustine went out among the people and preached to them about their sin until he brought them to tears, and they called it off. At Caesarea (Muratania), there was a similar festival called *Caterva*. Only here the customs were violent and bloody. The people actually battled each other. The city divided itself in half and for five to six days each side fought the other to the death. Whole families were divided. Again, he preached and by eliciting tears of repentance, he was able to bring that custom to an end once and for all.

When the Manichaean champion, Faustus, came to town in 392 Augustine challenged him to a debate which lasted two days. Countering all of Faustus's best arguments, he crushed him. As a result, Faustus left town in disgrace, Manichaeanism lost its influence in Hippo and many former Manichaeans became Christians.

B. His Audience

Augustine's audience was mixed and difficult. There were both learned scholars and ignorant peasants present. So, he determined to preach in provincial rather than scholarly or literary Latin. He said that it was better to have the schoolmasters laughing than to have the people not understand.

Pagans used to come and listen to Augustine's preaching out of sheer curiosity. Even the Manichaeans came, some to try to trick him. One day he saw a famous Manichaean in the audience, changed his sermon on the spot to meet this situation, and the man was converted.

Augustine's audience was demonstrative. They beat their breasts, cried, shouted out, clapped. Because there were many with little learning, Augustine frequently repeated materials. He took his stories largely from everyday life and, as a result, the common people heard him gladly. His preaching was so well received that he was constantly in demand and preached all over North Africa. In those times, the preacher also could be demonstrative, and it was not unusual for Augustine to be found pointing out people in the audience and crying himself.

C. Preparation

In a letter to Alypius, Augustine said that he did not write out his sermons. Elsewhere he claims that he wrote a sermon on the Trinity after he had preached it. His method was to jot down ideas while meditating and preach from these. His sermons were taken down in shorthand and revised slightly before publication.

Augustine dressed in ordinary street clothing, and, like the man himself, his 394 extant sermons are not ornate. Yet, many of the sermons are masterful and, even in their structure, clearly demonstrate the work of a superior preacher.

Many things may be learned from the study of Augustine's preaching. Obviously, the importance of solid content is one. But in the sermon that follows, several stylistic matters (particularly his use of parallelism, contrast and repetition) might be noted for study.

SERMON ON PSALM LXXXV.11

That day is called the birthday of the Lord on which the Wisdom of God manifested Himself as a speechless Child and the Word of God wordlessly uttered the sound of a human voice. His divinity, although hidden, was revealed by heavenly witness to the Magi and was announced to the shepherds by angelic voices. With yearly ceremony, therefore, we celebrate this day which saw the fulfillment of the prophecy: 'Truth is sprung out of the earth: and justice hath looked down from heaven.' Truth, eternally existing in the bosom of the Father, has sprung from the earth so that He might exist also in the bosom of a mother. Truth, holding the world in place, has sprung from the earth so that He might be carried in the hands of a woman. Truth, incorruptibly nourishing the happiness of the angels, has sprung from the earth in order to be fed by human milk. Truth, whom the heavens cannot contain, has sprung from the earth so that He might be placed in a manger. For whose benefit did such unparalleled greatness come in such lowliness? Certainly for no personal advantage, but definitely for our great good, if only we believe. Arouse yourself, O man; for you God has become man. 'Awake, sleeper, and arise from among the dead, and Christ will enlighten thee.' For you, I repeat, God has become man. If He had not thus been born in time, you would have been dead for all eternity. Never would you have been freed from sinful flesh, if He had not taken upon Himself the likeness of sinful flesh. Everlasting misery would have engulfed you, if He had not taken this merciful form. You would not have been restored to life, had He not submitted to your death; you would have fallen, had He not succored you; you would have perished, had He not come.

Let us joyfully celebrate the coming of our salvation and redemption. Let us celebrate the festal day on which the great and timeless One came from the great and timeless day to this brief span of our day. He 'has become for us . . . justice, and sanctification, and redemption; so that, just as it is written, "Let him who takes pride, take pride in the Lord." For, so that we might not resemble the proud Jews who, 'ignorant of the justice of God and seeking to establish their own, have not submitted to the justice of God,' when the Psalmist had said: 'Truth is sprung out of the earth,' he quickly added: 'and justice hath looked down from heaven.' He did this lest mortal frailty, arrogating this justice to itself, should call these blessings its own, and lest man should reject the justice of God in his belief that he is justified, that is, made just through his own efforts. 'Truth is sprung out of the earth' because Christ who said: 'I am the truth' was born of a virgin; and 'justice hath looked down from heaven' because, by believing in Him who was so born, man has been justified not by his own efforts but by God. 'Truth is sprung out of the earth' because 'the Word was made flesh,' and 'justice hath looked down from heaven' because 'every good and perfect gift is from above.' 'Truth is sprung out of the earth,' that is, His flesh was taken from Mary; and 'justice hath looked down from heaven' because 'no one can receive anything unless it is given to him from heaven.'

'Having been justified therefore by faith, let us have peace with God through our Lord Jesus Christ, through whom we also have access by faith unto that grace in which we stand and exult in the hope of the glory ... of God.' With these few words, which you recognize as those of the Apostle, it gives me pleasure, my brethren, to mingle a few passages of the psalm (which we are considering) and to find that they agree in sentiment. 'Having been justified by faith, let us have peace with God' because 'justice and peace have kissed'; 'through our Lord Jesus Christ' because 'truth is sprung out of the earth'; 'through whom we also have access by faith unto that grace in which we stand, and exult in the hope of the glory of God'—he does not say 'of our glory,' but 'of the glory of God' because justice has not proceeded from us but 'hath looked down from heaven.' Therefore, 'let him who takes pride, take pride in the Lord' not in himself. Hence, when the Lord whose birthday we are celebrating today was born of the Virgin, the announcement of the angelic choir was made in the words: 'Glory to God in the highest, and on earth peace among men of good will.' How can peace exist on earth unless it be because 'truth is sprung out of the earth,' that is, because Christ has been born in the flesh? Moreover, 'He Himself is our peace, he it is who has made both one' so that we might become men of good will, bound together by the pleasing fetters of unity. Let us rejoice, then, in this grace so that our glory may be the testimony of our conscience wherein we glory not in ourselves but in the Lord. Hence the Psalmist (in speaking of the Lord) has said: 'My glory and the lifter up of my head.' For what greater grace of God could have shone upon us than that, having an only-begotten Son, God should make Him the Son of Man, and thus, in turn, make the son of man the Son of God? Examine it as a benefit, as an inducement, as a token of justice, and see whether you find anything but a gratuitous gift of God.

HOMILY ON MATTHEW XVIII.15

On the words of the gospel, Matt. xviii. 15, "If thy brother sin against thee, go, shew him his fault between thee and him alone;" and of the words of Solomon, he that winketh with the eyes deceitfully, heapeth sorrow upon men; but he that reproveth openly, maketh peace.

Our Lord warns us not to neglect one another's sins, not by searching out what to find fault with, but by looking out for what to amend. For He said that his eye is sharp to cast out a mote out of his brother's eye, who has not a beam in his own eye. Now what this means, I will briefly convey to you, Beloved. A mote in the eye is anger; a beam in the eye is hatred. When therefore one who has hatred finds fault with one who is angry, he wishes to take a mote out of his brother's eye, but is hindered by the beam which he carries in his own eye. A mote is the beginning of a beam. For a beam in the course of its growth, is first a mote. By watering the mote, you bring it to a beam; by nourishing anger with evil suspicions, you bring it on to hatred.

Now there is a great difference between the sin of one who is angry, and the cruelty of one who holds another in hatred. For even with our children are we angry; but who is ever found to hate his children? Among the very cattle too, the cow in a sort of weariness will sometimes in anger drive away her sucking calf; but anon she embraces it with all the affection of a mother. She is in a way disgusted with it, when she butts at it; yet when she misses it, she will seek after it. Nor do we discipline our children otherwise, than with a degree of anger and indignation; yet we should not discipline them at all, but in love to them. So far then is every one who is angry from hating; that sometimes one would be rather convicted of hating, if he were not angry. For suppose a child wishes to play in some river's stream, by whose force he would be like to perish; if you see this, and patiently suffer it, this would be hating; your patient suffering him, is his death. How far better is it to be angry and correct him, than by not being angry to suffer him to perish! Above all things then is hatred to be avoided, and the beam to be cast out of the eye. Great is the difference indeed between one's exceeding due limits in some words through anger, which he afterwards wipes off by repenting of it; and the keeping an insidious purpose shut up in the heart. Great, lastly, the difference between these words of Scripture, "Mine eye is disordered because of anger." Whereas of the other it is said, "Whosoever hateth his brother is a murderer." Great is the difference between an eye disordered, and clean put out. A mote disorders, a beam puts clean out.

In order then that we may be able well to do and to fulfill what we have been admonished of to-day, let us first persuade ourselves to this, above all things to have no hate. For when there is no beam in thine own eye, thou seest rightly whatever may be in thy brother's eye; and art uneasy, till thou cast out of thy brother's eye what thou seest to hurt it. The light that is in thee, doth not allow thee to neglect thy brother's light. Whereas if thou hate, and wouldest correct him, how dost thou improve his light, when thou hast lost thine own light? For the same Scripture, where it is written, "Whosoever hateth his brother is a murderer," hath expressly told us this also. "He that hateth his brother is in darkness even until now." Hatred then is darkness. Now it cannot but be, that he who hateth another, should first injure himself. For him he endeavors to hurt outwardly, he lays himself waste inwardly. Now in proportion as our soul is of more value than our body, so much the more ought we to provide for it, that it be not hurt. But he that hateth another, doth hurt his own soul. And what would he do to him whom he hateth? What would he do? He takes away his money, can he take his faith away? he wounds his good fame, can he wound his conscience? Whatever injury he does, is but external; now observe what his injury to himself is? For he who hateth another is an enemy to himself within. But because he is not sensible of what harm he is doing to himself, he is violent against another, and that the more dangerously, that he is not sensible of the evil he is doing to himself; because by this very violence he has lost the power of perception. Thou art violent against thine enemy; by this violence of thine he is spoiled, and thou art wicked. Great is the difference between the two. He hath lost his money, thou thine innocence. Ask which hath suffered the heavier loss? He hath lost a thing that was sure to perish, and thou art become one who must now perish thyself.

Therefore ought we to rebuke in love; not with any eager desire to injure, but with an earnest care to amend. If we be so minded, most excellently do we practise that which we have been recommended to-day: "If thy brother shall sin against thee, rebuke him between thee and him alone." Why dost thou rebuke him? Because thou art grieved, that he should have sinned against thee? God forbid. If from love of thyself thou do it, thou doest nothing. If from love to him thou do it, thou doest excellently. In fact, observe in these words themselves, for the love of whom thou oughtest to do it, whether of thyself or him. "If he shall hear thee, thou hast gained thy brother." Do it for his sake then, that thou mayest "gain" him. If by so doing thou "gain" him, hadst thou not done it, he would have been lost. How is it then that most men disregard these sins, and say, "What great thing have I done? I have only sinned against man." Disregard them not. Thou hast sinned against man; but wouldest thou know that in sinning against man thou art lost. If he, against whom thou hast sinned, have "rebuked thee between thee and him alone," and thou hast listened to him, he hath "gained" thee. What can "hath gained thee," mean; but that thou hadst been lost, if he had not gained thee. For if thou wouldest not have been lost, how hath he gained thee? Let no man then disregard it, when he sins against a brother. For the Apostle saith in a certain place, "But when ye sin so against the brethren, and wound their weak conscience, ye sin against Christ;" for this reason, because we have been all made members of Christ. How dost thou not sin against Christ, who sinnest against a member of Christ?

Let no one therefore say, "I have not sinned against God, but against a brother. I have sinned against a man, it is a trifling sin, or no sin at all." It may be, thou sayest it is a trifling sin, because it is soon cured. Thou hast sinned against a brother; give him satisfaction, and thou art made whole. Thou didst a deadly thing quickly, but quickly too hast thou found a remedy. Who of us, my Brethren, can hope for the kingdom of heaven, when the Gospel says, "Whosoever shall say to his brother, Thou fool, shall be in danger of hell fire?" Exceeding terror! but behold in the same place the remedy: "If thou bring thy gift to the altar, and there rememberest that thy brother hath ought against thee, leave there thy gift before the altar." God is not angry that thou deferrest to lay thy gift upon the Altar. It is thee that God seeketh more than thy gift. For if thou come with a gift to thy God, bearing an evil mind against thy brother, He will answer thee, "Thou art lost, what hast thou brought Me? Thou bringest thy gift, and thou art thyself no proper gift for God. Christ seeketh him whom He hath redeemed with His Blood, more than what thou hast found in thy barn." So then, "Leave there thy gift before the altar, and go thy way, first be reconciled to thy brother, and so thou shalt come and offer thy gift." Lo that "danger of hell fire," how quickly dissolved it is! When thou wast not yet reconciled, thou offerest thy gift before the altar in all security.

But men are easy and ready enough to inflict injuries, and hard to seek for reconciliation. Ask pardon, says one, of him whom thou hast offended, of him whom thou hast injured. He answers, "I will not so humble myself." But now if thou despise thy brother, at least give ear to thy God. "He that humbleth himself shall be exalted." Wilt thou refuse to humble thyself, who hast already fallen? Great is the difference between one who humbleth himself, and one who lieth on the ground. Already dost thou lie on the ground, and wilt thou then not humble thyself? Thou mightest well say, I will not descend; if thou hadst first been unwilling to fall.

This then ought one to do who hath done an injury. And he who suffered one, what ought he to do? What we have heard to-day, "If thy brother shall sin against thee, rebuke him between thee and him alone." If thou shalt neglect this, thou art worse than he. He hath done an injury, and by doing an injury, hath stricken himself with a grievous wound; wilt thou disregard thy brother's wound? Wilt thou see him perishing, or already lost, and disregard his case? Thou art worse in keeping silence, than he in his reviling. Therefore when any one sins against us, let us take great care, not for ourselves, for it is a glorious thing to forget injuries; only forget thine own injury, not thy brother's wound. Therefore "rebuke him between thee and him alone," intent upon his amendment, but sparing his shame. For it may be that through shamefacedness he will begin to defend his sin, and so thou wilt make him whom thou desirest to amend, still worse. "Rebuke him" therefore "between him and thee alone. If he shall hear thee, thou hast gained thy brother;" because he would have been lost, hadst thou not done it. But "if he will not hear thee," that is, if he will defend his sin as if it were a just action, "take with thee one or two more, that in the mouth of two or three witnesses every word may be established; and if he will not hear them, refer it to the Church; but if he will not hear the Church, let him be unto thee as an heathen man and a publican." Reckon him no more amongst the number of thy brethren. But yet neither is his salvation on that account to be neglected. For the very heathen, that is the Gentiles and Pagans, we do not reckon among the number of brethren; but yet are we ever seeking their salvation. This then have we heard the Lord so advising, and with such great carefulness enjoining, that He even added this immediately, "Verily I say unto you, Whatsoever ye shall bind on earth, shall be bound in heaven; and whatsoever ye shall loose on earth, shall be loosed in heaven." Thou hast begun to hold thy brother for a publican; "thou bindest him on earth;" but see that thou bind him justly. For unjust bonds justice doth burst asunder. But when thou hast corrected, and been "reconciled to thy brother," thou hast "loosed him on earth." And when "thou shalt have loosed him on earth, he shall be loosed in heaven also." Thus thou doest a great thing, not for thyself, but for him; for a great injury had he done, not to thee, but to himself.

But since this is so, what is that which Solomon says, and which we heard first to-day out of another lesson, "He that winketh with the eyes deceitfully, heapeth sorrow upon men; but he that reproveth openly, maketh peace"? if then "he that reproveth openly, maketh peace;" how "rebuke him between him and thee alone"? We must fear, lest the divine precepts should be contrary to one another. But no: let us understand that there is the most perfect agreement in them, let us not follow the conceits of certain vain ones, who in their error think that the two Testaments in the Old and New Books are contrary to each other; that so we should think that there is any contradiction here, because one is in the book of Solomon, and the other in the Gospel. For if any one unskilful in, and a reviler of the divine Scriptures, were to say, "See where the two Testaments contradict each other. The Lord saith, 'Rebuke him between him and thee alone.' Solomon saith, 'He that reproveth openly maketh peace.' " Doth not the Lord then know what He hath commanded? Solomon would have the sinners' hard forehead bruised: Christ spareth his shame who blushes for his sins. For in the one place it is written, "He that reproveth openly maketh peace;" but in the other, "Rebuke him between him and thee alone;" not "openly," but apart and secretly. But wouldest thou know, whosoever thou art that thinkest such things, that the two Testaments are not opposed to each other, because the first of these passages is found in the book of Solomon, and the other in the Gospel? Hear the Apostle. And surely the Apostle is a Minister of the New Testament. Hear the Apostle Paul then, charging Timothy, and saying, "Them that sin rebuke before all, that others also may fear." So then not the book of Solomon, but an Epistle of Paul the Apostle seems to be at issue with the Gospel. Let us then without any prejudice to his honour lay aside Solomon for a while; let us hear the Lord Christ and His servant Paul. What sayest Thou, O Lord? "If thy brother sin against thee, rebuke him between him and thee alone." What sayest thou, O Apostle? "Them that sin rebuke before all, that others also may fear." What are we about? Are we listening to this controversy as judges? That be far from us. Yea, rather as those whose place is under the Judge, let us knock, that we may obtain, that it be opened to us; let us fly beneath the wings of our Lord God. For He did not speak in contradiction to His Apostle, seeing that He Himself spoke "in" him also, as he says, "Would ye receive a proof of Christ, who speaketh in me?" Christ in the Gospel, Christ in the Apostle: Christ therefore spake both; one by His own Mouth, the other by the mouth of His herald. For when the herald pronounces anything from the tribunal, it is not written in the records, "the herald said it;" but he is written as having said it, who commanded the herald what to say.

Let us then so give ear to these two precepts, Brethren, as that we may understand them, and let us settle ourselves in peace between them both. Let us but be in agreement with our own heart, and Holy Scripture will in no part disagree with itself. It is entirely true, both precepts are true; but we must make a distinction, that sometimes the one, sometimes the other must be done; that sometimes a brother must be "reproved between him and thee alone," sometimes a brother "must be reproved before all, that others also may fear." If we do sometimes the one, and sometimes the other, we shall hold fast the harmony of the Scriptures, and shall not err in fulfilling and obeying them. But a man will say to me, "When am I to do this one, and when the other? lest I 'reprove between me and him alone,' when I ought to 'reprove before all;' or 'reprove before all,' when I ought to reprove in secret."

You will soon see, Beloved, what we ought to do, and when; only I would we may not be slow to practise it. Attend and see: "If thy brother sin against thee, rebuke him between him and thee alone." Why? Because it is against thee that he hath sinned. What is that, "hath sinned against thee"? Thou knowest that he hath sinned. For because it was secret when he sinned against thee, seek for secresy, when thou dost correct his sin. For if thou only know that he hath sinned against thee, and thou wouldest "rebuke him before all," thou art not a reprover, but a betrayer. Consider how that "just man" Joseph spared his wife with such exceeding kindness, in so great a crime as he had suspected her of, before he knew by whom she had conceived; because he perceived that she was with child, and he knew that he had not come in unto her. There remained then an unavoidable suspicion of adultery, and yet because he only had perceived, he only knew it, what does the Gospel say of him? "Then Joseph being a just man, and not willing to make her a public example." The husband's grief sought no revenge; he wished to profit, not to punish the sinner. "And not willing to make her a public example, he was minded to put her away privily." But while he thought on these things, "behold, the Angel of the Lord appeared unto him," in sleep; and told him how it was, that she had not defiled her husband's bed, but that she had conceived of the Holy Ghost the Lord of them both. Thy brother then hath sinned against thee; if thou alone know it, then hath he really sinned against thee alone. For if in the hearing of many he hath done thee an injury, he hath sinned against them also whom he hath made witnesses of his iniquity. For I tell you, my dearly beloved Brethren, what you can yourselves recognise in your own case. When any one does my brother an injury in my hearing, God forbid that I should think that injury unconnected with myself. Certainly he has done it to me also; yea to me the rather, to whom he thought what he did was pleasing. Therefore those sins are to be reproved before all, which are committed before all; they are to be reproved with more secresy, which are committed more secretly. Distinguish times, and Scripture is in harmony with itself.

So let us act; and so must we act not only when the sin is committed against ourselves, but when the sin is so committed by any one as that it is unknown by the other. In secret ought we to rebuke, in secret to reprove him; lest if we would reprove him publicly, we should betray the man. We wish to rebuke and reform him; but what if his enemy is looking out to hear something that he may punish? For example, a Bishop knows of some one who has killed another, and no one else knows of him. I wish to reprove him publicly, but thou art seeking to prosecute him. Decidedly then I will neither betray him, nor neglect him; I will reprove him in secret; I will set the judgment of God before his eyes; I will alarm his bloodstained conscience; I will persuade him to repentance. With this charity ought we to be endued. And hence men sometimes find fault with us, as if we do not reprove; or they think that we know what we do not know, or that we hush up what we know. And it may be that what thou knowest, I know also; but I will not reprove in thy presence; because I wish to cure, not to act informer. There are men who commit adultery in their own houses, they sin in secret, sometimes they are discovered to us by their own wives, generally through jealousy, sometimes as seeking their husband's salvation; in such cases we do not betray them openly, but reprove them in secret. Where the evil has happened, there let the evil die. Yet do we not neglect that wound; above all things showing the man who is in such a sinful state, and bears such a wounded conscience, that that is a deadly wound which they who suffer from, sometimes by an unaccountable perverseness despise; and seek out testimonies in their favour, I know not whence, null certainly and void, saying, "God careth not for sins of the flesh." Where is that then which we have heard to-day, "Whoremongers and adulterers God will judge"? Lo! whosoever thou art that labourest under such a disease attend. Hear what God saith; not what thine own mind, in indulgence to thine own sins, may say, or what thy friend, thine enemy rather and his own too, bound in the same bond of iniquity with thee may say. Hear then what the Apostle saith, "Marriage is honourable in all, and the bed undefiled. But whoremongers and adulterers God will judge."

Come then, Brother, be reformed. Thou art afraid lest thine enemy should prosecute thee; and art thou not afraid lest God should judge thee? Where is thy faith? Fear whilst there is the time for fear. Far off indeed is the day of judgment; but every man's last day cannot be far off; for life is short. And since this shortness is ever uncertain, thou knowest not when thy last day may be. Reform thyself to-day, because of to-morrow. Let the reproof in secret be of service to thee now. For I am speaking openly, yet do I reprove in secret. I knock at the ears of all; but I accost the consciences of some. If I were to say, "Thou adulterer, reform thyself;" perhaps in the first place I might say what I had no knowledge of; perhaps suspect on a rash hearsay report. I do not then say, "Thou adulterer, reform thyself;" but "whosoever thou art among this people who art an adulterer, reform thyself." So the reproof is public; the reformation secret. This I know, that whoso feareth, will reform himself.

Let no one say in his heart, "God careth not for sin of the flesh." "Know ye not," saith the Apostle, "that ye are the temple of God, and the Spirit of God dwelleth in you? If any man defile the temple of God, him will God destroy." "Let no man deceive himself." But perhaps a man will say, "My soul is the temple of God, not my body," and will add this testimony also, "All flesh is as grass, and all the glory of man as the flower of grass." Unhappy interpretation! conceit meet for punishment! The flesh is called grass, because it dies; but take thou heed that that which dies for a time, rise not again with guilt. Wouldest thou ascertain a plain judgment on this point also? "Know ye not," says the same Apostle, "that your body is the temple of the Holy Ghost which is in you, which ye have of God?" Do not then any longer disregard sins of the body; seeing that your "bodies are the temples of the Holy Ghost which is in you, which ye have of God." If thou didst disregard a sin of the body, wilt thou disregard a sin which thou committest against a temple? Thy very body is a temple of the Spirit of God within thee. Now take heed what thou doest with the temple of God. If thou wert to choose to commit adultery in the Church within these walls, what wickedness could be greater? But now thou art thyself the temple of God. In thy going out, in thy coming in, as thou abidest in thy house, as thou risest up, in all thou art a temple. Take heed then what thou doest, take heed that thou offend not the Indweller of the temple, lest He forsake thee, and thou fall into ruins. "Know ye not," he says, "that your bodies" (and this the Apostle spake touching fornication, that they might not think lightly of sins of the body) "are the temples of the Holy Ghost which is in you, which ye have of God, and ye are not your own?" For "ye have been bought with a great price." If thou think so lightly of thine own body, have some consideration for thy price.

I know, and as I do every one knows, who has used a little more than ordinary consideration, that no man who has any fear of God omits to reform himself in obedience to His words, but he who thinks that he has longer time to live. This it is which kills so many, while they are saying, "To-morrow, To-morrow;" and suddenly the door is shut. He remains outside with the raven's croak, because he had not the moaning of the dove. "To-morrow, To-morrow;" is the raven's croak. Moan plaintively as the dove, and beat thy breast; but whilst thou art inflicting blows on thy breast, be the better for the beating; lest thou seem not to beat thy conscience, but rather with blows to harden it, and make an evil conscience more unyielding instead of better. Moan with no fruitless moaning. For it may be thou art saying to thyself, "God hath promised me forgiveness, whenever I reform myself I am secure; I read the divine Scripture, "In the day that the wicked man turneth away from his wickedness, and doeth that which is lawful and right, I will forget all his iniquities." I am secure then, whenever I reform myself, God will give me pardon for my evil deeds." What can I say to this? Shall I lift up my voice against God? Shall I say to God, Do not give him pardon? Shall I say, This is not written, God hath not promised this? If I should say ought of this, I should say falsely. Thou speakest well and truly; God hath promised pardon on thy amendment, I cannot deny it; but tell me, I pray thee; see, I consent, I grant, I acknowledge that God hath promised thee pardon, but who hath promised thee a to-morrow? Where thou dost read to me that thou shalt receive pardon, if thou reform thyself; there read to me how long thou hast to live. Thou dost confess, "I cannot read it there." Thou knowest not then how long thou hast to live. Reform thyself, and so be always ready. Be not afraid of the last day, as a thief, who will break up thy house as thou sleepest; but awake and reform thyself to-day. Why dost thou put it off till to-morrow? If thy life is to be a long one, let it be both long and good. No one puts off a good dinner, because it is to be a long one, and dost thou wish to have a long evil life? Surely if it is to be long, it will be all the better if it be good; if it is to be short, it is well that its good be as long as possible. But men neglect their life to such a degree, as that they are unwilling to have anything bad except it. You buy a farm, and you look out for a good one; you wish to marry a wife, you choose a good one; you wish for the birth of children, and you long for good ones; you bargain for shoes, and you do not wish for bad ones; and yet a bad life you do love. How hath thy life offended thee, that thou art willing to have it only bad; that amid all thy good things thou shouldest thyself alone be evil?

So then, my Brethren, if I should wish to reprove any of you individually in secret, perhaps he would listen to me. I reprove many of you now in public; all praise me; may some give attentive heed to me! I have no love for him who praises me with his voice, and with his heart despises me. For when thou dost praise, and not reform thyself, thou art a witness against thyself. If thou art evil, and thou art pleased with what I say, be displeased with thyself; because if thou art displeased with thyself as being evil, when thou dost reform, thou wilt be well pleased with thyself, which if I mistake not I said the day before yesterday. In all my words I set a mirror before you. Nor are they my words, but I speak at the bidding of the Lord, by whose terrors I refrain from keeping silence. For who would not rather choose to keep silence, and not to give account for you? But now I have undertaken the burden, and I cannot, and I ought not to shake it off my shoulders. When the Epistle to the Hebrews was being read, my Brethren, ye heard, "Obey them that have the rule over you, and submit yourselves: for they watch for your souls, as they that must give account, that they may do it with joy, and not with grief; for that is unprofitable for you." When do we it with joy? When we see man making progress in the words of God. When does the labourer in the field work with joy? When he looks at the tree, and sees the fruit; when he looks at the crop, and sees the prospect of abundance of corn in the floor; when he sees that he has not laboured in vain, has not bowed his back, and bruised his hands, and endured the cold and heat in vain. This is what he says, "That they may do it with joy, and not with grief; for that is unprofitable for you." Did he say, "unprofitable for them"? No. He said, "unprofitable for you." For when those who are set over you are saddened at your evil deeds, it is profitable for them; their very sadness is profitable for them; but it is unprofitable for you. But we do not wish that anything should be profitable for us, which for you is unprofitable. Let us then, Brethren, do good together in the Lord's field; that at the reward we may rejoice together.

LUTHER
(1483 - 1546)

There is little need to discuss the life of Martin Luther or his doctrinal teaching. These are well known and adequately handled in other places. Our concern is with Luther as a preacher.

In a real sense the Reformation was a revival of preaching. After a long, barren period in which sacerdotalism had gained ascendency, Reformation preaching was like water gushing from the rock. There had been no such preaching for centuries. Origen's allegorical method, coupled with the rise of a sterile scholasticism and a cultic sacerdotalism had all but killed preaching. But, at last, real exposition like that of Chrysostom—indeed, even better than Chrysostom's—was heard again!

The schoolmen had taken Origen's threefold level of interpretation and moved one step farther with it in what they called the *quadriga* or "fourfold rule." This was comprised of the literal, the allegorical, the moral, and the analogical senses. The literal had to do with historical acts, the moral with ethical acts of the listener formed as rules of conduct, the allegorical with the doctrine that the church is to believe, and the analogical with the invisible realities of heaven for which one is to look forward with hope.

Luther began his preaching in this tradition but at one point consciously abandoned it. Before 1521 he was still under the influence of scholastic rules of preaching and used the typical scholastic form. But in that year he consciously abandoned scholastic ways and developed what was for him a completely new method of preaching: the homily. He begins with the main point; when the time is up, he stops. However, his sermons usually have more unity than the simple homily. His method was similar to the developed homily used by some in the pre-Reformation period.

But Luther was never able to fully shake allegorical tendencies, and confessed that he found it a real struggle to do so. He once said, "When I was a monk, I was adept in allegory. I allegorized everything." So, from the standpoint of preaching, the Reformation was a conscious, deliberate return to Biblical, grammatical-historical preaching. One might say that the Antiochan school was finally about to win out over the Alexandrine.

An Expository Emphasis

We must not think of Luther as a mere rabble-rouser, or a firebrand. Yes, he can burn hotly, but usually his sermons are solidly grounded on careful exegesis. Remember, he translated the entire Bible into German and lectured on various books of the Bible. Of his lectures on the Psalms, K. Bauer said,

This is the first scholarly exegetical work of the protestant church, for its day a masterpiece. One has difficulty in comprehending how it could ever have been written.

For Luther, Kooiman writes, "The distance between the lecture desk and the pulpit was slight" (*Luther and the Bible*, 1961, p. 193). Modern distinctions between preaching and Biblical exposition were unknown to him. His preaching almost always involved exposition and his lectures were always homiletical as well. There are about 2000 sermons extant.

In emphasis, Luther's work was prophetic rather than systematic. His writings often took on more of the flavor of tracts for the time than institutes for the church. He may be profitably studied for his prophetic spirit and stance. The analysis of his sermons for persuasive styles and techniques is useful. In preaching, the use of direct address and dialogue was frequent. He even used imaginary dialogue between himself and his congregation and between himself and his opponents to make points live and to involve the congregation in what he had to say. Luther's use of dialogue provides a useful source for such study.

His preaching was his sharpest weapon in his battle with Rome. He proved by actual practice the claim that the Bible could be taught to the masses and understood by them. In other words, the effects of his preaching on the common man was the strongest refutation of the sacerdotal position. It was through preaching that he demonstrated the Reformation claim about the priesthood of all believers.

Luther's Theory of Preaching

Luther once wrote:

*When I ascend the pulpit I see no heads but imagine those before me to be all blocks. When I preach I sink myself deeply down; I regard neither doctors nor masters of which there are in the church above 40. But I have an eye to the multitude of young people, children and servants, of which there are more than 2,000. I preach to them. When he preaches on any article, a man must first distinguish it, then define, describe and show what it is; thirdly, he must produce sentences from the Scripture to prove and strengthen it; fourthly, he must explain it by examples; fifthly, he must adorn it with similitudes; lastly he must admonish and arouse the indolent, correct the disobedient, and reprove the authors of false doctrine. (Grenville Kleiser, *The World's Great Sermons, Vol. I, NY, 1908, p. 114).*

That is as clear a summary of his theory of preaching as I know.

Luther's style is direct. His sermons as a rule are not long. Simplicity and clarity were his aim. When he first preached, it was in a convent chapel. Here he could use all of the theological jargon he wanted. But when he became pastor of the town church at Wittenberg, he soon discovered that he "must make himself understood," as he said, "by raw Saxons."

So, he gathered collections of German proverbs and country sayings and used these as illustrations and a medium for his message. The conscious effort to be understood was so successful that people said it was impossible to misunderstand him. Possibly the most valuable use one could make of Luther's sermons is to study his use of language, examples and sayings.

Luther was an extemporaneous preacher. He used only a brief outline with a few cues and catchwords. The sermons were written out on Monday and do not always correspond closely with the notes taken by hearers on Sunday.

Introductions and conclusions were short, if used at all. But he preached every day, sometimes twice a day.

TO THE DIET AT WORMS

In obedience to your commands given me yesterday, I stand here, beseeching you, as God is merciful, so to deign mercifully to listen to this cause, which is, as I believe, the cause of justice and of truth. And if through inexperience I should fail to apply to any his proper title, or offend in any way against the manners of courts, I entreat you to pardon me as one not conversant with courts, but rather with the cells of monks, and claiming no other merit than that of having spoken and written with that simplicity of mind which regards nothing but the glory of God and the pure instruction of the people of Christ.

Two questions have been proposed to me: Whether I acknowledge the books which are published in my name, and whether I am determined to defend or disposed to recall them. To the first of these I have given a direct answer, in which I shall ever persist that those books are mine and published by me, except so far as they may have been altered or interpolated by the craft or officiousness of rivals. To the other I am now about to reply; and I must first entreat your Majesty and your Highnesses to deign to consider that my books are not all of the same description. For there are some in which I have treated the piety of faith and morals with simplicity so evangelical that my very adversaries confess them to be profitable and harmless and deserving the perusal of a Christian. Even the Pope's bull, fierce and cruel as it is, admits some of my books to be innocent, though even these, with a monstrous perversity of judgment, it includes in the same sentence. If, then, I should think of retracting these, should I not stand alone in my condemnation of that truth which is acknowledged by the unanimous confession of all, whether friends or foes?

The second species of my publications is that in which I have inveighed against the papacy and the doctrine of the papists, as of men who by their iniquitous tenets and examples have desolated the Christian world, both with spiritual and temporal calamities. No man can deny or dissemble this. The sufferings and complaints of all mankind are my witnesses, that, through the laws of the Pope and the doctrines of men, the consciences of the faithful have been insnared, tortured, and torn in pieces, while, at the same time, their property and substance have been devoured by an incredible tyranny, and are still devoured without end and by degrading means, and that too, most of all, in this noble nation of Germany. Yet it is with them a perpetual statute, that the laws and doctrines of the Pope be held erroneous and reprobate when they are contrary to the Gospel and the opinions of the Fathers.

If, then, I shall retract these books, I shall do no other than add strength to tyranny and throw open doors to this great impiety, which will then stride forth more widely and licentiously than it has dared hitherto; so that the reign of iniquity will proceed with entire impunity, and, notwithstanding its intolerable oppression upon the suffering vulgar, be still further fortified and established; especially when it shall be proclaimed that I have been driven to this act by the authority of your serene Majesty and the whole Roman Empire. What a cloak, blessed Lord, should I then become for wickedness and despotism!

In a third description of my writings are those which I have published against individuals, against the defenders of the Roman tyranny and the subverters of the piety taught by men. Against these I do freely confess that I have written with more bitterness than was becoming either my religion or my profession; for, indeed, I lay no claim to any especial sanctity, and argue not respecting my own life, but respecting the doctrine of Christ. Yet even these writings it is impossible for me to retract, seeing that through such retraction despotism and impiety would reign under my patronage, and rage with more than their former ferocity against the people of God.

Yet since I am but man and not God, it would not become me to go further in defence of my tracts than my Lord Jesus went in defence of his doctrine; who, when he was interrogated before Annas, and received a blow from one of the officers, answered: "If I have spoken evil, bear witness of the evil; but if well, why smitest thou me?" If then the Lord himself, who knew his own infallibility, did not disdain to require arguments against his doctrine even from a person of low condition, how much rather ought I, who am the dregs of the earth and the very slave of error, to inquire and search if there be any to bear witness against my doctrine! Wherefore, I entreat you, by the mercies of God, that if there be any one of any condition who has that ability, let him overpower me by the sacred writings, prophetical and evangelical. And for my own part, as soon as I shall be better instructed I will retract my errors and be the first to cast my books into the flames.

It must now, I think, be manifest that I have sufficiently examined and weighed, not only the dangers, but the parties and dissensions excited in the world by means of my doctrine, of which I was yesterday so gravely admonished. But I must avow that to me it is of all others the most delightful spectacle to see parties and dissensions growing up on account of the word of God, for such is the progress of God's word, such its ends and object. "Think not I am come to send peace on earth; I came not to send peace, but a sword. For I am come to set a man at variance against his father, and the daughter against her mother, and the daughter-in-law against her mother-in-law; and a man's foes shall be those of his own household."

Moreover we should reflect that our God is wonderful and terrible in his counsels; so that his work, which is now the object of so much solicitude, if we should found it in the condemnation of the word of God, may be turned by his providence into a deluge of intolerable calamity; and the reign of this young and excellent prince (in whom is our hope after God) not only should begin, but should continue and close under the most glowing auspices.

I could show more abundantly by reference to Scriptural examples—to those of Pharaoh, the King of Babylon, the kings of Israel—that they have brought about their own destruction by those very counsels of worldly wisdom which seemed to promise them peace and stability. For it is he who taketh the wise in their craftiness and removeth the mountains, and they know not, and overturneth them in his anger. So that it is the work of God to fear God. Yet I say not these things as if the great personages here present stood at all in need of my admonitions, but only because it was a service which I owed to my native Germany, and it was my duty to discharge it. And thus I commend myself to your serene Majesty and all the princes, humbly beseeching you not to allow the malice of my enemies to render me odious to you without a cause. I have done.

("Having delivered this address in German," says Doctor Waddington, "Luther was commanded to recite it in Latin. For a moment he hesitated; his breath was exhausted, and he was oppressed by the heat and throng of the surrounding multitude. One of the Saxon courtiers even advised him to excuse himself from obedience; but he presently collected his powers again, and repeated his speech with few variations and equal animation in the other language. His tone was that of supplication rather than remonstrance, and there was something of diffidence in his manner . . . . No sooner had he ceased than he was reminded, in a tone of reproach, that they were not assembled to discuss matters which had long ago been decided to councils, but that a simple answer was required of him to a simple question—whether he would retract or not. Then Luther continued—")

Since your most serene Majesty and the princes require a simple answer, I will give it thus: Unless I shall be convinced by proofs from Scripture or by evident reason—for I believe neither in Popes nor councils, since they have frequently both erred and contradicted themselves—I cannot choose but adhere to the word of God, which has possession of my conscience; nor can I possibly, nor will I ever make any recantation, since it is neither safe nor honest to act contrary to conscience! Here I stand; I cannot do otherwise; so help me God! Amen.

(Translated by Dr. George Waddington.)

SERMON ON LUKE 10:23-37

I hope that you rightly understand this Gospel, it being preached every year; we shall consider it again. First, the evangelist says that Christ took his disciples aside and said to them secretly, "Blessed are the eyes which see the things that ye see: for I tell you that many prophets and kings have desired to see those things which ye see, and have not seen them; and to hear those things which ye hear, and have not heard them." To see and hear, is to be understood in this place, simply of outward seeing and hearing; that is, that they saw Christ come in the flesh, heard his sermons and were present at those miracles that he did among the Jews. The Jews saw the same according to the flesh, and felt them also; yet they did not truly acknowledge him for Christ, as the apostles did. And especially Peter, who in the name of all the rest did confess him, saying, "Thou art Christ, the son of the living God." We grant, indeed, that there were some among the Jews who acknowledged him, as did the apostles, but the number of them was very small. That is why he takes his apostles apart to himself.

Many prophets and kings have seen Christ in the spirit; as the Lord himself says to the Jews concerning Abraham, "Your father Abraham rejoiced to see my day: and he saw it, and was glad" (John 8:56). The Jews thought that he had spoken of bodily seeing; but he spoke of spiritual seeing, by which all Christian hearts beheld him before he was born. Now, if Abraham saw him, undoubtedly many other prophets in whom the Holy Ghost was, saw him also. And although this seeing saved the holy fathers and prophets, yet they always with inward and hearty affection desire to see Christ in the flesh, as is plainly shown in the prophets. That is why the Lord says to his disciples, who saw him both in the flesh and in the spirit, "Blessed are the eyes which see the things which ye see." It is as if he had said: now is the acceptable year and time of grace; the matter is so weighty and precious that the eyes that see it are said to be blessed. Now the Gospel was preached openly and manifestly both by Christ and also by his apostles. So he here calls them all blessed who see and hear such grace as I have preached much and a long time to you. I would to God that you keep that which I have spoken fresh in memory.

When the Lord spoke these things, a certain lawyer stood up, showing himself, as he thought, to be some great one who, tempting the Lord, says, "Master, what shall I do to inherit eternal life?" This lawyer was endued with wisdom and not unskillful in the Scriptures, which even his answer declares. Yet in this place he is proved a fool. He is brought to shame and ignominy; Christ takes away all his glorying in one word. Believing that he had observed the whole law, and that he was a chief one, with respect to others, as undoubtedly he was, he thought himself sufficiently worthy by reason of his godliness and learning to carry on such a conversation with the Lord. But what does the Lord do in this case? The following text declares: "And he said unto him, what is written in the law? how readest thou? he answered and said, Thou shalt love the Lord thy God with all thy heart, and with all thy soul, and with all thy strength and with all thy mind, and thy neighbor as thyself. Then he said unto him, thou hast answered right; do this and thou shalt live." I think the Lord gave this good man a hard lesson; he deals very plainly with him, and puts him to shame openly, before all. He proves that he who thought that he had done all things had done nothing.

If I had time, many things might be said about the two commandments. They are the chief and greatest commandments in Moses, on which the whole law and all the prophets hang, as Christ himself says in Matthew. If we consider the commandments of Moses, we find that they have to do with love. This commandment, "Thou shalt have no other gods before me," we cannot declare or interpret in any other way than this: You must love God alone. So Moses expounded, where he says, "Hear, O Israel: the Lord our God is one Lord: and thou shalt love the Lord thy God with all thine heart, and with all thy soul, and with all thy might" (Deuteronomy 6:4,5) from which the lawyer got his answer. But the Jews think that this commandment extends no farther than that they should not set up or worship idols. And if they can say and witness that they have only one God, and worship none but him, they think they have observed this commandment. In the same way this lawyer understood it, but that was an evil and wrong understanding.

We must otherwise consider and understand this precept, "Thou shalt have no other gods before me." Thou, it saith, with all that you are, but especially all your heart, soul and strength. It speaks not of the tongue, not of the hand or the knees, but of the whole man, whatever you art and have. That no other god may be worshiped by me, it is necessary that I have the true and only God in my heart; that is, I must love him from my heart, so that I always depend upon him, trust in him, place my hope in him, have my pleasure, love and joy in him, and daily remember him. If we take pleasure in anything, we say, "It does me good inwardly at the heart," and if anyone speaks, or laughs, and doesn't mean it from his heart, we are apt to say, "He speaks or laughs, indeed, but it doesn't come from the heart." The love of the heart in the Scriptures signifies a vehement and special love that we ought to bear toward God. They who serve God with mouth, hands and knees only, are hypocrites, and God won't accept them because he will not have part, but the whole.

The Jews outwardly abstained from idolatry, and served God alone in mouth; but their hearts were far removed from him, being full of diffidence and unbelief. Outwardly they seemed to be very earnest in serving God, but within they were full of idolatry. So the Lord said unto them, "Woe unto you, scribes and Pharisees, hypocrites! for ye are like unto whited sepulchres, which indeed appear beautiful outward, but are within full of dead men's bones, and of all uncleanness. Even so ye also outwardly appear righteous unto men, but within ye are full of hypocrisy and iniquity" (Matthew 23:37). These are those wicked ones who glory in the outward thing, who go about to justify and make themselves good by their own works, after the manner of this lawyer. Consider how great the pride of this man was; he comes forth as though he could not be blessed or rebuked of the Lord. He thought, yea, it seemed to him, that the Lord would commend and praise his life before the people. He wasn't thinking about learning anything from the Lord, but sought only his own commendation. He would willingly have had Christ set forth his praise, toward him the eyes of all were bent, and who was an admiration to all. So all hypocrites outwardly pretend to excellent, great and weighty works.

They say that they have respect neither to glory nor praise, but in their hearts they are full of ambition, and wish that their holiness were known to the whole world. All those who most grievously offend against the first commandment are like this lawyer. They think that God is to be loved no more than the sound of the words, and that thereby it is fulfilled. The commandment therefore remains in their mouth, and floats above the heart but doesn't pierce it. I must go farther; I must so love God that I can be content to forsake all creatures for his sake, and if required, my body and life: I must love him above all things, for he is jealous, and cannot allow anything to be loved above him. But under him he permits us to love anything. Even as the husband allows his wife to love her maids, the house, household things and such, yet he doesn't allow her to love anything with that love wherewith she is bound to him, but will have her leave all such things for his sake. Again, the wife requires the same of her husband. In the same manner, God allows us to love his creatures since they are created and are good.

The sun, gold and silver, and whatever by nature is pleasant, procures our love, which makes it dear to us; neither is God offended at that. But that I should cleave to the creature, and love it equally with him, he will not allow; indeed, he will have me both deny and forsake all these things when he requires it of me, and will have me to be content even if I never see the sun, money or riches. The love of the creature must be far inferior to the love of the Creator. As he is the Sovereign, he insists that I love him above all other things, if he will not allow me to love anything equally with him, much less will he allow me to love anything above him. You see now what I think it is to love God with all the heart, with all the soul and with all the mind. To love God with all the heart is to love him above all creatures; that is, although creatures are very amiable and dear to me, and that I take great delight in them, yet must I so love them, that I condemn and forsake them if my Lord requires it of me.

To love God with all the soul is to give up our whole life and body at his pleasure; so that if the love of the creature or any creature or any temptation assail us or would overcome us, we may say, I had rather part with all these than forsake my God; whether he cast me off, or destroy me, or whatever through his permission shall come upon me. I had rather leave all things than him. Whatever I have and am, I will give up, but him I will not forsake. The soul, in the Scriptures, signifies the life of the body, and whatever is done by the five senses—as eating, drinking, sleeping, waking, seeing, hearing, smelling, tasting and whatever the soul accomplishes by the body. To love God with all the strength is, for his cause, to renounce all the members and limbs of the body, so that one will expose to peril both flesh and body, before he will commit that which is unjust against God. To love God with all the mind is to do nothing but what will please him.

You perceive now what is contained in this commandment of God. You, you, he says, and that wholly—not your hands, not your mouth, not your knees alone, but every part of you. They who do these things, as it is said, do truly fulfill it: but no man lives on earth that does so; we all do otherwise. So the law makes us all sinners; not so much as the least jot or point thereof is fulfilled by them that are most holy in this world. No man cleaves with all his heart to God, and leaves all things for his sake. How can it be that we should love God when his will is not settled in our mind? If I love God, I cannot but love his will also. If God sends sickness, poverty, shame and ignominy, it is his will, at which we murmur; our minds are carried here and there; we bear it very impatiently. We, like this Pharisee and lawyer, lead an honest life outwardly; we worship God, we serve him, we fast, we pray, we behave ourselves in outward appearance justly and holy. But God doesn't require that of us; he wants us to bend ourselves to do his will with pleasure and love, cheerfully and lovingly. Whatever the Lord says to the lawyer, he says to us all: that we have yet done nothing, but that all things remain yet to be done. All men are therefore guilty of death and subject to Satan. All men are liars, vain and filthy; and to whatever they pretend, it is worth nothing. We are wise in worldly matters, we scrape together money and goods, we speak pleasantly before men, and cunningly propound and set forth our case. What does God care about these things? He requires us to love him with our whole heart, which no man living is able to perform of himself; therefore it is inferred that we are all sinners, but especially those whose life has a goodly outward show only.

Having discussed the former part of the text, namely, the preaching of the law, now follows the other part, which is the preaching of the Gospel—which declares how we may fulfill the law, and how that that fulfilling takes place by it, which we shall learn from the Samaritan.

What does the lawyer do after the Lord had thus dealt with him? He, says the evangelist, willing to justify himself, spoke to the Lord, and asked him, "Who is my neighbor?" He asked not "Who is my God?" It is as if he said, "I owe nothing to God, neither do I want anything of him; indeed, it seems to me that I do not owe anything to man; nevertheless, I would like to know who is my neighbor." The Lord answering him, uses a powerful example in which he declares that we are all neighbors one to another—both he who gives a benefit and he who receives or needs one—although by the text it seems to appear that he only is a neighbor who bestows a benefit upon another. But the Scripture makes no difference: sometimes calling him our neighbor who bestows a benefit, and sometimes him that receives it.

By this example the Lord infers, "Go, and do thou likewise," so that the lawyer had offended not only God but also man, and was destitute of love both of God and his neighbor. This wretched man is brought into such a situation that he is found to be altogether evil, even from the head to the feet. How is it that he being so skillful in the Scripture, was not aware of this? He led a pharisaical, hypocritical and counterfeit life, which had no regard to his neighbor or to aid and help others; but sought thereby only glory and honor before men, and thought by negligent and dissolute living to get to heaven. But you have heard very often that a Christian life consists of this: that we deal with faith and the heart in things that pertain to God, and labor in life and words for our neighbors. But we must not wait until our neighbor seeks a benefit and requires something of us; it is our duty to prevent his asking, and of our own accord offer our liberality to him.

We will now see what is contained in the parable. The Samaritan, in this place, is without doubt our Lord Jesus Christ, who has declared his love toward God and man. Toward God, in descending from heaven, being made incarnate and fulfilling the will of his Father. Toward man, when, after baptism, he began to preach, to work miracles, to heal the sick. Neither was there any work that he did which concerned himself only, but all that he did was directed toward his neighbors; being made our minister, even though he is above all, and equal with God. But he did all these things knowing that they pleased God, and that it was the will of his Father. When he had fulfilled the commandment that he love God with all his heart, he committed his life and whatever he had to the will of his Father, saying: "Father, behold all that I have is thine; I leave for thy sake the glory and honor which I have had among men, yea, and all things, that the world may know how much I love thee."

This is that Samaritan, who, without being asked to do so, came and fulfilled the law. He alone fulfilled it, and that praise none can take from him. He alone deserved it, and to him alone it applies. He, being touched with pity, has compassion on the wounded man, binds up his wounds, brings him to an inn, and provides for him. This applies to us: the man who lies wounded, beaten, spoiled and half dead, is Adam; and we also. The thieves which wounded and left us in this deplorable situation are the devils. We are not able to help ourselves, and should we be left in this situation, we should die through anguish and distress; our wounds would become festered, and our afflictions exceedingly great.

This excellent parable is set before us to show us what we are, and what is the strength of our reason and free will. If that wretched man had attempted to help himself, his case would have been made worse; he would have hurt himself, he would have opened his wounds anew by exertion, and so would have fallen into greater calamity. Again, if he had been left lying, without assistance, his case would have been the same. So it is when we are left to ourselves; our efforts and endeavors amount to nothing. Numerous ways and different means have been invented to amend our lives and get to heaven. One man found out this way, another that; as a result innumerable sorts of orders have increased, letters of indulgences, pilgrimages to Saints, and so forth, which have always made the state of Christianity worse. This is the world, which is represented by this wounded man: he being laden with sins, fainting under a heavy burden and not able to help himself.

But the Samaritan who fulfilled the law is perfectly sound and whole. He does more than either the priest or Levite. He binds up his wounds, pours in oil and wine, sets him upon his own beast, brings him to an inn, makes provisions for him, and, when he departs, diligently commends him to the host, and leaves with him sufficient to pay his expenses—none of which either the priest or Levite did. By the priest is signified the holy fathers who flourished before Moses; the Levite is a representation of the priesthood of the Old Testament. All these could do nothing by their works, but passed by like unto this priest and Levite; wherefore, though I had all the good works of Noah, Abraham and all the faithful leaders, they would profit me nothing.

The priest and Levite saw the miserable man lying there wounded, but they could not help him; they saw him lie half dead, but could not give him any remedy. The holy fathers saw men drowned and plunged all over in sin; they also felt the sting and anguish of it, but they could make the case no better. These were the preachers of the law, which shows what the world is: namely, that it is full of sin, and lieth half dead and cannot help itself with its utmost strength and reason. But Christ is that true Samaritan, who is moved with the case of the miserable man: he binds up his wounds, and taking great care of him, pours in oil and wine, which is the pure Gospel. He pours in oil when grace is preached; when it is said, "O miserable man, this is your unbelief, this is your condemnation; thus you are wounded and sick. But I will show you a remedy: join yourself to this Samaritan, Christ the Saviour; he will help and aid you."

The nature of oil, as we know, is to make soft and mollify; so the sweet and gentle preaching of the Gospel makes the heart soft and tender toward God and our neighbors. Sharp wine signifies the cross of affliction, which follows: there is no cause for a Christian to seek the cross, for it sooner hangs over his head than he is aware of. As Paul witnesseth, "All that will live godly in Christ Jesus shall suffer persecution" (II Timothy 3:12). This is the emblem and badge of this King; and he that is ashamed of it, does not belong to him. Moreover, the Samaritan puts the wounded man upon his own beast: this is the Lord Jesus Christ, who supports us, and carries us upon his shoulders. There is scarce a more amiable and comfortable passage in the whole Scripture than that where Christ compares himself to a shepherd, who carrieth again the lost sheep upon his shoulders to the flock.

The inn is the state of Christianity in this world, in which we must remain for a short time; the host is the ministers and preachers of the Gospel, whose charge is to have care of us. This, therefore, is the sum of the text: the kingdom of Christ is a kingdom of mercy and grace; Christ bears our defects and infirmities; he takes our sins upon himself, and bears our fall willingly, we daily lie upon his neck. And he doesn't grow weary of carrying us. It is the duty of the preachers of this kingdom to comfort consciences, to handle them gently, to feed them with the Gospel, to bear the weak, to heal the sick; they ought fitly to apply the Word according to the need of everyone.

This is the duty of a true bishop and preacher, not to proceed by violence, as is the custom of some bishops at the present day, who vex, torment and cry out, "He that will not willingly do it, shall be compelled to do it." We must in no wise proceed in this manner; but a bishop or preacher ought to behave himself as a healer of the sick, who deals very tenderly with them, uttering very loving words, talking gently, and making every effort to do them good. A bishop or minister ought to consider his parish as a hospital, in which are such as are afflicted with different kinds of disease. If Christ be thus preached, faith and love come together, and fulfill the commandment of love.

CALVIN
(1509 - 1564)

Life

John Calvin, the son of an ecclesiastical lawyer, was born July 10, 1509 in Noyon, Picardy, France. He began to prepare for the ministry in Paris, but his father removed him from that course of study and sent him to law school at the University of Orleans where he studied from 1527-1528. He then transferred to the law school at the University of Bourges. While there, he preached in two village churches (Lignieres and Asnieres). His father died in 1531, and John went back to Paris. One year later, he published a commentary on Seneca's treatise, *De Clementia.* His brilliance was immediately recognized and his career seemed assured. But in 1533 he got into trouble. His friend Nicholas Cop was accused of teaching Lutheran doctrine in his rectoral address which, it is almost certain, Calvin wrote for him.

As a result, Calvin fled Paris, arriving in Basil, Switzerland in 1535. There, he published his first version of the *Institutes* in March 1536. The same month he went to Ferrara, Italy. Then, in 1536, he headed for Strasbourg by way of Geneva. The Protestant preacher Farel intercepted him and by means of a threat induced him to remain there as a pastor. The council minutes first speak of Farel and Calvin as preachers on July 3, 1537. Under the influence of factions that were opposed to his faithful, Biblical approach, he was exiled from Geneva from 1538-1541. During this exile, Calvin settled in Strasbourg where he became the pastor of a French church. He lectured or preached every day. At Strasbourg he was almost destitute; he took in lodgers and sold his books. But it was here, in August 1540, that he married a widow, Idelette de Bure, who was a member of the congregation.

By request, he returned to Geneva, arriving September 13, 1541. Calvin left a very interesting account of his first sermon after returning:

> Entirely omitting any mention of those matters which they all expected with certainty to hear, I gave a short account of our office . . . After this preface, I took up the exposition where I had stopped—by which I indicated that I had interrupted my office of preaching for a time rather than that I had given it up entirely.

On February 12, 1545, referring to the government and morality of Geneva, Calvin wrote to Viret: "Already I have broken ground upon the internal state of the city in ten sermons." This statement is significant. It shows clearly two things: Calvin intended to change the life of the entire city in which he was ministering and, secondly, he proposed to do it through preaching. Perhaps one of the reasons why preachers today have so little impact on their communities is because, unlike Calvin, they have no such vision and no such faith in God's blessing of the preaching of His Word. They think small and expect little.

Later the same year (November 4), he preached a "war sermon" when he heard that Papal forces had started a war in Germany against the Christians there. (His text was Psalm 115.) Just one week after, he preached a "victory" sermon (Psalm 124). These were his first two published sermons. It was Calvin's custom to preach without either notes or manuscript. They were taken down in note form, yet he may have written them out fully after preaching.

In 1546 he preached through Isaiah, and from 1546-48 he was in the Psalms. He was rebuked three times in 1548 for preaching about the City Council (note the contemporary, fearless nature of his preaching). In October 1549 he began to preach once a day, every other week. There are

2023 sermons in the public library of Geneva, only a few of which are available in modern English. Nearly all were taken down by his secretary. Calvin's asthma helped the secretary to get every word because it forced him to speak slowly and deliberately. He died May 27, 1564.

As a result of his ministry, Geneva was utterly transformed and remained a model of piety for over 150 years.

Calvin's Preaching Method

Calvin's commentaries were the fruit of his preaching and lecturing. In effect, you could say that the sermons were the commentaries applied. His sermons were mostly continuous expositions of Bible books, but they were not merely a running commentary with application. They were well-developed, modified homilies. Now and then he interrupted these expositions for occasional sermons. The average length of the Old Testament expository passages from which he preached was just under five verses, and the average for the New Testament was two to three verses. Unlike a number of his followers today, Calvin believed in short sermons.

Behind his preaching was careful preparation. He slept little and worked long. One sermon format that he used consisted of:
1. Prayer
2. Recapitulation of the previous sermon
3. Exegesis and exposition of the first point in the passage
4. Application of this and exhortation to duty
5. #3 and #4 repeated as many times as there were additional points
6. Summary and prayer

Sometimes the sermons lack unity. One in Job on patience abruptly shifts to a discussion of angels. If Calvin had not had so much to say, and if he had not said it so well, this format, repeated sermon after sermon might well have grown boring. Introductions and conclusions were often like this: "We saw yesterday . . . , " "We have seen this morning . . . , " "We will have to save the rest for tomorrow . . . . "

However, there is another feature of Calvin's sermons which deserves attention. There are sermons in which Calvin shows such great concern to preach relevantly that the text, while undergirding his remarks at every point, hardly appears at all. In these sermons—as well as in the more expository ones—Calvin always preaches from his text to the congregation. Unlike so many modern preachers, he preached not about David, Job, Paul or Peter, but about *God* and the *listener*. A good example of this sort of preaching is Calvin's first sermon on the book of Titus. Here, you can see how he began with the congregation *not* with the text.

Calvin's sermons carry frequent remarks like: "The Holy Spirit here says to us . . . . " No one listening to his preaching would ever get the idea that the Bible was a Book dealing with persons and times long ago and far away. As he preached it, the listener would recognize that the Bible was addressed to the persons seated before him every bit as truly as it was to its first recipients.

This is an extremely important matter that points up the critical difference between good Reformation preaching and most of the inferior preaching of today. Modern preachers—especially those who purport to be Calvinists—have followed a modified form of the scholastic-Puritan *lecture* sermon rather than the true *preaching* style of the reformers. They might do well to follow Calvin's example of preaching *to* the congregation *about* God *from* the Bible, rather than preach *about the Bible* and people who lived long ago and far away.

If anything in the preaching stance of Calvin and the other reformers accounts for the difference in results between then and now, this is it. (For more on the whole matter of stance in preaching and the distinction between the preaching and the lecture stance, see my book *Preaching with Purpose*.)

Calvin's congregation included scholars, leaders and preachers from all over the western world (eg., John Knox), many of whom were refugees. He was a preacher's preacher. Yet, unlike what might be expected if you have read only his *Institutes* or his commentaries, Calvin did not preach to scholars in a scholastic manner. His concern was first of all for them as persons. For instance, in his sermon on II Timothy 4:1,2 he says, "... it is not enough to preach the law of God and the promises, and whatever else is contained in the holy Scripture, as though a man should teach in a school; but we must apply, threaten and exhort."

Calvin cared about how the congregation listened and advised them not to eat too much breakfast before coming to the service.

Calvin's Style

Calvin's forte was clarity and content, both of which should be studied along with his expository method. Fairbairn declared, "Modern oratory may be said to have begun with Calvin, and indeed, to be his creation." Parker wrote, "Alone among his contemporaries Calvin writes and preaches in the modern style." Bossert says, "He approximates the prose of the seventeenth century." He spoke extemporaneously and said that written sermons hindered the power of God. Out of this conviction, Calvin even went so far as to criticize preachers in the Church of England for using manuscripts.

According to these accounts, Calvin is the first, great modern preacher. Calvin's sermons should be studied not only for content and clarity, but also for simplicity. He studiously avoided using periodic sentences, scholastic syllogisms, enthymemes and other rhetorical devices calculated to impress the hearer. In other words, the classical rhetoric and, especially, the Aristotelian-scholastic rhetoric was laid aside and a more Biblical style of preaching was developed.

There was also a soberness in his preaching. Beza, who knew him well, said, *Tot verba tot pondera*—"Every word weighed a pound." When preaching, Calvin rarely quotes. He walks, rarely soars. He seldom uses extended examples or anecdotes. He can assail his opponents with vigor and vividness, however. His metaphors are frequently mixed, and his imagery is full, coming primarily from the military, legal, scholastic areas and from the workshop, nature and animals.

A careful, precise use of words with a scarcity of adjectives characterized his preaching. With his command of nouns and verbs he needed few adjectives. There was a frequent use of colloquialisms and proverbs, many relating to country life, although Calvin's language is not so vigorous or colorful as Luther's.

William Perkins's *Arte of Prophecying* (1592) is an attempt to systematize Calvin's preaching methods, but English speaking preachers never adopted them except, perhaps, in the area of style. By the end of the 17th century the Reformation sermon and the expository homily largely lost out in England. Sadly, Puritanism reverted to the deadening, scholastic methodology of which, in modified forms, we have become the unfortunate heirs.

SERMON ON ENDURING PERSECUTION

"Let us go forth out of the tents after Christ, bearing his reproach." (Hebrews 12:13)

All the exhortations which can be given us to suffer patiently for the name of Jesus Christ, and in defense of the gospel, will have no effect if we do not feel assured of the cause for which we fight. For when we are called to part with life it is absolutely necessary to know on what grounds. The firmness necessary we cannot possess unless it be founded on certainty of faith.

It is true that persons may be found who will foolishly expose themselves to death in maintaining some absurd opinions and reveries conceived by their own brain, but such impetuosity is more to be regarded as frenzy than as Christian zeal; and, in fact, there is neither firmness nor sound sense in those who thus, at a kind of haphazard, cast themselves away. But, however this may be, it is in a good cause only that God can acknowledge us as his martyrs. Death is common to all, and the children of God are condemned to ignominy and tortures just as criminals are; but God makes the distinction between them, inasmuch as he cannot deny his truth.

On our part, then, it is requisite that we have sure and infallible evidence of the doctrine which we maintain; and hence, as I have said, we cannot be rationally impressed by any exhortations which we receive to suffer persecution for the gospel, if no true certainty of faith has been imprinted in our hearts. For to hazard our life upon a peradventure is not natural, and though we were to do it, it would only be rashness, not Christian courage. In a word, nothing that we do will be approved of God if we are not thoroughly persuaded that it is for him and his cause we suffer persecution and the world is our enemy.

Now, when I speak of such persuasion, I mean not merely that we must know how to distinguish between true religion and the abuses or follies of men, but also that we must be thoroughly persuaded of the heavenly life, and the crown which is promised us above, after we shall have fought here below. Let us understand, then, that both of these requisites are necessary, and cannot be separated from each other. The points, accordingly, with which we must commence, are these: We must know well what our Christianity is, what the faith which we have to hold and follow—what the rule which God has given us; and we must be so well furnished with such instructions as to be able boldly to condemn all the falsehoods, errors, and superstitions which Satan has introduced to corrupt the pure simplicity of the doctrine of God. Hence we ought not to be surprised that, in the present day, we see so few persons disposed to suffer for the gospel, and that the greater part of those who call themselves Christians know not what it is. For all are as it were lukewarm, and, instead of making it their business to hear or read, count it enough to have had some slight taste of Christian faith. This is the reason why there is so little decision, and why those who are assailed immediately fall away. This fact should stimulate us to inquire more diligently into divine truth, in order to be well assured with regard to it.

Still, however, to be well informed and grounded is not the whole that is necessary. For we see some who seem to be thoroughly imbued with sound doctrine, and who, notwithstanding, have no more zeal or affection than if they had never known any more of God than some fleeting fancy. Why is this? Just because they have never comprehended the majesty of the holy Scriptures. And, in fact, did we, such as we are, consider well that it is God who speaks to us, it is certain that we would listen more attentively and with greater reverence. If we would think that in reading Scripture we are in the school of angels, we would be far more careful and desirous to profit by the doctrine which is propounded to us.

We now see the true method of preparing to suffer for the gospel. First, we must have profited so far in the school of God as to be decided in regard to true religion and the doctrine which we are to hold; and we must despise all the wiles and impostures of Satan, and all human inventions, as things not only frivolous but also carnal, inasmuch as they corrupt Christian purity; therein differing, like true martyrs of Christ, from the fantastic persons who suffer for mere absurdities. Second, feeling assured of the good cause, we must be inflamed, accordingly, to follow God whithersoever he may call us: his word must have such authority with us as it deserves, and, having withdrawn from this world, we must feel as it were enraptured in seeking the heavenly life.

But it is more than strange that, though the light of God is shining more brightly than it ever did before, there is a lamentable want of zeal! If the thought does not fill us with shame, so much the worse. For we must shortly come before the great Judge, where the iniquity which we endeavor to hide will be brought forward with such upbraidings that we shall be utterly confounded. For, if we are obliged to bear testimony to God according to the measure of the knowledge which he has given us, to what is it owing, I would ask, that we are so cold and timorous in entering into battle, seeing that God has so fully manifested himself at this time that he may be said to have opened to us and displayed before us the great treasures of his secrets? May it not be said that we do not think we have to do with God? For had we any regard to his majesty we would not dare to turn the doctrine which proceeds from his mouth into some kind of philosophic speculation. In short, it is impossible to deny that it is to our great shame, not to say fearful condemnation, that we have so well known the truth of God and have so little courage to maintain it!

Above all, when we look to the martyrs of past times, well may we detest our own cowardice! The greater part of those were not persons much versed in holy Scripture, so as to be able to dispute on all subjects. They knew that there was one God, whom they behoved to worship and serve; that they had been redeemed by the blood of Jesus Christ, in order that they might place their confidence of salvation in him and in his grace; and that, all the inventions of men being mere dross and rubbish, they ought to condemn all idolatries and superstitions. In one word, their theology was in substance this: There is one God, who created all the world, and declared his will to us by Moses and the Prophets, and finally by Jesus Christ and his apostles; and we have one sole Redeemer, who purchased us by his blood, and by whose grace we hope to be saved; all the idols of the world are cursed, and deserve execration.

With a system embracing no other points than these, they went boldly to the flames or to any other kind of death. They did not go in twos or threes, but in such bands that the number of those who fell by the hands of tyrants is almost infinite. We, on our part, are such learned clerks, that none can be more so (so at least we think), and, in fact, so far as regards the knowledge of Scripture, God has so spread it out before us that no former age was ever so highly favored. Still, after all, there is scarcely a particle of zeal. When men manifest such indifference it looks as if they were bent on provoking the vengeance of God.

What, then, should be done in order to inspire our breasts with true courage? We have, in the first place, to consider how precious the Confession of our Faith is in the sight of God. We little know how much God prizes it, if our life, which is nothing, is valued by us more highly. When it is so, we manifest a marvellous degree of stupidity. We cannot save our life at the expense of our confession without acknowledging that we hold it in higher estimation than the honor of God and the salvation of our souls.

A heathen could say that "it was a miserable thing to save life by giving up only things which made life desirable!" And yet he and others like him never knew for what end men are placed in the world and why they live in it. It is true they knew enough to say that men ought to follow virtue, to conduct themselves honestly and without reproach; but all their virtues were mere paint and smoke. We know far better what the chief aim of life should be, namely, to glorify God, in order that he may be our glory. When this is not done, woe to us! And we cannot continue to live for a single moment upon the earth without heaping additional curses on our heads. Still we are not ashamed to purchase some few days to languish here below, renouncing the eternal kingdom by separating ourselves from him by whose energy we are sustained in life.

Were we to ask the most ignorant, not to say the most brutish persons in the world, why they live, they would not venture to answer simply that it is to eat and drink and sleep; for all know that they have been created for a higher and holier end. And what end can we find if it be not to honor God, and allow ourselves to be governed by him, like children by a good parent; so that after we have finished the journey of this corruptible life we may be received into his eternal inheritance? Such is the principal, indeed the sole end. When we do not take it into account, and are intent on a brutish life, which is worse than a thousand deaths, what can we allege for our excuse? To live and not know why is unnatural. To reject the causes for which we live, under the influence of a foolish longing for a respite of some few days, during which we are to live in the world while separated from God—I know not how to name such infatuation and madness.

But as persecution is always harsh and bitter, let us consider how and by what means Christians may be able to fortify themselves with patience, so as unflinchingly to expose their life for the truth of God. The text which we have read out, when it is properly understood, is sufficient to induce us to do so. The Apostle says, "Let us go forth from the city after the Lord Jesus, bearing his reproach." In the first place he reminds us, although the swords should not be drawn over us nor the fires kindled to burn us, that we cannot be truly united to the Son of God while we are rooted in this world. Wherefore, a Christian, even in repose, must always have one foot lifted to march to battle, and not only so, but he must have his affections withdrawn from the world, although his body is dwelling in it. Grant that this at first sight seems to us hard, still we must be satisfied with the words of St. Paul, "We are called and appointed to suffer." As if he had said, Such is our condition as Christians; this is the road by which we must go if we would follow Christ.

Meanwhile, to solace our infirmity and mitigate the vexation and sorrow which persecution might cause us, a good reward is held forth: In suffering for the cause of God we are walking step by step after the Son of God and have him for our guide. Were it simply said that to be Christians we must pass through all the insults of the world boldly, to meet death at all times and in whatever way God may be pleased to appoint, we might apparently have some pretext for replying, It is a strange road to go at a peradventure. But when we are commanded to follow the Lord Jesus, his guidance is too good and honorable to be refused. Now, in order that we may be more deeply moved, not only is it said that Jesus Christ walks before us as our Captain, but that we are made conformable to his image; as St. Paul speaks in the eighth chapter to the Romans, "God hath ordained all those whom he hath adopted for his children, to be made conformable to him who is the pattern and head of all."

Are we so delicate as to be unwilling to endure anything? Then we must renounce the grace of God by which he has called us to the hope of salvation. For there are two things which cannot be separated,—to be members of Christ and to be tried by many afflictions. We certainly ought to prize such a conformity to the Son of God much more than we do. It is true that in the world's judgment there is disgrace in suffering for the gospel. But since we know that unbelievers are blind, ought we not to have better eyes than they? It is ignominy to suffer from those who occupy the seat of justice, but St. Paul shows us by his example that we have to glory in scourgings for Jesus Christ, as marks by which God recognises us and avows us for his own. And we know what St. Luke narrates of Peter and John, namely, that they rejoiced to have been "counted worthy to suffer infamy and reproach for the name of the Lord Jesus."

Ignominy and dignity are two opposites: so says the world which, being infatuated, judges against all reason, and in this way converts the glory of God into dishonor. But, on our part, let us not refuse to be vilified as concerns the world, in order to be honored before God and his angels. We see what pains the ambitious take to receive the commands of a king, and what a boast they make of it. The Son of God presents his commands to us, and every one stands back! Tell me, pray, whether in so doing are we worthy of having anything in common with him? There is nothing here to attract our sensual nature, but such, notwithstanding, are the true escutcheons of nobility in the heavens. Imprisonment, exile, evil report, imply in men's imagination whatever is to be vituperated; but what hinders us from viewing things as God judges and declares them, save our unbelief? Wherefore let the Name of the Son of God have all the weight with us which it deserves, that we may learn to count it honor when he stamps his marks upon us. If we act otherwise our ingratitude is insupportable.

Were God to deal with us according to our deserts, would he not have just cause to chastise us daily in a thousand ways? Nay, more, a hundred thousand deaths would not suffice for a small portion of our misdeeds! Now, if in his infinite goodness he puts all our faults under his foot and abolishes them, and, instead of punishing us according to our demerit, devises an admirable means to convert our afflictions into honor and a special privilege, inasmuch as through them we are taken into partnership with his Son, must it not be said, when we disdain such a happy state, that we have indeed made little progress in Christian doctrine?

Accordingly St. Peter, after exhorting us to walk so purely in the fear of God as "not to suffer as thieves, adulterers, and murderers," immediately adds, "If we must suffer as Christians, let us glorify God for the blessing which he thus bestows upon us." It is not without cause he speaks thus. For who are we, I pray, to be witnesses of the truth of God, and advocates to maintain his cause? Here we are poor worms of the earth, creatures full of vanity, full of lies, and yet God employs us to defend his truth—an honor which pertains not even to the angels of heaven! May not this consideration alone well inflame us to offer ourselves to God to be employed in any way in such honorable service?

Many persons, however, cannot refrain from pleading against God, or, at least, from complaining against him for not better supporting their weakness. It is marvellously strange, they say, how God, after having chosen us for his children, allows us to be so trampled upon and tormented by the ungodly. I answer: Even were it not apparent why he does so, he might well exercise his authority over us and fix our lot at his pleasure. But when we see that Jesus Christ is our pattern, ought we not, without inquiring further, to esteem it great happiness that we are made like to him? God, however, makes it very apparent what the reasons are for which he is pleased that we should be persecuted. Had we nothing more than the consideration suggested by St. Peter, we were disdainful indeed not to acquiesce in it. He says, "Since gold and silver, which are only corruptible metals, are purified and tested by fire, it is but reasonable that our faith, which surpasses all the riches of the world, should be tried."

It were easy indeed for God to crown us at once without requiring us to sustain any combats; but as it is his pleasure that until the end of the world Christ shall reign in the midst of his enemies, so it is also his pleasure that we, being placed in the midst of them, shall suffer their oppression and violence till he deliver us. I know, indeed, that the flesh kicks when it is to be brought to this point, but still the will of God must have the mastery. If we feel some repugnance in ourselves it need not surprise us; for it is only too natural for us to shun the cross. Still let us not fail to surmount it, knowing that God accepts our obedience, provided we bring all our feelings and wishes into captivity and make them subject to him.

When the prophets and apostles went to death it was not without feeling within some inclination to recoil. "They will lead thee whither thou wouldst not," said our Lord Jesus Christ to Peter. When such fears of death arise within us, let us gain the mastery over them, or rather let God gain it; and meanwhile let us feel assured that we offer him a pleasing sacrifice when we resist and do violence to our inclinations for the purpose of placing ourselves entirely under his command. This is the principal war in which God would have his people to be engaged. He would have them strive to suppress every rebellious thought and feeling which would turn them aside from the path to which he points. And the consolations are so ample that it may well be said we are more than cowards if we give way.

In ancient times vast numbers of people, to obtain a simple crown of leaves, refused no toil, no pain, no trouble; nay, it even cost them nothing to die, and yet every one of them fought for a peradventure, not knowing whether he was to gain or lose the prize. God holds forth to us the immortal crown by which we may become partakers of his glory. He does not mean us to fight at haphazard, but all of us have a promise of the prize for which we strive. Have we any cause, then, to decline the struggle? Do we think it has been said in vain, "If we die with Jesus Christ we shall also live with him?" Our triumph is prepared, and yet we do all we can to shun the combat.

THE PROPER USE OF SCRIPTURE

_____

_____

_____

_____

_____

_____

_____

_____

_____

_____

_____

_____

_____

_____

_____

_____

_____

_____

_____

_____

"All scripture is given by inspiration of God, and is profitable for doctrine, for reproof, for correction, for instruction in righteousness: That the man of God may be perfect, thoroughly furnished unto all good works"—2 Timothy 3:16-17.

The Word of God being called our spiritual sword, there is need of our being armed with it: for in this world the devil continually fighteth against us, endeavoring to deceive, and draw us into sin. Therefore, St. Paul saith the Word of God deserveth such reverence that we ought to submit ourselves to it without gainsaying. He likewise informeth us what profit we receive from it; which is another reason why we should embrace it with reverence and obedience. There have been some fantastical men at all times who would wish to bring the Holy Scripture into doubt; although they were ashamed to deny that the Word of God ought to be received without contradiction. There have always been wicked men who have frankly confessed that the Word of God hath such a majesty in it that all the world ought to bow before it; and yet they continue to blaspheme and speak evil against God.

Where is the Word of God to be found, unless we see it in the law, and in the prophets, and in the gospel? There it is that God hath set forth His mind to us. To the end, therefore, that men may not excuse themselves, St. Paul plainly showeth us that if we will do homage to God, and live in subjection to Him, we must receive that which is contained in the law and the prophets. And that no man might take the liberty to choose what he pleaseth, and so obey God in part, he saith, the whole Scripture hath this majesty of which he speaketh, and that it is all profitable. To be short, St. Paul informeth us, that we must not pick and call the Scripture to please our own fancy, but must receive the whole without exception. Thus we see what St. Paul's meaning is in this place; for when he speaketh of the Holy Scripture, he doth not mean that which he was then writing, neither that of the other apostles and evangelists, but the Old Testament.

Thus we perceive that his mind was that the law and the prophets should always be preached in the church of Christ; for it is a doctirne that must, and will, remain forever. Therefore, those that would have the law laid aside, and never spoken of again, are not to be regarded. They have made it a common proverb in their synagogues and taverns, saying, "we need neither the law nor the prophets any more": and this is as common a thing among them as among the Turks.

But St. Paul bridleth the Christian, and telleth us, that if we will prove our faith and obedience toward God, the law and the prophets must reign over us; we must regulate our lives by them; we must know that it is an abiding and an immortal truth; not flitting nor changeable; for God gave not a temporal doctrine to serve but for a season, for His mind was that it should be in force in these days and that the world should sooner perish, and heaven and earth decay, than the authority thereof to fail. Thus we see St. Paul's meaning is that we should suffer ourselves to be governed by the Holy Scripture, and seek for wisdom no where else.

We must observe (as hath already been said) that he giveth us no liberty to choose what we list, but he will have us to be obedient to God in all respects, approving what is contained in the Holy Scripture. Now let us notice the two points which are here set forth. He saith first, *All scripture is given by inspiration of God;* and then addeth, and *is profitable.* These remarks St. Paul maketh upon the Holy Scripture, to induce us to love it, and to show that it is worthy to be received with great humility. When he saith it is given by the inspiration of God, it is to the end that no mortal man should endeavor to control His almighty power. Shall miserable creatures make war against God, and refuse to accept the Holy Scripture? What is the cause of this? It is not forged by men (saith St. Paul); there is no earthly thing in it.

Whosoever will not show himself a rebel against God, and set Him at nought, must submit himself to the Holy Scripture. St. Paul addeth in the second place, besides the reverence which we owe to God by doing Him homage, we must confess, moreover, that He sought our profit and salvation, when it pleased Him to teach us by the Holy Scripture: for He will not have us busy ourselves with unprofitable things. Therefore, if we be diligent in reading the Holy Scripture, we shall perceive that there is nothing contained in it but what is good and fit for us, from which we may obtain some benefit.

How unthankful we are, if we accept not the blessings which God offereth so freely! After St. Paul had magnified the Holy Scripture, showing that the majesty of God appeareth in it, he would also give us some taste, that we might come to it with an affection and desire to profit thereby, knowing that it was God's design, and the end be aimed at. Let us always remember that the Holy Scripture will never be of any service to us, unless we be persuaded that God is the author of it. When we read Moses, or any of the prophets, as the history of mortal men, do we feel a liveliness of the spirit of God inflaming us? No, no; it is far from it.

Therefore the Holy Scripture will be lifeless, and without force, until we know it is God that speaketh in it, and thereby revealeth His will to man; for St. Paul saith, *the Holy Scripture is given by inspiration of God.* The *pope* will boast that all he hath put forth is from God: thus we see that by using the name of God for a cloak and covering, the world hath been deceived, and kept in ignorance from the beginning. For there never was any poison of false doctrine, but that it was put into a golden cup; that is to say, was hid under this honorable title: *that God spake to man.*

If we are content to be governed by the will of God, our faith will be rightly sealed; so that we may perceive that it is not the illusion of Satan, neither a fable invented by men. I mean those things contained in the Holy Scripture, which were spoken by God, who is the author of them. Let us consider the infinite goodness of our God, in that it hath pleased Him to seal up His truth in our hearts, and cause us to feel the virtue of it; while unbelievers are left in their ignorance, to despise the authority of the Holy Scripture.

We may gather from what St. Paul saith that there is no authority in the church of God but what is received from Him. If then we admit of a doctrine, it must not be borrowed from the authority or wisdom of men, but we must know that it came from God. This is a notable point; for God will prove thereby whether we be His people or not. He is our King indeed, because we have no laws nor ordinances except from Him; our souls are not guided by chance, for He ruleth over us, and we are subject to His yoke. If this be not the case, we do not show that God governs us, though we make ever so formal pretensions; they are but false shows.

St. Paul doth not inform us, in order to prove the Holy Scripture to be an undoubted truth, that Moses was an excellent man; he doth not say that Isaiah was very eloquent: he declareth nothing of them whereby he may raise the credit of their persons; but he saith, they were instruments in the hands of God: their tongues were guided by the Holy Ghost: they spake nothing of their own, but it was God that spake by them. We must not consider them as uninspired men, but as servants of the living God; as faithful stewards of the treasures committed to them.

If these things had been observed, men would not have come into such horrible confusion, as the papists are at this day. For upon what is their faith grounded, except upon men? There is nothing but hypocrisy in all their doings. It is true, they declare God's name, but in the mean time observe their own ceremonies. But St. Paul requireth us to confine ourselves to the Holy Scripture because God speaketh there, and not man. Thus we see, he excludeth all human authority: God must have the preeminence above all creatures whatsoever; they must submit themselves to Him, and not presume to encroach upon His sovereignty. When we go into the pulpit, we ought to be assured that it is God that sent us, and that we bring the message which He committed to us.

Let him that speaketh, speak according to the Word of God: that is, let him show that he doth not thrust himself in rashly, nor patch up with any of his own works, but that he holdeth forth the truth of God in its purity; he must make his doctrine edifying to the people, that God may be honored thereby. Seeing the doctrine of men is here cast down, let us banish it from the church of Christ, that it may never be admitted again. Therefore, let us beware and keep ourselves steadfast in the simplicity of the gospel: for our Lord hath been so gracious, as to reveal His will to us by the law and the prophets: then let us hold fast that which we have received, and not suffer men to bind our consciences, and frame articles of faith for us according to their will.

St. Paul saith *all Scripture is profitable.* Therefore, if the Holy Scripture be profitable, we are very unthankful in not applying ourselves to the study of it. Who is there among us that doth not desire profit and salvation? And where can it be found, except in the Holy Scripture? Woe be unto us then, if we hear not the Word of God, who seeketh nothing but our happiness. Moreover, we must not read the Holy Scripture in order to support our own notions, and favorite sentiments; but submit ourselves unto the doctrine contained therein, agreeably to the whole contents of it; for it is all profitable.

When I expound the Holy Scripture, I must always compass myself by it, that those who hear me, may be profited by the doctrine held forth, and receive edification thereby. If I have not this affection, if I do not edify those that hear me, I commit sacrilege, and profane the Word of God. Those also who read the Holy Scripture, or come to hear the sermon, if they seek any foolish speculations, if they come hither to recreate themselves, they are guilty of profaning the gospel. If we divert the Holy Scripture from its proper use, and seek questions in it, without endeavoring to profit by it, we pollute it.

St. Paul hath taught us that we must come to God with earnest desires, seeing He seeketh nothing but our profit and salvation. He showeth us also that we must not pollute the Holy Scripture, to make it serve our own fancy; but knowing it is God's mind that it should be made profitable to us, we must come thither to be taught: yea, and taught in that which will be profitable for our salvation. Now it remaineth for us severally to examine and see what this profit is: if St. Paul had pronounced but this one word, the sense might have been somewhat obscure: but he openeth it so plainly that we cannot mistake his meaning; for he saith, "The scripture is profitable for doctrine, for reproof, for correction, for instruction in righteousness; that the man of God may be perfect, thoroughly furnished unto all good works."

St. Paul doth not set forth a single use of the Holy

Scripture, but when he hath spoken of the doctrine, he addeth, *to reprove, correct, and instruct.* And why so? It is not enough for God to show us what is good, because we are so cold that we should hardly preceive it: therefore He must needs stir us up to an earnestness: we must know that He speaketh to us, and that we are bound to obey. Thus we see there is no dead doctrine in the Holy Scripture; but there are reproofs and corrections to stir us up, that we may come to God.

St. Paul saith *all Scripture is profitable for doctrine:* and then addeth, *to reprove, correct,* &c. Why beginneth he with this word *doctrine?* Because it is the natural order; for if we are not taught to say, this is the truth, exhortation will be of no use: therefore, we must first of all be made sensible that that which is taught us is good, and true, and right. Thus the word *doctrine* signifieth that we must be instructed in the truth, that we must be thoroughly resolved in it, and so edified by it, that we doubt not its authenticity. St. Paul informeth us, that this doctrine is to know Jesus Christ, and put our whole trust in Him; to live soberly, righteously, and godly.

When we call upon God by prayer and supplication, we must put our trust in Him, and look to the heavenly life whereunto he calleth us: we must mortify all our wicked affections, and conform ourselves to His righteousness. The doctrine of the gospel, in few words, is this: to know God, and put our whole trust in Him: and to know by what means He is our Savior: namely, in the person of our Lord Jesus Christ, His only begotten Son, who died for our justification. This is the way whereby we are reconciled to God, and cleansed from all sin; from which proceedeth the confidence we have to call upon Him, knowing that He will not cast us off, when we come in the name of Him who is appointed our advocate.

When we consider that there is nothing but sin and wickedness in us, we must learn to be displeased with ourselves, and serve God fervently, with a pure heart: this is the doctrine contained in the Holy Scripture. We must understand the meaning of St. Paul, when he saith *to reprove*: that is, if we would be well instructed in the school of God, we must confess ourselves guilty; we must be pricked to the heart; we must be reproved for our faults. When the Word of God is rightly expounded, the faithful are not only edified, but if an unbeliever come into the church and hear the doctrine of God he is reproved and judged. By this we understand that although the unbeliever may be wrapped in darkness, and pleased with his own ignorance, yet when God so enlighteneth him that he seeth the misery and wickedness in which he hath lived, when he seeth his deplorable situation, while giving ear to the Word of God, he perceiveth the heavens open, as it were, and that man was not made for this life only, but to be exalted to a higher station.

Thus unbelievers are convicted.

And to make it more clear, St. Paul addeth the secrets of the heart are then disclosed; for we know while the Word of God is buried, no man taketh heed to himself; our hearts are in darkness. What then must we do? We must apply the Word of God to our use, and be awakened out of sleep: we must no more forget God, nor the salvation of our own souls; we must search the very depth of our hearts, and examine our whole lives; that we may be ashamed of our filthiness, and become our own judges, to avoid the condemnation that is ready at the hand of God. Thus we understand what St. Paul meaneth by the word *reproof*.

It is not enough for men to lay the blessings of God before us, and say, this is God's will; but we must be awakened to think upon it in good earnest, and look narrowly to ourselves: yea, and to draw near to God, as if He had summoned us to appear before His judgment seat: we must bring all to light, that we may be ashamed of our evil deeds: and when we breathe into this heavenly air, we must be careful not to turn aside from the right way.

It is not enough to be thus *reproved*, but *correction* must be added likewise: we must be chastised, as it were, by the Word of God, to the end we may be reformed. We must forsake our sins; we must be sharply dealt with, that they may be plucked out by the roots, and separated from us. Thus, when we have been roused to think upon God, we feel condemned before Him, while our sins are laid open to view; and we become guilty in the sight of both God and man. Moreover, we must be drawn to it by force; if we have been drunk with delicacies, if we have indulged ourselves in folly and vanity, and have thereby been deceived, the corrections must be quick and severe, that we may give God the honor, and suffer Him to reform us, and bring us into subjection to His will.

When a father seeth his children conduct themselves improperly and viciously, he thinketh it not enough to say, why do you so? but he will say, you wretched creatures, have I brought you up, and hitherto fostered you, to recompense me thus? doth it become you to do me this dishonor after I have used you so gently? you deserve to be given into the hands of the hangman. So it is with us: when God seeth that we are more rebellious against Him than disobedient children are against earthly parents, hath He not occasion to be angry with us? Not that there are any unruly passions in Him, but He useth this earnestness that we may be brought into subjection, and learn to obey Him.

Now we may judge whether it would be enough for a man, when he would expound the Holy Scripture, to discourse upon it as though it were a mere history; for if it were so, that which St. Paul saith concerning it is unprofitable: it would be sufficient for him to have said, to preach the gospel, we need only say, *thus spake God.* The office of a good and faithful shepherd is not barely to expound the Scripture, but he must use earnestness, and sharpness, to give force and virtue to the Word of God. St. Paul saith in another place that the shepherds of the church must be earnest, even to be importunate; and not only show the people what is good, but reprove them.

It is true, he saith it must be done meekly, mildly, and patiently: but however it be, corrections must be used. Men must not say, this is too hard to be borne, you must not deal after this sort; let those who cannot suffer reproof, seek another master beside God, for they are not worthy to hear His Word. The world would gladly be spared; and we see many who are ready to burst with rage when they are threatened and corrected. They say that they wish to be won by mildness. Then let them go to the devil's school; he will flatter, yea, and destroy them.

But as for the faithful, after they have received the doctrine, they must humble themselves, and be willing to receive reproof: they must be exhorted when they have done amiss: they must be reproved for their sins and offences that they may be purged from all iniquity. In this manner we must behave ourselves, if we wish to be instructed in the doctrine of God. St. Paul addeth, *the Scripture is profitable for instruction in righteousness; that the man of God may be perfect, thoroughly furnished unto all good works.* When he saith that the Holy Scripture is profitable to instruct in righteousness, he shutteth out whatsoever man might bring; showing that we shall not become righteous by observing the works introduced by man.

We see how the papists torment themselves in vain; observing whatsoever is enjoined upon them by men. In what consists their righteousness? upon what is it grounded? It is grounded upon this: *the church so commandeth.* But St. Paul showeth that there is neither religion nor doctrine, except in that which is contained in the Holy Scripture; yea, and in that only is righteousness. Do they then follow that which God hath commanded? No; for they go entirely contrary to it. Therefore, if we wish to have our lives well framed, let us not ground ourselves upon the works of men, but let us follow that which God enjoins upon us.

If we regulate our lives by the instructions contained in the Holy Scripture, we shall be justified thereby: but the doctrine of men is but folly, and an abomination to God. Then let us remember it is not without cause that St. Paul saith, *to instruct in righteousness.* Again, he giveth us to understand that to be good divines, we must live holy lives. The Word of God is not given to teach us how to talk, to make us eloquent and subtle, but to reform our lives, that the world may know we are the servants of God. If we wish to know whether a man profiteth by the gospel or not, let us mark his life: men may know how to talk, they may make a fair profession of godliness, and yet not have their lives correspond with the written Word of God.

St. Paul informeth us that we must make the Word of God our counsellor, that we may walk uprightly, and form our lives by it: thus, *the man of God may be perfect, and furnished unto all good works.* In this manner we must be instructed in righteousness, and reject the inventions of men, for with them God is not well pleased. Men wish to serve God according to their own notions, and therefore bring their own works into the account; but God will not allow them. St. Paul, seeing such impudent boldness in men, that they cannot keep themselves within the bounds which God hath set them, points out the disease, that it may be healed: he saith, if we have the Word of God in our hearts, we shall be upright in life, and furnished unto all good works.

Men may boast as much as they please that their works are virtuous and holy; but when they shall appear before the heavenly judge, all will be as chaff. When we mix our inventions with that which God hath commanded, we injure all: Therefore we may conclude that whatever things are forged by men are nothing but corruptions. The papists call these good works: to fast upon a saint's eve; to eat no flesh upon Friday; to keep Lent; to serve saints; to go from altar to altar, and chapel to chapel, to attend mass; to go on pilgrimage, &c. They have forged so many laws and statutes that a man cannot understand them. But we must at last appear before the great judge, to give an account of all our actions.

It is said here that we shall be furnished unto all good works, if we profit by the Holy Scripture. But what will come of the traditions and inventions of the papists in which the Word of God seemeth to be buried? They make not one hundredth part as much of the Word of God, as they do of men's traditions. Therefore let us not deceive ourselves willingly, considering we shall have the measure of our perfection: God shutteth out whatsoever is added to the Holy Scripture, and showeth that it shall not be reckoned or received by Him; therefore men make their items in vain; it will but double their condemnation.

A man might ask, of what use is the gospel, seeing there is so much uprightness in the law and the prophets? This may be easily answered: the gospel was not given to add any thing to the law or the prophets. Let us read the New Testament: we shall not find one syllable added to either; it is only setting forth that which was taught before more plainly. It is true that God hath been more gracious to us than to the fathers who lived before the coming of our Lord Jesus Christ, matters being more clearly set forth to us, although there is nothing added. So then, when St. Paul saith that we shall find uprightness and perfect righteousness in the law and in the prophets, it diminisheth not the gospel.

There is an agreement in all the Holy Scripture; of the *Old*, and *New* Testament. The doctrine which was contained in the law has been expounded so familiarly to us by the apostles since Jesus Christ that we cannot say we must do this or that, but we must confine ourselves to that which was commanded from the beginning. God hath made known His will in such clear terms, and hath given so many reasons why we should believe it, that we must be convinced of its truth, unless we are monsters in wickedness. Therefore, if we will profit by the Holy Scripture, we must study holiness of life, knowing that God will not be served after our own fancy; for He hath given us a certain rule whereby we should regulate our lives, and such a one as cannot be found fault with. Let us then direct our hearts, thoughts, and affections, to that which is contained in the Holy Scripture; and then the heavenly judge will receive us. We must be the more induced to these things, because our good God draweth so nigh, and setteth forth His will in such a plain manner to us, that we cannot excuse ourselves, unless we cleave wholly to Him.

LATIMER
(1485 - 1555)

Sketch of Latimer's Life

Hugh Latimer was born in 1485, two years after Luther. He was burned at the stake in 1555. Raised on an English farm, Latimer was a zealous Roman Catholic and studied at Cambridge. For his B.D. degree, he preached against the views of Melanchthon. After this sermon, Thomas Bilney came up to him, explained justification by faith and led him to personal faith in Christ. Slowly—there was much vacillation on Latimer's part—through Bilney's help, he came to the full Reformation position. Bilney and he would walk together and hold bull sessions so often that, long after his death, the fields where they walked were called "Heretics Hill."

Latimer was an expert in canon law. He decided in favor of Henry VIII's marriage plans to Katherine of Aragon, and was given a royal chaplaincy as a reward. In 1535 he became bishop of Worchester. Here, he preached boldly against abuses and sin wherever it was found. He was forced out in 1539 and given peaceful retirement under Edward VI. But when Mary came to the throne, he, Cranmer and Ridley were arrested and thrown into the Tower of London. He was examined at Oxford, but refused to recant. After a year in prison, on October 16, 1555, he was burned at the stake together with Ridley. It was to Ridley, a younger man, that he made the famous prophetic statement:

> Be of good comfort, master Ridley and play the man. We shall
> this day light such a candle by God's grace in England, as I
> trust shall never be put out.

The great emphasis of his ministry was to get the gospel and the Bible to people in language they could understand. Others were afraid that if the people had the Bible in their language, they would misunderstand it and all sorts of damage would be done. Latimer thought that was nonsense and, like Luther, by the effects of his preaching proved them wrong. His favorite topic was the necessity for preaching. Latimer was a jovial man of wit. He was known far and wide for his quick answers, his frankness, his memorable speech and his friendliness. Again and again he successfully met challenges from learned opponents who were out to get him. He has been called the father of English preaching. What a glorious history English preaching might have known if it had been modeled in attitude and style after him!

Attitude, or mood, is an element worth study in Latimer's sermons. While striking at sin every bit as fiercely as the Puritans (and probably far more successfully), there was a likableness about him, and a mood in his sermons of encouragement and enthusiasm, that disappeared from later English preaching. Though the styles of the two men were quite different, there is something of a similar mood in Chrysostom. Both men were loved. Children used to follow Latimer through the streets.

Content

Latimer preached mainly from the New Testament (at least the few extant sermons indicate this). But he made many Old Testament allusions and frequently used Old Testament examples as illustrations. This practice has its problems: the Old Testament should be used authoritatively, not illustratively. Other material was gleaned from farm life and everyday affairs. Like the sermons of many great preachers, Latimer's sermons were homey and designed to be graphic, understandable and memorable to the common man.

Latimer preached justification by faith alone. He said, "Faith only justifieth; this proposition is most true and certain." He further declared: "Faith is the hand wherewith we take hold on everlasting life" (sermon on John 15:12). Yet, he was balanced; in the same sermon he was careful to observe that there are evidences of faith: "Love is a child of faith," and continuing, he insisted, "Sirs, I tell you, unless restitution is made, look for no salvation."

Latimer preached with force, and fearlessly spoke against specific sins in the lives of the highest and the lowest. In one sermon he says, "I had occasion of late to speak of picking and stealing." When he preached before the king, his friends urged him to be discreet, but he spared none, and showed deference to no one. He was the most famous preacher of his day.

Organization

The organization of Latimer's sermons was in some respects weak. He often rambled. His preaching was largely deductive (from the abstract and general to the concrete and particular), hortatory and persuasive in form (rarely did he teach in any formal sense of the word). In concert with his basically persuasive preaching, the bones in his messages did not protrude. But, at points within the sermon itself, his approach was more inductive.

One preaching method that Latimer developed early and used often thereafter was to cast the entire sermon into the mold of an image. Others since Latimer have attempted this with more or less success. He was a master of the technique. The sermons on the *Card* and on the *Ploughers* as well as the sermon on love (included in this textbook) use the figure of the livery of Christ throughout, and are examples of this. His introductions were often topical and occasional and fairly long. Conclusions were brief, usually consisting of a summary and exhortation. Hortatory elements appeared throughout the sermon.

Style

Blench calls Latimer "the greatest pulpit exponent of the colloquial style in the century." Along with this went humor and a rich, pungent language. Latimer's tendency was to choose from among those words that are emotionally freighted. He was a master of the barb and used sarcasm to make his point. He had a vivid imagination and used it well in Christ's service. A study of any one of these elements would be of significance in sermon analysis.

Latimer's humorous reference to "strawberry prelates," who, like the red berry, preach only seasonally, became a figure of speech among the common people. Many such sayings of his were widely quoted. His language was vivid and memorable. Listen to this:

I grant you may both laugh and make good cheer, and yet there remain a bag of rusty malice, twenty years old, in thy neighbor's bosom.

Latimer even used visual aids. Once he produced a new silver shilling and read on it, "The fear of the Lord is the beginning of wisdom." At Saint Paul's he took into the pulpit a Roman Catholic image called the *Rood of Grace* (rood =crucifix) and showed the congregation that it was able to roll its eyes, shake its head, open and shut its mouth and perform other supposed miracles by pulling strings. He then threw the image out of the church door in defiance of the claim by the members of the congregation from which it came that eight oxen couldn't move it. From this incident, a popular song arose:

The sweet rod of Ramsbury
Twenty miles from Malmesbury
Was oftimes put in fear;
And now at last
He hath bridling [proud image?] cast
And is gone, I know not where.

How many popular songs are composed about preaching today?

There are many personal reminiscences used illustratively in his sermons. In them, for instance, you learn about Latimer's childhood on the farm, how he learned to shoot, et cetera. He also speaks of his school days, years at the university, and his conversion.

Latimer was careful to adapt to each audience. "Now if I should preach in the country, among the unlearned, I would tell what propitiatory, expiatory and remissory mean" (from the sermon on the ploughers). There is an instance of a bishop who appeared unexpectedly in the congregation seeking evidence against Latimer. On the spot he changed his sermon and preached to the bishop about the duties of bishops!

Latimer prepared carefully, but preached extemporaneously. He usually preached twice on Sundays, and crowds gathered to hear him. There are accounts of crowds so large that they destroyed benches, and we have records of the costs of repairs after Latimer's preaching at Saint Margaret's, Westminster. People were radically changed as the result of his preaching, and many made restitution of money. Indeed, even the king received funds that were long due him. While Latimer had his faults, he reminds one of what the Apostle Peter might have been like once he entered into his ministry. He is a man too often neglected. Many modern preachers could benefit greatly from a thorough study of Latimer's preaching.

SERMON ON CHRISTIAN LOVE

"This is my commandment, that ye love one another, as I have loved you." (John 15:12)

Seeing the time is so far spent, we will take no more in hand at this time than this one sentence; for it will be enough for us to consider this well and to bear it away with us. "This I command unto you, that ye love one another." Our Saviour himself spake these words at his last supper: it was the last sermon that he made unto his disciples before his departure; it is a very long sermon. For our Saviour, like as one that knows he shall die shortly, is desirous to spend that little time he has with his friends, in exhorting and instructing them how they should lead their lives. Now, among other things that he commanded this was one: "This I command unto you, that ye love one another." The English expresses as though it were but one, "This is my commandment." I examined the Greek, where it is in the plural number, and very well; for there are many things that pertain to a Christian man, and yet all those things are contained in this one thing, that is, Love. He lappeth up all things in love.

Our whole duty is contained in these words, "Love together." Therefore St. Paul saith, "He that loveth another fulfilleth the whole law;" so it appeareth that all things are contained in this word Love. This Love is a precious thing; our Saviour saith, "By this shall all men know that ye are my disciples, if ye shall love one another."

So Christ makes love his cognizance, his badge, his livery. Like as every lord commonly gives a certain livery to his servants, whereby they may be known that they pertain unto him; and so we say, yonder is this lord's servants, because they wear his livery: so our Saviour, who is the Lord above all lords, would have his servants known by their liveries and badge, which badge is love alone. Whosoever now is endued with love and charity is his servant; him we may call Christ's servant; for love is the token whereby you may know that such a servant pertaineth to Christ; so that charity may be called the very livery of Christ. He that hath charity is Christ's servant: he that hath not charity is the servant of the devil. For as Christ's livery is love and charity, so the devil's livery is hatred, malice, and discord.

But I think the devil has a great many more servants than Christ has; for there are a great many more in his livery than in Christ's livery; there are but very few who are endued with Christ's livery; with love and charity, gentleness and meekness of spirit; but there are a great number that bear hatred and malice in their hearts, that are proud, stout, and lofty; therefore the number of the devil's servants is greater than the number of Christ's servants.

Now St. Paul shows how needful this love is. I speak not of carnal love, which is only animal affection; but of this charitable love which is so necessary that, when a man hath it, without all other things it will suffice him. Again, if a man have all other things and lacketh that love, it will not help him; it is all vain and lost. St. Paul used it so: "Though I speak with tongues of men and angels, and yet had no love, I were even as sounding brass or as a tinkling cymbal. And though I could prophesy and understand all secrets and all knowledge; yea, if I had all faith, so that I could move mountains out of their places, and yet had no love, I were nothing. And though I bestowed all my goods to feed the poor, and though I gave my body even that I were burned, and yet had no love, it profiteth me nothing."

These are godly gifts, yet St. Paul calls them nothing when a man hath them without charity; which is a great commendation, and shows the great need of love, insomuch that all other virtues are in vain when this love is absent. And there have been some who thought that St. Paul spake against the dignity of faith; but you must understand that St. Paul speaks here, not of the justifying faith wherewith we receive everlasting life, but he understands by this word "faith" the gift to do miracles, to remove hills: of such a faith he speaks. This I say to confirm this proposition. Faith only justifieth: this proposition is most true and certain. And St. Paul speaks not here of this lively justifying faith; for this right faith is not without love, for love cometh and floweth out of faith, love is a child of faith; for no man can love except he believe, so that they have two several offices, they themselves being inseparable.

St. Paul has an expression in the thirteenth chapter of the First Epistle to the Corinthians, which, according to the outward letter, seems much to the dispraise of this faith, and to the praise of love; these are his words: "Now abideth faith, hope, and love, even these three; but the chiefest of these is love."

There are some learned men who expound the greatness of which St. Paul speaketh here as if meant for eternity. For when we come to God, then we believe no more, but rather see with our eyes face to face how he is; yet for all that, love remains still; so that love may be called the chiefest because she endureth forever. And though she is the chiefest, yet we must not attribute unto her the office which pertains unto faith only. Like as I cannot say, the mayor of Stamford must make me a pair of shoes because he is a greater man than the shoemaker is; for the mayor, though he is the greater man, yet it is not his office to make shoes; so, though love be greater, yet it is not her office to save. Thus much I thought good to say against those who fight against the truth.

Now, when we would know who are in Christ's livery or not, we must learn it of St. Paul, who most evidently described charity, which is the very livery, saying, "Love is patient, she suffereth long." Now whosoever fumeth and is angry, he is out of this livery: therefore let us remember that we do not cast away the livery of Christ our master. When we are in sickness or any manner of adversities, our duty is to be patient, to suffer willingly, and to call upon him for aid, help and comfort; for without him we are not able to abide any tribulation. Therefore we must call upon God, he has promised to help: therefore let me not think him to be false or untrue in his promises, for we cannot dishonor God more than by not believing or trusting in him. Therefore let us beware above all things of dishonoring God; and so we must be patient, trusting and most certainly believing that he will deliver us when it seems good to him, who knows the time better than we ourselves.

"Charity is gentle, friendly, and loving; she envieth not." They that envy their neighbor's profit when it goes well with him, such fellows are out of their liveries, and so out of the service of God; for to be envious is to be the servant of the devil.

"Love doth not frowardly, she is not a provoker;" as there are some men who will provoke their neighbor so far that it is very hard for them to be in charity with them; but we must wrestle with our affections; we must strive and see that we keep this livery of Christ our master; for "the devil goeth about as a roaring lion seeking to take us at a vantage," to bring us out of our liveries, and to take from us the knot of love and charity.

"Love swelleth not, is not puffed up;" but there are many swellers nowadays, they are so high, so lofty, insomuch that they despise and condemn all others: all such persons are under the governance of the devil. God rules not them with his good Spirit; the evil spirit has occupied their hearts and possessed them.

"She doth not dishonestly; she seeketh not her own; she doth all things to the commodity of her neighbors." A charitable man will not promote himself with the damage of his neighbor. They that seek only their own advantage, forgetting their neighbors, they are not of God, they have not his livery. Further, "charity is not provoked to anger; she thinketh not evil." We ought not to think evil of our neighbor as long as we see not open wickedness; for it is written, "You shall not judge;" we should not take upon us to condemn our neighbor. And surely the condemners of other men's works are not in the livery of Christ. Christ hateth them.

"She rejoiceth not in iniquity;" she loveth equity and godliness. And again, she is sorry to hear of falsehood, of stealing, or such like, which wickedness is now at this time commonly used. There never was such falsehood among Christian men as there is now at this time; truly I think, and they that have experience report it so, that among the very infidels and Turks there is more fidelity and uprightness than among Christian men. For no man setteth anything by his promise, yea, and writings will not serve with some, they are so shameless that they dare deny their own handwriting: but, I pray you, are those false fellows in the livery of Christ? Have they his cognizance? No, no; they have the badge of the devil, with whom they shall be damned world without end except they amend and leave their wickedness.

"She suffereth all things; she believeth all things." It is a great matter that should make us to be grieved with our neighbor; we should be patient when our neighbor doth wrong, we should admonish him of his folly, earnestly desiring him to leave his wickedness, showing the danger that follows, namely, everlasting damnation. In such wise we should study to amend our neighbor, and not to hate him or do him a foul turn again, but rather charitably study to amend him: whosoever now does so, he has the livery and cognizance of Christ; he shall be known at the last day for his servant.

"Love believeth all things." It appears daily that they who are charitable and friendly are most deceived; because they think well of every man, they believe every man, they trust their words, and therefore are most deceived in this world, among the children of the devil. These and such like things are the tokens of the right and godly love: therefore they that have this love are soon known, for this love cannot be hid in corners, she has her operation: therefore all that have her are well enough, though they have no other gifts besides her. Again, they that lack her, though they have many other gifts besides, yet it is to no other purpose, it does them no good: for when we shall come at the great day before him, not having this livery (that is, love) with us, then we are lost; he will not take us for his servants, because we have not his cognizance. But if we have this livery; if we wear his cognizance here in this world; that is, if we love our neighbor, help him in his distress, are charitable, loving, and friendly unto him,—then shall we be known at the last day: but if we be uncharitable toward our neighbor, hate him, seek our own advantage with his damage, then we shall be rejected of Christ and so damned world without end.

Our Saviour saith here in this gospel, "I command you these things:" he speaketh in the plural number, and lappeth it up in one thing, which is, that we should love one another, much like St. Paul's saying in the thirteenth [chapter] to the Romans, "Owe nothing to any man, but love one another." Here St. Paul lappeth up all things together, signifying unto us that love is the consummation of the law; for this commandment,

"Thou shalt not commit adultery," is contained in this law of love: for he that loveth God will not break wedlock, because wedlock-breaking is a dishonoring of God and serving of the devil. "Thou shalt not kill." He that loveth will not kill, he will do no harm. "Thou shalt not steal." He that loveth his neighbor as himself will not take away his goods. I had of late occasion to speak of picking and stealing, where I showed unto you the danger wherein they are that steal their neighbors' goods from them, but I hear nothing yet of restitution. Sirs, I tell you, except restitution is made, look for no salvation.

And it is a miserable and heinous thing to consider that we are so blinded with this world that, rather than we would make restitution, we will sell unto the devil our souls which are bought with the blood of our Saviour Christ. What can be done more to the dishonoring of Christ than to cast our souls away to the devil for the value of a little money?—the soul which he has bought with his painful passion and death! But I tell you those that will do so, and that will not make restitution when they have done wrong, or have taken away their neighbor's goods, they are not in the livery of Christ, they are not his servants; let them go as they will in this world, yet for all that they are foul and filthy enough before God; they stink before his face; and therefore they shall be cast from his presence into everlasting fire; this shall be all their good cheer that they shall have, because they have not the livery of Christ, nor his cognizance, which is love. They remember not that Christ commanded us, saying, "This I command you, that ye love one another." This is Christ's commandment. Moses, the great prophet of God, gave many laws, but he gave not the spirit to fulfil the same laws: but Christ gave this law, and promised unto us that when we call upon him he will give us his Holy Ghost, who shall make us able to fulfil his laws, though not so perfectly as the law requires, but yet to the contentation of God and to the protection of our faith: for as long as we are in this world we can do nothing as we ought to do, because our flesh leadeth us, which is ever bent against the law of God; yet our works which we do are well taken for Christ's sake, and God will reward them in heaven.

Therefore our Saviour saith, "My yoke is easy, and my burden is light," because he helpeth to bear them; else indeed we should not be able to bear them. And in another place he saith his commandments are not heavy; they are heavy to our flesh, but, being qualified with the Spirit of God, to the faithful which believe in Christ, to them, I say, they are not heavy; for, though their doings are not perfect, yet they are well taken for Christ's sake.

You must not be offended because the Spirit commends love so highly, for he that commends the daughter commends the mother; for love is the daughter and faith is the mother: love floweth out of faith; where faith is, there is love; but yet we must consider their offices; faith is the hand wherewith we take hold on everlasting life.

Now let us enter into ourselves and examine our own hearts whether we are in the livery of God or not: and when we find ourselves to be out of this livery let us repent and amend our lives, so that we may come again to the favor of God and spend our time in this world to his honor and glory, forgiving our neighbors all such things as they have done against us.

And now to make an end: mark here who gave this precept of love—Christ our Saviour himself. When and at what time? At his departing, when he should suffer death. Therefore these words ought the more to be regarded, seeing he himself spake them at his last departing from us. May God of his mercy give us grace so to walk here in this world, charitably and friendly with one another, that we may attain the joy which God hath prepared for all those that love him. Amen.

EDWARDS
(1703 - 1758)

Sketch of His Life

Jonathan Edwards was educated by his father, Timothy, a preacher. Jonathan was a precocious child. At the age of twelve he wrote a famous essay on spiders after studying their habits for days in the field. He was sent to Yale for further education at the age of thirteen. In his time, Yale was a new, frontier school. Jonathan graduated in 1720. In 1722 he supplied a small Presbyterian church in New York City for eight months. From 1724-1726 he tutored at Yale. In 1727 he was ordained and became an assistant to his grandfather, Solomon Stoddard, at the Congregational church of Northhampton, Massachusetts, which was on the frontier. Stoddard died two years later and Jonathan became the pastor of this 600 member church.

His preaching was well-respected and in six months he gained an additional 300 members. Five years later, his fame had spread all over New England. During the years 1734/35 there was a great revival centered in and around his church. He remained the pastor of the Northhampton congregation for twenty-four years.

In June 1750, the church dismissed him. The occasion for this was his conclusion that the halfway covenant people must be excluded from the communion. There were other problems, though. He didn't do pastoral work or counseling and had been pretty rough on the young people. These and other such complaints were probably at the root of his dismissal.

Actually, the change of policy with reference to the halfway covenant amounted to an initial challenge to this whole institution. His grandfather had permitted people who were not yet ready to profess faith in Christ to have their children baptized and partake of the Lord's table. He considered these ordinances a means of grace to lead them to Christ. Jonathan had gone along with this practice for some time, but, at length, came to see the error of it.

The halfway covenant had been instituted originally to counter the baneful results of the doctrine of preparation that was held by Stoddard and many other Puritans. According to this doctrine, one had to prepare himself for regeneration by doing the sorts of things that are listed in Alleine's *Alarm to the Unconverted*, a handbook of preparationism. There were many people who purportedly were doing all of these things but did not think that they had yet been regenerated. Since they knew nothing else to do, they were simply waiting for the Spirit to regenerate them. In the meanwhile, children were being born to them. Stoddard allowed them to partake of the Lord's supper and to bring their children for baptism on the basis of their sincerity. The error behind the entire problem was preparationism itself. Rather than directing the unconverted to repent and believe the gospel, they urged people to prepare themselves for regeneration in the false hope that such preparation would make their regeneration more likely. Thus, contrary to all Biblical teaching, works of righteousness were held forth as a meritorious cause of regeneration. Preparationism killed the Reformed church in England, in Scotland and in New England. It led to a deadly, subjective, introspective and works-for-salvation type of preaching.

Following his dismissal, Edwards became a missionary to the Stockbridge Indians among whom he served for seven years. In 1757, he became president of Princeton, but died the next year after contracting smallpox from the vaccination.

Content

Edwards's preaching was Calvinistic but advanced beyond the scholastic-Puritan type in both form and content. However, like other Puritan preaching it was experiential in nature and concerned with the psychology of conversion. He clearly preached hell-fire and damnation. However, not all of his sermons were like "Sinners in the Hands of an Angry God." He spoke often about sweetness, light and beauty. A study of fifteen sermons, reveals the use of 374 Biblical quotations (an average of twenty-five per sermon).

His preaching goals are set forth in his farewell sermon: "I have not only endeavored to awaken you, that you might be moved with fear, but I have used my utmost endeavor to win you." Like many Puritans, Edwards was preoccupied with discovering the steps of conversion. His sermons were molded by his theories about this. As his statement of goals indicates, he was also concerned about motivation. He studied and commented on the effects of the revival. In this, he was something of an empiricist (cf. also his work on spiders).

Edwards's sermons were rigidly organized; there was no digression. The exposition was brief, usually accurate. Then came a statement of the teaching (usually called "doctrine"). This, was followed by application (called "use") which was, by far, the larger part of the sermon. The organization was logical, and consisted of points and sub-points. He used a deductive plan. There were frequent summaries.

Style

The style was simple and unadorned. Early, he resolved "to extricate all questions from least confusion or ambiguity of words, so that the ideas shall be left naked." Most of his words are short, a majority of one syllable. One study showed that 82 percent were five letter words or less; 25 percent were three letter words, 23 percent two letter words. The average was four letters. The sentences seem long in print, but have many short, separable clauses.

Edwards's powerful use of the second person should be studied. He learned to write his sermons in an oral style that was appropriate to his day. There was vivid imagery, rhetorical parallelism, use of rhetorical questions, use of question clusters and simple language in them (all of which might be studied with profit). Illustrative material mostly came from colonial life. There are references to occasional events. As a rule, he used logical argument based on Biblical authority.

Delivery

Edwards's voice was pleasant, but weak. He was tall, graceful and slender. It was said that his eyes were so piercing that when he did lift them from the written page, men shuddered. On one occasion, when a church bell came loose and fell, some wag declared that he "looked off the bell-rope in the steeple, so that the bell fell with a crash."

Sermons, at first, were written and read from a pack of 4" x 4" notes close to his eyes in order to read the small scrawl which filled the entire page. At times he interjected impromptu material, "often with greater pathos and attended with a more sensible effect on his hearers as any part that he had written" (*Observer*, quoted in Hitchcock).

When George Whitefield visited, he persuaded Edwards to preach without such slavish dependence on manuscripts. So, after 1746, he depended only on outlines which became more and more sketchy in nature. There are more than 1200 of his sermons in the library at Yale.

Effects

The preaching of Jonathan Edwards produced results that are almost without parallel. Men grasped the railings of pews to keep from sinking into hell. During the famous sermon, "Sinners in the Hands of an Angry God," people cried aloud for mercy and some clung to the columns of the building when he described the spider hanging over the open mouth of hell by one slender thread. It was this kind of preaching that brought about the Great Awakening.

But there were also bad effects. The emotional responses were not always positive. Some were so carried away that they tried to commit suicide, and a few succeeded. Some of Edwards's messages left people in despair, without hope. He, himself, wrote: "Satan seemed to be more let loose and raged in a dreadful manner. The first instance wherein it appeared, was a person putting an end to his own life by cutting his throat . . . and many who seemed to be under no melancholy, some pious persons . . . had it urged upon them as if somebody had spoke to them, 'Cut your own throat, now is a good opportunity.'" Yet there were lasting good effects of the Great Awakening. Eighty-five years later (1835) two English ministers visited the town for the expressed purpose of discovering whether the effects had continued and concluded that they had. In the sermon that follows, note especially, the relentless manner in which he pursues the listener.

WRATH UPON THE WICKED TO THE UTTERMOST

"To fill up their sins alway: for the wrath is come upon them to the uttermost." (I Thess. ii, 16)

In verse 14 the Apostle commends the Christian Thessalonians that they became the followers of the churches of God in Judea, both in faith and in sufferings; in faith in that they received the word, not as the word of man, but as it is in truth the "word of God"; in sufferings in that they had suffered like things of their own countrymen, as they had of the Jews. Upon which the Apostle sets forth the persecuting, cruel, and perverse wickedness of that people "who both killed the Lord Jesus and their own prophets, and have," says he, "persecuted us; and they please not God, and are contrary to all men, forbidding us to speak to the Gentiles, that they might be saved." Then come in the words of the text, "To fill up their sins alway; for the wrath is come upon them to the uttermost."

In these words we may observe two things:

To what effect was the heinous wickedness and obstinacy of the Jews, namely, to fill up their sins. God hath set bounds to every man's wickedness; he suffers men to live, and to go on in sin, till they have filled up their measure, and then cuts them off. To this effect was the wickedness and obstinacy of the Jews; they were exceedingly wicked and thereby filled up the measure of their sins a great pace. And the reason why they were permitted to be so obstinate under the preaching and miracles of Christ and of the apostles, and under all the means used with them, was that they might fill up the measure of their sins. This is agreeable to what Christ said, "Wherefore ye be witnesses unto yourselves, that ye are the children of them which killed the prophets. Fill ye up then the measure of your fathers."

The punishment of their wickedness: "The wrath is come upon them to the uttermost." There is a connection between the measure of men's sin and the measure of punishment. When they have filled up the measure of their sin then is filled up the measure of God's wrath.

The degree of their punishment is the uttermost degree. This may respect both a national and personal punishment. If we take it as a national punishment, a little after the time when the epistle was written, wrath came upon the nation of the Jews to the uttermost in their terrible destruction by the Romans, when, as Christ said, "was great tribulation, such as never was since the beginning of the world to that time." That nation had before suffered many of the fruits of divine wrath for their sins; but this was beyond all, this was their highest degree of punishment as a nation. If we take it as a personal punishment, then it respects their punishment in hell. God often punishes men very dreadfully in this world, but in hell "wrath comes on them to the uttermost." By this expression is also denoted the certainty of this punishment. For though the punishment was then future, yet it is spoken of as present: "The wrath is come upon them to the uttermost." It was as certain as if it had already taken place. God, who knows all things, speaks of things that are not as though they were; for things present and things future are equally certain with him. It also denotes the near approach of it. The wrath is come; that is, it is just at hand; it is at the door; as it proved with respect to that nation; their terrible destruction by the Romans was soon after the Apostle wrote this epistle.

Doctrine. When those that continue in sin shall have filled up the measure of their sin, then wrath will come upon them to the uttermost.

There is a certain measure that God hath set to the sin of every wicked man. God says concerning the sin of man, as he says to the raging waves of the sea, Hitherto shalt thou come and no further. The measure of some is much greater than of others. Some reprobates commit but a little sin in comparison with others, and so are to endure proportionably a smaller punishment. There are many vessels of wrath, but some are smaller and others greater vessels; some will contain comparatively but little wrath, others a greater measure of it. Sometimes, when we see men go to dreadful lengths and become very heinously wicked, we are ready to wonder that God lets them alone. He sees them go on in such audacious wickedness and keeps silence, nor does anything to interrupt them, but they go smoothly on and meet with no hurt. But sometimes the reason why God lets them alone is because they have not filled up the measure of their sins. When they live in dreadful wickedness they are but filling up the measure which God hath limited for them. This is sometimes the reason why God suffers very wicked men to live so long; because their iniquity is not full: "The iniquity of the Amorites is not yet full." For this reason also God sometimes suffers them to live in prosperity. Their prosperity is a snare to them and an occasion of their sinning a great deal more. Wherefore God suffers them to have such a snare because he suffers them to fill up a larger measure. So, for this cause, he sometimes suffers them to live under great light and great means and advantages, at the same time to neglect and misimprove all. Everyone shall live till he hath filled up his measure.

While men continue in sin they are filling the measure set them. This is the work in which they spend their whole lives; they begin in their childhood, and if they live to grow old in sin they still go on with this work. It is the work with which every day is filled up. They may alter their business in other respects; they may sometimes be about one thing and sometimes about another; but they never change from this work of filling up the measure of their sins. Whatever they put their hands to, they are still employed in this work. This is the first thing that they set themselves about when they awake in the morning, and the last thing they do at night. They are all the while treasuring up wrath against the day of wrath and the revelation of the righteous judgment of God.

It is a gross mistake of some natural men who think that when they read and pray they do not add to their sins, but, on the contrary, think they diminish their guilt by these exercises. They think that instead of adding to their sins they do something to satisfy for their past offences, but, instead of that, they do but add to the measure by their best prayers and by those services with which they themselves are most pleased.

When once the measure of their sins is filled up then wrath will come upon them to the uttermost. God will then wait no longer upon them. Wicked men think that God is altogether such an one as themselves, because when they commit such wickedness he keeps silence. "Because judgment against an evil work is not executed speedily, therefore the heart of the children of men is fully set in them to do evil." But when once they shall have filled up the measure of their sins judgment will be executed; God will not bear with them any longer. Now is the day of grace, and the day of patience, which they spend in filling up their sins; but when their sins shall be full then will come the day of wrath, the day of the fierce anger of God. God often executes his wrath on ungodly men in a less degree in this world. He sometimes brings afflictions upon them, and that in wrath. Sometimes he expresses his wrath in very sore judgments; sometimes he appears in a terrible manner, not only outwardly, but also in the inward expressions of it on their consciences. Some, before they died, have had the wrath of God inflicted on their souls in degrees that have been intolerable. But these things are only forerunners of their punishment, only slight foretastes of wrath. God never stirs up all his wrath against wicked men while in this world; but when once wicked men shall have filled up the measure of their sins then wrath will come upon them to the uttermost, and that in the following respects:

Wrath will come upon them without any restraint or moderation in the degree of it. God doth always lay, as it were, a restraint upon himself; he doth not stir up his wrath; he stays his rough wind in the day of his east wind; he lets not his arm light down on wicked men with its full weight. But when sinners shall have filled up the measure of their sins there will be no caution, no restraint. His rough wind will not be stayed nor moderated. The wrath of God will be poured out like fire. He will come forth, not only in anger, but in the fierceness of his anger; he will execute wrath with power, so as to show what his wrath is and make his power known. There will be nothing to alleviate his wrath; his heavy wrath will lie on them without anything to lighten the burden or to keep off in any measure the full weight of it from pressing the soul. His eye will not spare, neither will he regard the sinner's cries and lamentations, however loud and bitter. Then shall wicked men know that God is the Lord; they shall know how great that majesty is which they have despised and how dreadful that threatened wrath is which they have so little regarded.

Then shall come on wicked men that punishment which they deserve. God will exact of them the uttermost farthing. Their iniquities are marked before him; they are all written in his book; and in the future world he will reckon with them and they must pay all the debt. Their sins are laid up in store with God; they are sealed up among his treasures, and them he will recompense, even recompense into their bosoms. The consummate degree of punishment will not be executed till the day of judgment; but the wicked are sealed over to this consummate punishment immediately after death; they are cast into hell, and there bound in chains of darkness to the judgment of the great day, and they know that the highest degree of punishment is coming upon them. Final wrath will be executed without any mixture; all mercy, all enjoyments will be taken away. God sometimes expresses his wrath in this world; but here good things and evil are mixed together; in the future there will be only evil things.

Wrath will then be executed without any merciful circumstances. The judgments which God executes on ungodly men in this world are attended with many merciful circumstances. There is much patience and long-suffering, together with judgment; judgments are joined with continuance of opportunity to seek mercy. But in hell there will be no more exercises of divine patience. The judgments which God exercises on ungodly men in this world are warnings to them to avoid greater punishments; but the wrath which will come upon them when they shall have filled up the measure of their sin will not be of the nature of warnings. Indeed they will be effectually awakened and made thoroughly sensible by what they shall suffer; yet their being awakened and made sensible will do them no good. Many a wicked man hath suffered very awful things from God in this world which have been a means of saving good; but that wrath which sinners shall suffer after death will be no way for their good. God will have no merciful design in it; neither will it be possible that they should get any good by that or by anything else.

Wrath will so be executed as to perfect the work to which wrath tends, namely, utterly to undo the subject of it. Wrath is often so executed in this life as greatly to distress persons and bring them into great calamity; yet not so as to complete the ruin of those who suffer it; but in another world it will be so executed as to finish their destruction and render them utterly and perfectly undone; it will take away all comfort, all hope, and all support. The soul will be, as it were, utterly crushed; the wrath will be wholly intolerable. It must sink, and will utterly sink, and will have no more strength to keep itself from sinking than a worm would have to keep itself from being crushed under the weight of a mountain. The wrath will be so great, so mighty and powerful as wholly to abolish all manner of welfare: "But on whomsoever it shall fall it will grind him to powder."

When persons shall have filled up the measure of their sin that wrath will come upon them which is eternal. Though men may suffer very terrible and awful judgments in this world, yet those judgments have an end. They may be long continued, yet they commonly admit of relief. Temporal distresses and sorrows have intermissions and respite and commonly by degrees abate and wear off; but the wrath that shall be executed when the measure of sin shall have been filled up will have no end. Thus it will be to the uttermost as to its duration; it will be of so long continuance that it will be impossible it should be longer. Nothing can be longer than eternity.

When persons shall have filled up the measure of their sin then wrath will come upon them to the uttermost of what is threatened. Sin is an infinite evil, and the punishment which God hath threatened against it is very dreadful. The threatenings of God against the workers of iniquity are very awful; but these threatenings are never fully accomplished in this world. However dreadful things some men may suffer in this life, yet God never fully executes his threatenings for so much as one sin till they have filled up the whole measure. The threatenings of the law are never answered by anything that any man suffers here. The most awful judgment in this life doth not answer God's threatenings, either in degree or in circumstances or in duration. If the greatest sufferings that ever are endured in this life should be eternal, it would not answer the threatening. Indeed temporal judgments belong to the threatenings of the law; but these are not answered by them; they are but foretastes of the punishment. "The wages of sin is death." No expressions of wrath that are suffered before men have filled up the measure of their sin are its full wages. But then God will reckon with them and will recompense into their bosoms the full deserved sum.

The use I would make of this doctrine is of warning to natural men to rest no longer in sin and to make haste to flee from it. The things which have been said under this doctrine may well be awakening, awful considerations to you. It is awful to consider whose wrath it is that abides upon you and of what wrath you are in danger. It is impossible to express the misery of a natural condition. It is like being in Sodom with a dreadful storm of fire and brimstone hanging over it just ready to break forth and to be poured down upon it. The clouds of divine vengeance are full and just ready to burst. Here let those who yet continue in sin in this town consider particularly:

Under what great means and advantages you continue in sin. God is now favoring us with very great and extraordinary means and advantages in that we have such extraordinary tokens of the presence of God among us; his spirit is so remarkably poured out and multitudes of all ages and all sorts are converted and brought home to Christ. God appears among us in the most extraordinary manner, perhaps, that ever he did in New England. The children of Israel saw many mighty works of God when he brought them out of Egypt; but we, at this day, see works more mighty and of a more glorious nature.

We who live under such light have had loud calls, but now above all. Now is the day of salvation. The fountain hath been set open among us in an extraordinary manner and hath stood open for a considerable time. Yet you continue in sin, and the calls that you have hitherto had have not brought you to be washed in it. What extraordinary advantages have you lately enjoyed to stir you up! How hath everything in the town of late been of that tendency! Those things which used to be the greatest hindrances have been removed. You have not the ill examples of immoral persons to be a temptation to you. There is not now that vain worldly talk and ill company to divert you and to be a hindrance to you which there used to be. Now you have multitudes of good examples set before you; there are many now all around you who, instead of diverting and hindering you, are earnestly desirous of your salvation and willing to do all that they can to move you to flee to Christ: they have a thirsting desire for it. The chief talk in the town has of late been about the things of religion and has been such as hath tended to promote and not hinder your souls' good. Everything all around you hath tended to stir you up; and will you yet continue in sin?

Some of you have continued in sin till you are far advanced in life. You were warned when you were children, and some of you had awakenings then; however, the time went away. You became men and women, and then you were stirred up again; you had the strivings of God's Spirit; and some of you have fixed the times when you would make thorough work of seeking salvation. Some of you, perhaps, determined to do it when you should be married and settled in the world; others when you should have finished such a business and when your circumstances should be so and so altered. Now these times have come and are past, yet you continue in sin.

Many of you have had remarkable warnings of Providence. Some of you have been warned by the deaths of near relations; you have stood by and seen others die and go into eternity; yet this hath not been effectual. Some of you have been near death yourselves, have been brought nigh the grave in sore sickness, and were full of your promises how you would behave yourselves if it should please God to spare your lives. Some of you have very narrowly escaped death by dangerous accidents; but God was pleased to spare you, to give you a further space to repent; yet you continue in sin.

Some of you have seen times of remarkable outpourings of the Spirit of God in this town in times past, but it had no good effect on you. You had the strivings of the Spirit of God, too, as well as others. God did not pass so by your door but that he came and knocked; yet you stood it out. Now God hath come again in a more remarkable manner than ever before, and hath been pouring out his Spirit for some months in its most gracious influence: yet you remain in sin until now. In the beginning of this awakening you were warned to flee from wrath and to forsake your sins. You were told what a wide door there was open, what an accepted time it was, and were urged to press into the kingdom of God. And many did press in; they forsook their sins and believed in Christ, but you, when you had seen it, repented not that you might believe him.

Then you were warned again, and still others have been pressing and thronging into the kingdom of God. Many have fled for refuge and have laid hold on Christ: yet you continue in sin and unbelief. You have seen multitudes of all sorts, of all ages, young and old, flocking to Christ, and many of about your age and your circumstances; but you still are in the same miserable condition in which you used to be. You have seen persons daily flocking to Christ, as doves to their windows. God hath not only poured out his Spirit on this town, but also on other towns around us, and they are flocking in there as well as here. This blessing spreads further and further; many, far and near, seem to be setting their faces Zion-ward; yet you who live here, where this work first began, continue behind still; you have no lot nor portion in this matter.

How dreadful the wrath of God is when it is executed to the uttermost. To make you in some measure sensible of that, I desire you to consider whose wrath it is. The wrath of a king is the roaring of a lion, but this is the wrath of Jehovah, the Lord God Omnipotent. Let us consider, what can we rationally think of it? How dreadful must be the wrath of such a Being when it comes upon a person to the uttermost, without any pity, or moderation, or merciful circumstances! What must be the uttermost of his wrath who made heaven and earth by the word of his power;

who spake and it was done, who commanded and it stood fast! What must his wrath be who commandeth the sun and it rises not, and sealeth up the stars! What must his wrath be who shaketh the earth out of its place and causeth the pillars of heaven to tremble! What must his wrath be who rebuketh the sea and maketh it dry, who removeth the mountains out of their places and overturneth them in his anger? What must his wrath be whose majesty is so awful that no man could live in the sight of it? What must the wrath of such a Being be when it comes to the uttermost, when he makes his majesty appear and shine bright in the misery of wicked men? And what is a worm of the dust before the fury and under the weight of this wrath, which the stoutest devils cannot bear, but utterly sink and are crushed under it?

Consider how dreadful the wrath of God is sometimes in this world, only in a little taste or view of it. Sometimes, when God only enlightens conscience to have some sense of his wrath, it causes the stout-hearted to cry out; nature is ready to sink under it, when indeed it is but a little glimpse of divine wrath that is seen. This hath been observed in many cases. But if a slight taste and apprehension of wrath be so dreadful and intolerable, what must it be when it comes upon persons to the uttermost? When a few drops or a little sprinkling of wrath is so distressing and overbearing to the soul, how must it be when God opens the flood-gates and lets the mighty deluge of his wrath come pouring down upon men's guilty heads and brings in all his waves and billows upon their souls? How little of God's wrath will sink them! "When his wrath is kindled but a little, blessed are all they that put their trust in him."

Consider, you know not what wrath God may be about to execute upon wicked men in this world. Wrath may, in some sense, be coming upon them in the present life, to the uttermost, for aught we know. When it is said of the Jews, "the wrath is come upon them to the uttermost," respect is had, not only to the execution of divine wrath on that people in hell, but that terrible destruction of Judea and Jerusalem, which was then near approaching by the Romans. We know not but the wrath is now coming, in some peculiarly awful manner, on the wicked world. God seems, by the things which he is doing among us, to be coming forth for some great thing. The work which hath been lately wrought among us is no ordinary thing. He doth not work in his usual way, but in a way very extraordinary; and it is probable that it is a forerunner of some very great revolution. We must not pretend to say what is in the womb of Providence, or what is in the book of God's secret decrees; yet we may and ought to discern the signs of these times.

Though God be now about to do glorious things for his church and people, yet it is probable that they will be accompanied with dreadful things to his enemies.

It is the manner of God, when he brings about any glorious revolution for his people, at the same time to execute very awful judgments on his enemies.

"Rejoice, O ye nations, with his people; for he will avenge the blood of his servants, and will render vengeance to his adversaries, and will be merciful unto his land and to his people."

"Say ye to the righteous, it shall be well with him: for they shall eat the fruit of their doings. Woe unto the wicked, it shall be ill with him: for the reward of his hands shall be given him."

"Therefore, thus saith the Lord God, Behold, my servants shall eat, but ye shall be hungry: behold, my servants shall drink, but ye shall be thirsty: behold, my servants shall rejoice, but ye shall be ashamed: behold, my servants shall sing for joy of heart, but ye shall cry for sorrow of heart and shall howl for vexation of spirit."

We find in Scripture that where glorious times are prophesied to God's people there are at the same time awful judgments foretold to his enemies. What God is now about to do, we know not; but this we may know, that there will be no safety to any but those who are in the ark. Therefore it behooves all to haste, and flee for their lives, to get into a safe condition, to get into Christ; then they need not fear, though the earth be removed and the mountains carried into the midst of the sea; though the waters thereof roar and be troubled; though the mountains shake with the swelling thereof: for God will be their refuge and strength; they need not be afraid of evil tidings; their hearts may be fixed, trusting in the Lord.

WHITEFIELD
(1714 - 1770)

Sketch of His Life

The Evangelical Revival began under George Whitefield, who preached unabashed, evangelistic Calvinism. Wesley had begun on the same course, but defected to Arminianism because he retained preconversion opinions on predestination and the extent of the atonement. Lloyd-Jones called Whitefield "the greatest preacher and orator of the 18th century."

Whitefield had a good education, including work in Greek and Latin, as well as studying public speaking. It was at Oxford that he met the Wesleys. He was ordained at the age of 22 to the Anglican ministry and became popular almost at once. More than one-third of his ministry was carried on in the United States; and while in the United States, he began an orphanage in Savannah, Georgia. He crossed the Atlantic 13 times (no easy task in those days). After a fruitful, thirty-four year ministry, he died in New England.

Benjamin Franklin said, "I knew him intimately upwards of thirty years. His integrity, disinterestedness and indefatigable zeal in prosecuting every good work I have never seen excelled, and shall never see excelled." Sometimes he was so exhausted he had to be lifted on and off his horse. He preached about thirteen sermons a week, a total of more than 18,000 sermons in all. There are seventy-five sermons extant.

Content

He was a Calvinistic Methodist. Remember that the revivals in America and England were begun by Calvinistic preaching. Wesley declared his defection from Calvinism in the "Free Grace" sermon and Whitefield urged him not to publish it. Wesley replied in a nasty way and published it. As a result, the two were estranged (1741). After this, Whitefield was once asked if he thought that he would see Wesley in heaven. He said, "No. He'll be so close to the throne and we so far, we'll hardly get a sight of him." Later, however, they were reconciled (though not in belief), and Wesley preached a notable memorial sermon upon the occasion of Whitefield's death.

Whitefield's sermons contained Biblical, doctrinal and evangelistic materials. There are repeated references to authors that show his knowledge of the best writers in theology and preaching. Whitefield studied sermons, and preached frequently from the Old Testament.

Organization

His structure, though often rather loose, followed a modified Puritan plan. There was ordinarily the introduction, a division of the subject, an application and the conclusion. Explanations of the context often end in a statement of purpose.

Style

Whitefield's preaching was bold and direct, two outstanding features of his sermons that are worthy of analysis. He preached personally throughout much of the sermon; application was not tacked on to the end. Bolingbroke said, "He has the most commanding eloquence I have ever heard in any person."

Whitefield was dramatic and used imagery well. When he described a sinking ship, men rose from the pews to man the lifeboat. He was emotional and inspirational. His power of description is unequaled. Accounts of his preaching consistently say that the congregation "saw," "felt" and "heard" as he preached. People shivered. Punshon says that David Hume was so caught up in Whitefield's preaching that "he forgot to sneer." Chesterfield sprang forward to catch a blind beggar that Whitefield pictured poised on the edge of a cliff. This power to make preaching so real and vivid as to deeply involve the congregation is a feature worthy of analysis. We saw the same thing in Edwards's preaching.

Delivery

Whitefield was called the "Demosthenes of the pulpit." His voice was very powerful. Whitefield did much outdoor preaching in the fields and in the city streets. Crowds of 25,000 to 35,000 often gathered and could hear easily. When Whitefield was preaching in Philadelphia, Franklin backed up from city hall to Front Street, all the while able to hear him clearly. Franklin calculated that 35,000 people in a circle around him would have no difficulty hearing him. Once, on board a ship crossing the Atlantic, he preached so loudly that not only could those on his ship hear, but those on a ship traveling alongside could, too.

It was said of him that he could make you laugh or cry by the way he said "Mesopotamia." Garrick, the famous actor, praised his gestures and claimed that "his face was language." He once declared that he would give $500 if he could say "Oh" like Whitefield. He urged actors to attend Whitefield's meetings and learn from him. There was pathos and feeling in his sermons; sometimes he wept.

Soon after he began, Whitefield became an extemporaneous preacher. In his journal of February 2, 1739 (he was ordained in 1736), he wrote, "This is the first time that I have preached without notes ... but I find myself now, as it were, constrained to do it." The next day he wrote, "I find I gain greater light and knowledge by preaching extempore, so that I fear I should quench the Spirit did I not go on to speak as He gives me utterance."

Effects

The colliers (coal miners) at Kingswood (near Bristol), where he began his field preaching, also wept—so freely that the tears streaming down their cheeks cut white furrows through the coal dust on their faces. The Great Awakening in England began under his preaching and was furthered in America as well. As the result of his preaching, hundreds of new congregations were formed in a half dozen different denominations. Franklin said, "It was wonderful to see the change soon made by his preaching in the manners of the inhabitants of Philadelphia. From being thoughtless or indifferent about religion, it seemed as if the world were growing religious." On one occasion, when Whitefield was appealing for money for his orphanage in Georgia, Franklin determined not to give anything. Then, as Whitefield spoke, he decided to give his coppers. As he continued, he determined to give his silver. But by the time the plate was passed, he gave his coppers, his silver and his gold!

After Whitefield had finished preaching on his last night on earth, the crowd begged him for more. So he preached from the stairs of the house where he was staying till the candle burned down, then went to bed and died. The Lord granted His servant the privilege of continuing to do what he loved to do most—preaching the Word—to the very end.

ON THE METHOD OF GRACE

"They have healed also the hurt of the daughter of my people slightly, saying, Peace, peace; when there is no peace." (Jeremiah 6:14)

As God can send a nation of people no greater blessing than to give them faithful, sincere, and upright ministers, so the greatest curse that God can possibly send upon a people in this world is to give them over to blind, unregenerate, carnal, lukewarm, and unskilful guides. And yet, in all ages, we find that there have been many wolves in sheep's clothing, many that daubed with untempered mortar, that prophesied smoother things than God did allow. As it was formerly, so it is now; there are many that corrupt the word of God and deal deceitfully with it. It was so in a special manner in the prophet Jeremiah's time; and he, faithful to his Lord, faithful to that God who employed him, did not fail from time to time to open his mouth against them, and to bear a noble testimony to the honor of that God in whose name he from time to time spake. If you will read his prophecy, you will find that none spake more against such ministers than Jeremiah, and here especially in the chapter out of which the text is taken he speaks very severely against them. He charges them with several crimes; particularly he charges them with covetousness: "For," says he, in the thirteenth verse, "from the least of them even to the greatest of them, every one is given to covetousness; and from the prophet even unto the priest, every one dealeth falsely."

And then, in the words of the text, in a more special manner, he exemplifies how they had dealt falsely, how they had behaved treacherously to poor souls: says he, "They have healed also the hurt of the daughter of my people slightly, saying, Peace, peace, when there is no peace." The prophet, in the name of God, had been denouncing war against the people; he had been telling them that their house should be left desolate, and that the Lord would certainly visit the land with war. "Therefore," says he, in the eleventh verse, "I am full of the fury of the Lord; I am weary with holding in; I will pour it out upon the children abroad, and upon the assembly of young men together; for even the husband with the wife shall be taken, the aged with him that is full of days. And their houses shall be turned unto others, with their fields and wives together; for I will stretch out my hand upon the inhabitants of the land, saith the Lord."

The prophet gives a thundering message, that they might be terrified and have some convictions and inclinations to repent; but it seems that the false prophets, the false priests, went about stifling people's convictions, and when they were hurt or a little terrified, they were for daubing over the wound, telling them that Jeremiah was but an enthusiastic preacher, that there could be no such thing as war among them, and saying to people, Peace, peace, be still, when the prophet told them there was no peace.

The words, then, refer primarily unto outward things,

but I verily believe have also a further reference to the soul, and are to be referred to those false teachers who, when people were under conviction of sin, when people were beginning to look towards heaven, were for stifling their convictions and telling them they were good enough before. And, indeed, people generally love to have it so; our hearts are exceedingly deceitful and desperately wicked; none but the eternal God knows how treacherous they are.

How many of us cry, Peace, peace, to our souls, when there is no peace! How many are there who are now settled upon their lees, that now think they are Christians, that now flatter themselves that they have an interest in Jesus Christ; whereas if we come to examine their experiences we shall find that their peace is but a peace of the devil's making—it is not a peace of God's giving—it is not a peace that passeth human understanding.

It is a matter, therefore, of great importance, my dear hearers, to know whether we may speak peace to our hearts. We are all desirous of peace; peace is an unspeakable blessing; how can we live without peace? And, therefore, people from time to time must be taught how far they must go and what must be wrought in them before they can speak peace to their hearts. This is what I design at present, that I may deliver my soul, that I may be free from the blood of all those to whom I preach—that I may not fail to declare the whole counsel of God. I shall, from the words of the text, endeavor to show you what you must undergo and what must be wrought in you before you can speak peace to your hearts.

But before I come directly to this give me leave to premise a caution or two.

And the first is, that I take it for granted you believe religion to be an inward thing; you believe it to be a work in the heart, a work wrought in the soul by the power of the Spirit of God. If you do not believe this, you do not believe your Bibles. If you do not believe this, though you have got your Bibles in your hand, you hate the Lord Jesus Christ in your heart; for religion is everywhere represented in Scripture as the work of God in the heart. "The kingdom of God is within us," says our Lord; and, "he is not a Christian who is one outwardly; but he is a Christian who is one inwardly." If any of you place religion in outward things, I shall not perhaps please you this morning; you will understand me no more when I speak of the work of God upon a poor sinner's heart than if I were talking in an unknown tongue.

I would further premise a condition, that I would by no means confine God to one way of acting. I would by no means say that all persons, before they come to have a settled peace in their hearts, are obliged to undergo the same degrees of conviction. No; God has various ways of bringing his children home; his sacred Spirit bloweth when, and where, and how it listeth. But, however, I will venture to affirm this: that before ever you can speak peace to your heart, whether by shorter or longer continuance of your convictions, whether in a more pungent or in a more gentle way, you must undergo what I shall hereafter lay down in the following discourse.

First, then, before you can speak peace to your hearts, you must be made to see, made to feel, made to weep over, made to bewail, your actual transgressions against the law of God. According to the covenant of works, "the soul that sinneth it shall die;" cursed is that man, be he what he may, be he who he may, that continueth not in all things that are written in the book of the law to do them.

We are not only to do some things, but we are to do all things, and we are to continue so to do, so that the least deviation from the moral law, according to the covenant of works, whether in thought, word, or deed, deserves eternal death at the hand of God. And if one evil thought, if one evil word, if one evil action deserves eternal damnation, how many hells, my friends, do every one of us deserve whose whole lives have been one continued rebellion against God! Before ever, therefore, you can speak peace to your hearts, you must be brought to see, brought to believe, what a dreadful thing it is to depart from the living God.

And now, my dear friends, examine your hearts, for I hope you came hither with a design to have your souls made better. Give me leave to ask you, in the presence of God, whether you know the time, and if you do not know exactly the time, do you know there was a time when God wrote bitter things against you, when the arrows of the Almighty were within you? Was ever the remembrance of your sins grievous to you? Was the burden of your sins intolerable to your thoughts? Did you ever see that God's wrath might justly fall upon you, on account of your actual transgressions against God? Were you ever in all your life sorry for your sins? Could you ever say, My sins are gone over my head as a burden too heavy for me to bear? Did you ever experience any such thing as this? Did ever any such thing as this pass between God and your soul? If not, for Jesus Christ's sake, do not call yourselves Christians; you may speak peace to your hearts, but there is no peace. May the Lord awaken you, may the Lord convert you, may the Lord give you peace, if it be his will, before you go home!

But, further, you may be convinced of your actual sins, so as to be made to tremble, and yet you may be strangers to Jesus Christ, you may have no true work of grace upon your hearts. Before ever, therefore, you can speak peace to your hearts, conviction must go deeper; you must not only be convinced of your actual transgressions against the law of God, but likewise of the foundation of all your transgressions. And what is that? I mean original sin, that original corruption each of us brings into the world with us, which renders us liable to God's wrath and damnation. There are many poor souls that think themselves fine reasoners, yet they pretend to say there is no such thing as original sin; they will charge God with injustice in imputing Adam's sin to us; although we have got the mark of the beast and of the devil upon us, yet they tell us we are not born in sin. Let them look abroad into the world and see the disorders in it, and think, if they can, if this is the paradise in which God did put man. No! everything in the world is out of order.

I have often thought, when I was abroad, that if there were no other argument to prove original sin, the rising of wolves and tigers against man, nay, the barking of a dog against us, is a proof of original sin. Tigers and lions durst not rise against us if it were not for Adam's first sin: for when the creatures rise up against us it is as much as to say, "You have sinned against God, and we take up our Master's quarrel. If we look inwardly, we shall see enough of lusts and man's temper contrary to the temper of God. There is pride, malice, and revenge in all our hearts; and this temper cannot come from God; it comes from our first parent, Adam, who, after he fell from God, fell out of God into the devil.

However, therefore, some people may deny this, yet when conviction comes, all carnal reasonings are battered down immediately, and the poor soul begins to feel and see the fountain from which all the polluted streams do flow. When the sinner is first awakened, he begins to wonder, How came I to be so wicked? The Spirit of God then strikes in, and shows that he has no good thing in him by nature; then he sees that he is altogether gone out of the way, that he is altogether become abominable, and the poor creature is made to lie down at the foot of the throne of God and to acknowledge that God would be just to damn him, just to cut him off, though he never had committed one actual sin in his life.

Did you ever feel and experience this, any of you—to justify God in your damnation—to own that you are by nature children of wrath, and that God may justly cut you off, though you never actually had offended him in all your life? If you were ever truly convicted, if your hearts were ever truly cut, if self were truly taken out of you, you would be made to see and feel this. And if you have never felt the weight of original sin, do not call yourselves Christians. I am verily persuaded original sin is the greatest burden of a true convert; this ever grieves the regenerate soul, the sanctified soul. The indwelling of sin in the heart is the burden of a converted person; it is the burden of a true Christian. He continually cries out: "Oh! who will deliver me from this body of death, this indwelling corruption in my heart?" This is that which disturbs a poor soul most. And, therefore, if you never felt this inward corruption, if you never saw that God might justly curse you for it, indeed, my dear friends, you may speak peace to your hearts, but I fear, nay, I know, there is no true peace.

Further, before you can speak peace to your hearts you must not only be troubled for the sins of your life, the sins of your nature, but likewise for the sins of your best duties and performances.

When a poor soul is somewhat awakened by the terrors of the Lord, then the poor creature, being born under the covenant of works, flies directly to a covenant of works again. And as Adam and Eve hid themselves among the trees of the garden and sewed fig-leaves together to cover their nakedness, so the poor sinner when awakened flies to his duties and to his performances, to hide himself from God, and goes to patch up a righteousness of his own. Says he, I will be mighty good now—I will reform—I will do all I can; and then certainly Jesus Christ will have mercy on me. But before you can speak peace to your heart you must be brought to see that God may damn you for the best prayer you ever put up; you must be brought to see that all your duties—all your righteousness—as the prophet elegantly expresses it—put them all together, are so far from recommending you to God, are so far from being any motive and inducement to God to have mercy on your poor soul, that he will see them to be filthy rags, a menstruous cloth—that God hates them, and cannot away with them, if you bring them to him in order to recommend you to his favor.

My dear friends, what is there in our performances to recommend us unto God? Our persons are in an unjustified state by nature, we deserve to be damned ten thousand times over; and what must our performances be? We can do no good thing by nature: "They that are in the flesh cannot please God."

You may do things materially good, but you cannot do a thing formally and rightly good; because nature cannot act above itself. It is impossible that a man who is unconverted can act for the glory of God; he cannot do anything in faith, and "whatsoever is not of faith is sin."

After we are renewed, yet we are renewed but in part, indwelling sin continues in us, there is a mixture of corruption in every one of our duties; so that after we are converted, were Jesus Christ only to accept us according to our works, our works would damn us, for we cannot put up a prayer but it is far from that perfection which the moral law requireth. I do not know what you may think but I can say that I cannot pray but I sin—I cannot preach to you or to any others but I sin—I can do nothing without sin; and, as one expresseth it, my repentance wants to be repented of, and my tears to be washed in the precious blood of my dear Redeemer.

Our best duties are as so many splendid sins. Before you can speak peace to your heart you must not only be sick of your original and actual sin, but you must be made sick of your righteousness, of all your duties and performances. There must be a deep conviction before you can be brought out of your self-righteousness; it is the last idol taken out of our heart. The pride of our heart will not let us submit to the righteousness of Jesus Christ. But if you never felt that you had no righteousness of your own, if you never felt the deficiency of your own righteousness, you cannot come to Jesus Christ.

There are a great many now who may say, Well, we believe all this; but there is a great difference betwixt talking and feeling. Did you ever feel the want of a dear Redeemer? Did you ever feel the want of Jesus Christ, upon the account of the deficiency of your own righteousness? And can you now say from your heart, Lord, thou mayest justly damn me for the best duties that ever I did perform? If you are not thus brought out of self, you may speak peace to yourselves, but yet there is no peace.

But then, before you can speak peace to your souls, there is one particular sin you must be greatly troubled for, and yet I fear there are few of you think what it is; it is the reigning, the damning sin of the Christian world, and yet the Christian would seldom or never think of it.

And pray what is that?

It is what most of you think you are not guilty of—and that is, the sin of unbelief. Before you can speak peace to your heart, you must be troubled for the unbelief of your heart. But can it be supposed that any of you are unbelievers here in this churchyard, that are born in Scotland, in a reformed country, that go to church every Sabbath? Can any of you that receive the sacrament once a year—Oh, that it were administered oftener!—can it be supposed that you who had tokens for the sacrament, that you who keep up family prayer, that any of you do not believe in the Lord Jesus Christ?

I appeal to your own hearts, if you would not think me uncharitable, if I doubted whether any of you believed in Christ; and yet I fear upon examination, we should find that most of you have not so much faith in the Lord Jesus Christ as the devil himself. I am persuaded the devil believes more of the Bible than most of us do. He believes the divinity of Jesus Christ; that is more than many who call themselves Christians do; nay, he believes and trembles, and that is more than thousands amongst us do.

My friends, we mistake a historical faith for a true faith, wrought in the heart by the Spirit of God. You fancy you believe because you believe there is such a book as we call the Bible—because you go to church; all this you may do and have no true faith in Christ. Merely to believe there was such a person as Christ, merely to believe there is a book called the Bible, will do you no good, more than to believe there was such a man as Caesar or Alexander the Great. The Bible is a sacred depository. What thanks have we to give to God for these lively oracles! But yet we may have these and not believe in the Lord Jesus Christ.

My dear friends, there must be a principle wrought in the heart by the Spirit of the living God. Did I ask you how long it is since you believed in Jesus Christ, I suppose most of you would tell me you believed in Jesus Christ as long as ever you remember—you never did misbelieve. Then, you could not give me a better proof that you never yet believed in Jesus Christ, unless you were sanctified early, as from the womb; for they that otherwise believe in Christ know there was a time when they did not believe in Jesus Christ.

You say you love God with all your heart, soul, and strength. If I were to ask you how long it is since you loved God, you would say, As long as you can remember; you never hated God, you know no time when there was enmity in your heart against God. Then, unless you were sanctified very early, you never loved God in your life.

My dear friends, I am more particular in this, because it is a most deceitful delusion, whereby so many people are carried away, that they believe already. Therefore it is remarked of Mr. Marshall, giving account of his experiences, that he had been working for life, and he had ranged all his sins under the ten commandments, and then, coming to a minister, asked him the reason why he could not get peace. The minister looked to his catalogue, Away, says he, I do not find one word of the sin of unbelief in all your catalogue. It is the peculiar work of the Spirit of God to convince us of our unbelief—that we have got no faith. Says Jesus Christ, "I will send the Comforter; and when he is come, he will reprove the world" of the sin of unbelief; "of sin," says Christ, "because they believe not on me."

Now, my dear friends, did God ever show you that you had no faith? Were you ever made to bewail a hard heart of unbelief? Was it ever the language of your heart, Lord, give me faith; Lord, enable me to lay hold on thee; Lord, enable me to call thee my Lord and my God? Did Jesus Christ ever convince you in this manner? Did he ever convince you of your inability to close with Christ, and make you to cry out to God to give you faith? If not, do not speak peace to your heart. May the Lord awaken you and give you true, solid peace before you go hence and be no more!

Once more, then: before you can speak peace to your heart, you must not only be convinced of your actual and original sin, the sins of your own righteousness, the sin of unbelief, but you must be enabled to lay hold upon the perfect righteousness, the all-sufficient righteousness, of the Lord Jesus Christ; you must lay hold by faith on the righteousness of Jesus Christ, and then you shall have peace. "Come," says Jesus, "unto me, all ye that are weary and heavy laden, and I will give you rest."

This speaks encouragement to all that are weary and heavy laden; but the promise of rest is made to them only upon their coming and believing, and taking him to be their God and their all. Before we can ever have peace with God we must be justified by faith through our Lord Jesus Christ, we must be enabled to apply Christ to our hearts, we must have Christ brought home to our souls, so as his righteousness may be made our righteousness, so as his merits may be imputed to our souls. My dear friends, were you ever married to Jesus Christ? Did Jesus Christ ever give himself to you? Did you ever close with Christ by a lively faith, so as to feel Christ in your hearts, so as to hear him speaking peace to your souls? Did peace ever flow in upon your hearts like a river? Did you ever feel that peace that Christ spoke to his disciples? I pray God he may come and speak peace to you. These things you must experience.

I am now talking of the invisible realities of another world, of inward religion, of the work of God upon a poor sinner's heart. I am now talking of a matter of great importance, my dear hearers; you are all concerned in it, your souls are concerned in it, your eternal salvation is concerned in it. You may be all at peace, but perhaps the devil has lulled you asleep into a carnal lethargy and security, and will endeavor to keep you there till he get you to hell, and there you will be awakened; but it will be dreadful to be awakened and find yourselves so fearfully mistaken, when the great gulf is fixed, when you will be calling to all eternity for a drop of water to cool your tongue and shall not obtain it.

CHRIST THE BELIEVER'S WISDOM, RIGHTEOUS-NESS, SANCTIFICATION AND REDEMPTION

"But of him are ye in Christ Jesus, who of God is made unto us wisdom, and righteousness, and sanctification, and redemption." (I Cor. 1:30)

Of all the verses in the book of God, this which I have now read to you, is, I believe, one of the most comprehensive: what glad tidings does it bring to believers! what precious privileges are they herein invested with! how are they here led to the fountain of them all, I mean, the love, the everlasting love of God the Father! 'Of him are ye in Christ Jesus, who of God is made unto us wisdom, righteousness, sanctification, and redemption.'

Without referring you to the context, I shall from the words,

First, Point out to you the fountain, from which all those blessings flow, that the elect of God partake of in Jesus Christ, 'Who of God is made unto us'. And,

Secondly, I shall consider what these blessings are, 'Wisdom, righteousness, sanctification, and redemption'.

First, I would point out to you the fountain, from which all those blessings flow, that the elect of God partake of in Jesus, 'who of God is made unto us', the Father, he it is who is spoken of here. Not as though Jesus Christ was not God also; but God the Father is the fountain of the Deity; and if we consider Jesus Christ acting as Mediator, God the Father is greater than he; there was an eternal contract between the Father and the Son: 'I have made a covenant with my chosen, and I have sworn unto David my servant'; now David was a type of Christ, with whom the Father made a covenant, that if he would obey and suffer, and make himself a sacrifice for sin, he should 'see his seed, he should prolong his days, and the pleasure of the Lord should prosper in his hands'. This compact our Lord refers to, in that glorious prayer recorded in the 17th chapter of John; and therefore he prays for, or rather demands with a full assurance, all that were given to him by the Father: 'Father, I will that they also whom thou hast given me, be with me where I am.' For this same reason, the apostle breaks out into praises of God, even the Father of our Lord Jesus Christ; for he loved the elect with an everlasting love, or, as our Lord expresses it, 'before the foundation of the world'; and, therefore, to shew them to whom they were beholden for their salvation, our Lord, in the 25th of Matthew, represents himself saying, 'Come, ye blessed children of my Father, receive the kingdom prepared for you from the foundation of the world'. And thus, in reply to the mother of Zebedee's children, he says, 'It is not mine to give, but it shall be given to them for whom it is prepared of the Father'. The apostle therefore, when here speaking of the Christian's privileges, lest they should sacrifice to their own drag, or think their salvation was owing to their own faithfulness, or improvement of their own free-will, reminds them to look back on the everlasting love of God the Father; 'who of God is made unto us', etc.

Would to God this point of doctrine was considered more, and people were more studious of the covenant of redemption between the Father and the Son! we should not then have so much disputing against the doctrine of election, or hear it condemned (even by good men) as a doctrine of devils. For my own part, I cannot see how true humbleness of mind can be attained without a knowledge of it; and though I will not say, that every one who denies election is a bad man, yet I will say, with that sweet singer, Mr. Trail, it is a very bad sign: such a one, whoever he be, I think cannot truly know himself; for, if we deny election, we must, partly at least, glory in ourselves; but our redemption is so ordered, that no flesh should glory in the Divine presence; and hence it is, that the pride of man opposes this doctrine, because, according to this doctrine, and no other, 'he that glories, must glory only in the Lord'. But what shall I say? Election is a mystery that shines with such resplendent brightness, that, to make use of the words of one who has drunk deeply of electing love, it dazzles the weak eyes even of some of God's dear children; however, though they know it not, all the blessings they receive, all the privileges they do or will enjoy, through Jesus Christ, flow from the everlasting love of God the Father: 'But of him are you in Christ Jesus, who of God is made unto us, wisdom, righteousness, sanctification, and redemption.'

Secondly, I come to shew what these blessings are, which are here, through Christ, made over to the elect. And,

1: *First*, Christ is made to them *Wisdom*; but wherein does true wisdom consist? Were I to ask some of you, perhaps you would say, in indulging the lust of the flesh, and saying to your souls, eat, drink, and be merry: but this is only the wisdom of brutes; they have as good a gust and relish for sensual pleasures, as the greatest epicure on earth. Others would tell me, true wisdom consisted in adding house to house, and field to field, and calling lands after their own names: but this cannot be true wisdom; for riches often take to themselves wings, and fly away, like an eagle towards heaven. Even wisdom itself assures us, 'that a man's life doth not consist in the abundance of the things which he possesses'; vanity, vanity, all these things are vanity; for, if riches leave not the owner, the owners must soon leave them; 'for rich men must also die, and leave their riches for others'; their riches cannot procure them redemption from the grave, whither we are all hastening apace.

But perhaps you despise riches and pleasure, and therefore place wisdom in the knowledge of books: but it is possible for you to tell the numbers of the stars, and call them all by their names, and yet be mere fools; learned men are not always wise; nay, our common learning, so much cried up, makes men only so many accomplished fools; to keep you therefore no longer in suspense, and withal to humble you, I will send you to a heathen to school, to learn what true wisdom is: 'Know thyself', was a saying of one of the wise men of Greece; this is certainly true wisdom, and this is that wisdom spoken of in the text, and which Jesus Christ is made to all elect sinners— they are made to know themselves, so as not to think more highly of themselves than they ought to think. Before, they were darkness; now, they are light in the Lord; and in that light they see their own darkness; they now bewail themselves as fallen creatures by nature, dead in trespasses and sins, sons and heirs of hell, and children of wrath; they now see that all their righteousnesses are but as filthy rags; that there is no health in their souls; that they are poor and miserable, blind and naked; and that there is no name given under heaven, whereby they can be saved, but that of Jesus Christ. They see the necessity of closing with a Saviour, and behold the wisdom of God in appointing him to be a Saviour; they are also made willing to accept of salvation upon our Lord's own terms, and receive him as their all in all: thus Christ is made to them wisdom.

2: *Secondly, Righteousness*, 'Who of God is made unto us, wisdom, righteousness': Christ's whole personal righteousness is made over to, and accounted theirs. They are enabled to lay hold on Christ by faith, and God the Father blots out their transgressions, as with a thick cloud: their sins and their iniquities he remembers no more; they are made the righteousness of God in Christ Jesus, 'who is the end of the law for righteousness to every one that believeth'. In one sense, God now sees no sin in them; the whole covenant of works is fulfilled in them; they are actually justified, acquitted, and looked upon as righteous in the sight of God; they are perfectly accepted in the beloved; they are complete in him; the flaming sword of God's wrath, which before moved every way, is now removed, and free access given to the tree of life; they are enabled to reach out the arm of faith, and pluck, and live for evermore. Hence it is that the apostle, under a sense of this blessed privilege, breaks out into this triumphant language; 'It is Christ that justifies, who is he that condemns?' Does sin condemn? Christ's righteousness delivers believers from the guilt of it: Christ is their Saviour, and is become a propitiation for their sins: who therefore shall lay any thing to the charge of God's elect? Does the law condemn? By having Christ's righteousness imputed to them, they are dead to the law, as a covenant of works; Christ has fulfilled it for them, and in their stead. Does death threaten them? They need not fear: the sting of death is sin, the strength of sin is the law; but God has given them the victory by imputing to them the righteousness of the Lord Jesus.

And what a privilege is here! Well might the angels at the birth of Christ say to the humble shepherds, 'Behold, I bring you glad tidings of great joy'; unto you that believe in Christ 'a Saviour is born'. And well may angels rejoice at the conversion of poor sinners; for the Lord is their righteousness; they have peace with God through faith in Christ's blood, and shall never enter into condemnation. O believers! (for this discourse is intended in a special manner for you) lift up your heads; 'rejoice in the Lord always; again I say, rejoice'. Christ is made to you, of God, righteousness, what then should you fear? You are made the righteousness of God in him; you may be called, 'The Lord our righteousness'. Of what then should you be afraid? What shall separate you henceforward from the love of Christ? 'Shall tribulation, or distress, or persecution, or famine, or nakedness, or peril, or sword? No, I am persuaded, neither death, nor life, nor angels, nor principalities, nor powers, nor things present, nor things to come, nor height, nor depth, nor any other creature, shall be able to separate you from the love of God, which is in Christ Jesus our Lord', who of God is made unto you righteousness.

This is a glorious privilege, but this is only the beginning of the happiness of believers: For,

3:*Thirdly*, Christ is not only made to them righteousness, but sanctification; by sanctification, I do not mean a bare hypocritical attendance on outward ordinances, though rightly informed Christians will think it their duty and privilege constantly to attend on all outward ordinances. Nor do I mean by sanctification a bare outward reformation, and a few transient convictions, or a little legal sorrow; for all this an unsanctified man may have; but, by sanctification I mean a total renovation of the whole man: by the righteousness of Christ, believers come legally, by sanctification they are made spiritually, alive; by the one they are entitled to, by the other they are made meet for, glory. They are sanctified, therefore, throughout, in spirit, soul, and body.

Their understandings, which were dark before, now become light in the Lord; and their wills, before contrary to, now become one with the will of God; their affections are now set on things above; their memory is now filled with divine things; their natural consciences are now enlightened; their members, which were before instruments of uncleanness, and of iniquity into iniquity, are now new creatures: 'old things are passed away, all things are become new', in their hearts: sin has now no longer dominion over them; they are freed from the power, though not the indwelling and being, of it; they are holy both in heart and life, in all manner of conversation; they are made partakers of a divine nature, and from Jesus Christ, they receive grace; and every grace that is in Christ, is copied and transcribed into their souls; they are transformed into his likeness; he is formed within them; they dwell in him, and he in them; they are led by the Spirit, and bring forth the fruits thereof; they know that Christ is their Emmanuel, God with and in them; they are living temples of the Holy Ghost. And therefore, being a holy habitation unto the Lord, the whole Trinity dwells and walks in them; even here, they sit together with Christ in heavenly places, and are vitally united to him, their Head, by a living faith; their Redeemer, their Maker, is their husband; they are flesh of his flesh, bone of his bone; they talk, they walk with him, as a man talketh and walketh with his friend; in short, they are one with Christ, even as Jesus Christ and the Father are one.

Thus is Christ made to believers sanctification. And O what a privilege is this! to be changed from beasts into saints, and from a devilish, to be made partakers of a divine nature; to be translated from the kingdom of Satan, into the kingdom of God's dear Son! to put off the old man, which is corrupt, and to put on the new man, which is created after God, in righteousness and true holiness! O what an unspeakable blessing is this! I almost stand amazed at the contemplation thereof. Well might the apostle exhort believers to rejoice in the Lord; indeed they have reason always to rejoice; yea, to rejoice on a dying bed; for the kingdom of God is in them; they are changed from glory to glory, even by the Spirit of the Lord: well may this be a mystery to the natural, for it is a mystery even to the spiritual man himself, a mystery which he cannot fathom. Does it not often dazzle your eyes, O ye children of God, to look at your own brightness, when the candle of the Lord shines out, and your Redeemer lifts up the light of his blessed countenance upon your souls? Are not you astonished, when you feel the love of God shed abroad in your hearts by the Holy Ghost, and God holds out the golden sceptre of his mercy, and bids you ask what you will, and it shall be given you? Does not that peace of God, which keeps and rules your hearts, surpass the utmost limits of your understandings? And is not the joy you feel unspeakable? Is it not full of glory? I am persuaded it is; and in your secret communion, when the Lord's love flows in upon your souls, you are as it were swallowed up in, or, to use the apostle's phrase, 'filled with all the fullness of God'. Are not you ready to cry out with Solomon, 'And will the Lord, indeed, dwell thus with men!' How is it that we should be thus thy sons and daughters, O Lord God Almighty!

If you are children of God, and know what it is to have fellowship with the Father and the Son; if you walk by faith, and not by sight; I am assured this is frequently the language of your hearts.

But look forward, and see an unbounded prospect of eternal happiness lying before thee, O believer! what thou hast already received are only the first-fruits, like the cluster of grapes brought out of the land of Canaan; only an earnest and pledge of yet infinitely better things to come: the harvest is to follow; thy grace is hereafter to be swallowed up in glory. Thy great Joshua, and merciful High-Priest, shall administer an abundant entrance to thee into the land of promise, that rest which awaits the children of God: for Christ is not only made to believers wisdom, righteousness, and sanctification, but also *redemption*.

But, before we enter upon the explanation and contemplation of this privilege.

Firstly, Learn hence the great mistake of those writers and clergy, who, notwithstanding they talk of sanctification and inward holiness, (as indeed sometimes they do, though in a very loose and superficial manner,) yet they generally make it the *cause*, whereas they should consider it as the *effect*, of our justification. 'Of him are ye in Christ Jesus, who of God is made unto us, wisdom, righteousness, (and then) sanctification.' For Christ's righteousness, or that which Christ has done in our stead without us, is the sole cause of our acceptance in the sight of God, and of all holiness wrought in us: to this, and not to the light within, or any thing wrought within, should poor sinners seek for justification in the sight of God: for the sake of Christ's righteousness alone, and not any thing wrought in us, does God look favourably upon us; our sanctification at best, in this life, is not complete: though we be delivered from the power, we are not freed from the in-being of sin; but not only the dominion, but the in-being of sin, is forbidden, by the perfect law of God: for it is not said, thou shalt not give way to lust, but 'thou shalt not lust'. So that whilst the principle of lust remains in the least degree in our hearts, though we are otherwise never so holy, yet we cannot, on account of that, hope for acceptance with God. We must first, therefore, look for a righteousness without us, even the righteousness of our Lord Jesus Christ: for this reason the apostle mentions it, and puts it before sanctification, in the words of the text. And whosoever teacheth any other doctrine, doth not preach the truth as it is in Jesus.

Secondly, From hence also, the Antinomians and formal hypocrites may be confuted, who talk of Christ without, but know nothing, experimentally, of a work of sanctification wrought within them. Whatever they may pretend to, since Christ is not in them, the Lord is not their righteousness, and they have no well-grounded hope of glory: for though sanctification is not the cause, yet it is the effect of our acceptance with God; 'Who of God is made unto us righteousness and sanctification'. He, therefore, that is really in Christ, is a new creature; it is not going back to a covenant of works, to look into our hearts, and, seeing that they are changed and renewed, from thence form a comfortable and well grounded assurance of the safety of our states: no, but this is what we are directed to in scripture; by our bringing forth the fruits, we are to judge whether or no we ever did truly partake of the Spirit of God. 'We know (says John) that we are passed from death unto life, because we love the brethren.' And however we may talk of Christ's righteousness, and exclaim against legal preachers, yet, if we be not holy in heart and life, if we be not sanctified and renewed by the Spirit in our minds, we are self-deceivers, we are only formal hypocrites: for we must not put asunder what God has joined together; we must keep the medium between the two extremes; not insist so much on the one hand upon Christ without, as to exclude Christ within, as an evidence of our being his, and as a preparation for future happiness; nor, on the other hand, so depend on inherent righteousness or holiness wrought in us, as to exclude the righteousness of Jesus Christ without us. But,

4: *Fourthly,* Let us now go on, and take a view of the other link, or rather the end, of the believer's golden chain of privileges, *Redemption.* But we must look very high; for the top of it, like Jacob's ladder, reaches heaven, where all believers will ascend, and be placed at the right hand of God. 'Who of God is made unto us, wisdom, righteousness, sanctification, and *redemption.*'

This is a golden chain indeed! and, what is best of all, not one link can ever be broken asunder from another. Was there no other text in the book of God, this single one sufficiently proves the final perseverance of true believers: for never did God yet justify a man, whom he did not sanctify; nor sanctify one, whom he did not completely redeem and glorify: no! as for God, his way, his work, is perfect; he always carried on and finished the work he begun; thus it was in the first, so it is in the new creation; when God says, 'Let there be light,' there is light, that shines more and more unto the perfect day, when believers enter into their eternal rest, as God entered into his. Those whom God has justified, he has in effect glorified: for as a man's worthiness was not the cause of God's giving him Christ's righteousness; so neither shall his unworthiness be a cause of his taking it away; God's gifts and callings are without repentance; and I cannot think they are clear in the notion of Christ's righteousness, who deny the final perseverance of the saints; I fear they understand justification in that low sense, which I understood it in a few years ago, as implying no more than remission of sins: but it not only signifies remission of sins past, but also a *federal right* to all good things to come. If God has given us his only Son, how shall he not with him freely give us all things? Therefore, the apostle, after he says, 'Who of God is made unto us righteousness', does not say, perhaps he may be made to us sanctification and redemption: but, 'he is made': for there is an eternal, indissoluble connexion between these blessed privileges. As the obedience of Christ is imputed to believers, so his perseverance in that obedience is to be imputed to them also; and it argues great ignorance of the covenant of grace and redemption, to object against it.

By the word *redemption*, we are to understand, not only a complete deliverance from all evil, but also a full enjoyment of all good both in body and soul: I say, both in body and soul; for the Lord is also for the body; the bodies of the saints in this life are temples of the Holy Ghost; God makes a covenant with the dust of believers; after death, though worms destroy them, yet, even in their flesh shall they see God. I fear, indeed, there are some Sadducees in our days, or at least heretics, who say, either, that there is no resurrection of the body, or that the resurrection is past already, namely, in our regeneration: Hence it is, that our Lord's coming in the flesh, at the day of judgment, is denied; and consequently, we must throw aside the sacrament of the Lord's supper. For why should we remember the Lord's death until he come to judgment, when he is already come to judge our hearts, and will not come a second time? But all this is only the reasoning of unlearned, unstable men, who certainly know not what they say, nor whereof they affirm. That we must follow our Lord in the regeneration, be partakers of a new birth, and that Christ must come into our hearts, we freely confess; and we hope, when speaking of these things, we speak no more than what we know and feel: but then it is plain, that Jesus Christ will come, hereafter, to judgment, and that he ascended into heaven with the body which he had here on earth; for says he, after his resurrection, 'Handle me, and see; a spirit has not flesh and bones, as you see me have'. And it is plain, that Christ's resurrection was an earnest of ours: for says the apostle, 'Christ is risen from the dead, and become the first-fruits of them that sleep; and as in Adam all die, and are subject to mortality; so all that are in Christ, the second Adam, who represented believers as their federal head, shall certainly be made alive, or rise again with their bodies at the last day'.

Here then, O believers! is one, though the lowest, degree of that redemption which you are to be partakers of hereafter; I mean, the redemption of your bodies: for this corruptible must put on incorruption, this mortal must put on immortality. Your bodies, as well as souls, were given to Jesus Christ by the Father; they have been companions in watching, and fasting, and praying: your bodies, therefore, as well as souls, shall Jesus Christ raise up at the last day. Fear not, therefore, O believers, to look into the grave: for to you it is not other than a consecrated dormitory, where your bodies shall sleep quietly until the morning of the resurrection; when the voice of the archangel shall sound, and the trump of God give the general alarm, 'Arise, ye dead, and come to judgment'; earth, air, fire, water, shall give up your scattered atoms, and both in body and soul shall you be ever with the Lord. I doubt not, but many of you are groaning under crazy bodies, and complain often that the mortal body weighs down the immortal soul; at least this is my case; but let us have a little patience, and we shall be delivered from our earthly prisons; ere long, these tabernacles of clay shall be dissolved, and we shall be clothed with our house which is from heaven; hereafter, our bodies shall be spiritualized, and shall be so far from hindering our souls through weakness, that they shall become strong; so strong, as to bear up under an exceeding and eternal weight of glory; others again may have deformed bodies, emaciated also with sickness, and worn out with labour and age; but wait a little, until your blessed change by death comes; then your bodies shall be renewed and made glorious, like unto Christ's glorious body: of which we may form some faint idea, from the account given us of our Lord's transfiguration on the mount, when it is said, 'His raiment became bright and glistening, and his face brighter than the sun.' Well then may a believer break out in the apostle's triumphant language, 'O death, where is thy sting! O grave, where is thy victory!'

But what is the redemption of the body, in comparison of the redemption of the better part, our souls? I must, therefore say to you believers, as the angel said to John, 'Come up higher'; and let us take as clear a view as we can, at such a distance, of the redemption Christ has purchased for, and will shortly put you in actual possession of. Already you are justified, already you are sanctified, and thereby freed from the guilt and dominion of sin: but, as I have observed, the being and indwelling of sin yet remains in you; God sees it proper to leave some Amalekites in the land, to keep his Israel in action. The most perfect Christian, I am persuaded, must agree, according to one of our Articles, 'That the corruption of nature remains even in the regenerate; that the flesh lusteth always against the spirit, and the spirit against the flesh'. So that believers cannot do things for God with that perfection they desire; this grieves their righteous souls day by day, and, with the holy apostle, makes them cry out, 'Who shall deliver us from the body of this death!' I thank God, our Lord Jesus Christ will, but not completely before the day of our dissolution; then will the very being of sin be destroyed, and an eternal stop put to inbred, indwelling corruption. And is not this a great redemption? I am sure believers esteem it so: for there is nothing grieves the heart of a child of God so much, as the remains of indwelling sin. Again, believers are often in heaviness through manifold temptations; God sees that it is needful and good for them so to be; and though they may be highly favoured, and wrapt up in communion with God, even to the third heavens; yet a messenger of Satan is often sent to buffet them, lest they should be puffed up with the abundance of revelations. But be not weary, be not faint in your minds: the time of your complete redemption draweth nigh. In heaven the wicked one shall cease from troubling you, and your weary souls shall enjoy an everlasting rest; his fiery darts cannot reach those blissful regions: Satan will never come any more to appear with, disturb, or accuse the sons of God, when once the Lord Jesus Christ shuts the door. Your righteous souls are now grieved, day by day, at the ungodly conversation of the wicked; tares now grow up among the wheat; wolves come in sheep's clothing: but the redemption spoken of in the text, will free your souls from all anxiety on these accounts; hereafter you shall enjoy a perfect communion of saints; nothing that is unholy or unsanctified shall enter into the holy of holies, which is prepared for you above: this, and all manner of evil whatsoever, you shall be delivered from, when your redemption is hereafter made complete in heaven; not only so, but you shall enter into the full enjoyment of all good. It is true, all saints will not have the same degree of happiness, but all will be as happy as their hearts can desire. Believers, you shall judge the evil, and familiarly converse with good, angels: you shall sit down with Abraham, Isaac, Jacob, and all the spirits of just men made perfect; and, to sum up all your happiness in one word, you shall see God the Father, Son, and Holy Ghost; and, by seeing God, be more and more like unto him, and pass from glory to glory, even to all eternity.

But I must stop: the glories of the upper world crowd in so fast upon my soul, that I am lost in the contemplation of them. Brethren, the redemption spoken of is unutterable; we cannot here find it out; eye hath not seen, nor ear heard, nor has it entered into the hearts of the most holy men living to conceive, how great it is. Were I to entertain you whole ages with an account of it, when you come to heaven, you must say, with the queen of Sheba, 'Not half, no, not one thousandth part was told us'. All we can do here, is to go upon mount Pisgah, and, by the eye of faith, take a distant view of the promised land: we may see it, as Abraham did Christ, afar off, and rejoice in it; but here we only know in part. Blessed be God, there is a time coming, when we shall know God, even as we are known, and God be all in all. Lord Jesus, accomplish the number of thine elect! Lord Jesus, hasten thy kingdom!

And now, where are the scoffers of these last days, who count the lives of Christians to be madness, and their end to be without honour? Unhappy men! you know not what you do. Were your eyes open, and had you senses to discern spiritual things, you would not speak all manner of evil against the children of God, but you would esteem them as the excellent ones of the earth, and envy their happiness: your souls would hunger and thirst after it: you also would become fools for Christ's sake. You boast of wisdom; so did the philosophers of Corinth: but your wisdom is the foolishness of folly in the sight of God. What will your wisdom avail you, if it does not make you wise unto salvation? Can you, with all your wisdom, propose a more consistent scheme to build your hopes of salvation on, than what has been now laid before you? Can you, with all the strength of natural reason, find out a better way of acceptance with God, than by the righteousness of the Lord Jesus Christ? Is it right to think your own works can in any measure deserve or procure it? If not, why will you not believe in him? Why will you not submit to his righteousness? Can you deny that you are fallen creatures? Do not you find that you are full of disorders, and that these disorders make you unhappy? Do not you find that you cannot change your own hearts? Have you not resolved many and many a time, and have not your corruptions yet dominion over you? Are you not bondslaves to your lusts, and led captive by the devil at his will? Why then will you not come to Christ for sanctification? Do you not desire to die the death of the righteous, and that your future state may be like theirs; I am persuaded you cannot bear the thoughts of being annihilated, much less of being miserable for ever. Whatever you may pretend, if you speak truth, you must confess, that conscience breaks in upon you in more sober intervals whether you will or not, and even constrains you to believe that hell is no painted fire. And why then will you not come to Christ? He alone can procure you everlasting redemption. Haste, haste away to him, poor beguiled sinners. You lack wisdom; ask it of Christ. Who knows but he may give it you? He is able: for he is the wisdom of the Father; he is that wisdom which was from everlasting. You have no righteousness; away, therefore, to Christ: 'He is the end of the law for righteousness to every one that believeth.' You are unholy: flee to the Lord Jesus: He is full of grace and truth; and of his fullness all may receive that believe in him. You are afraid to die; let this drive you to Christ: he has the keys of death and hell: in him is plenteous redemption; he alone can open the door which leads to everlasting life.

Let not, therefore, the deceived reasoner boast any longer of his pretended reason. Whatever you may think, it is the most reasonable thing in the world not to believe on Jesus Christ, whom God has sent. Why, why will you die? Why will you not come unto him, that you may have life? 'Ho! every one that thirsteth, come unto the waters of life, and drink freely: come, buy without money and without price.' Were these blessed privileges in the text to be purchased with money, you might say, we are poor, and cannot buy: or, were they to be conferred only on sinners of such a rank or degree, then you might say, how can such sinners as we, expect to be so highly favoured? But they are to be freely given of God to the worst of sinners. 'To us', says the apostle, to me a persecutor, to you Corinthians, who were 'unclean, drunkards, covetous persons, idolators.' Therefore, each poor sinner may say then, why not unto me? Has Christ but one blessing? What if he has blessed millions already, by turning them away from their iniquities; yet he still continues the same: he lives for ever to make intercession, and therefore will bless you, even you also. Though, Esau-like, you have been profane, and hitherto despised your heavenly Father's birth-right; even now, if you believe, 'Christ will be made to you of God, wisdom, righteousness, sanctification, and redemption'.

But I must turn again to believers, for whose instruction, as I observed before, this discourse was particularly intended. You see, brethren, partakers of the heavenly calling, what great blessings are treasured up for you in Jesus Christ your Head, and what you are entitled to by believing on his name. Take heed, therefore, that ye walk worthy of the vocation wherewith ye are called. Think often how highly you are favoured; and remember, you have not chosen Christ, but Christ has chosen you. Put on (as the elect of God) humbleness of mind, and glory, but let it be only in the Lord; for you have nothing but what you have received of God. By nature ye were foolish, as legal, as unholy, and in as damnable a condition, as others. Be pitiful, therefore, be courteous; and, as sanctification is a progressive work, beware of thinking you have already attained. Let him that is holy be holy still; knowing, that he who is most pure in heart, shall hereafter enjoy the clearest vision of God. Let indwelling sin be your daily burden; and not only bewail and lament, but see that you subdue it daily by the power of divine grace; and look up to Jesus continually to be the finisher, as well as author, of your faith. Build not on your own faithfulness, but on God's unchangeableness. Take heed of thinking you stand by the power of your own free will. The everlasting love of God the Father, must be your only hope and consolation; let this support you under all trials. Remember that God's gifts and callings are without repentance; that Christ having once loved you, will love you to the end. Let this constrain you to obedience, and make you long and look for that blessed time, when he shall not only be your wisdom, and righteousness, and sanctification, but also complete and everlasting redemption.

Glory be to God in the highest!

BONAR
(1808 - 1889)

Horatius Bonar was born on December 19, 1808 in Edinburgh, Scotland, one of three sons who inherited the traditions of a long line of famous preachers. He attended grade schools there and later graduated from the famous university of the same city. He became a fast friend of Thomas Chalmers and went along with him in the disruption that led to the formation of the Free Presbyterian church.

Before his ordination in 1837, Bonar did mission work in Leith. From that year he served the congregation of the first North parish church of Kelso until, under the disruption, he formed a new church in the city where he continued to minister until 1866. Under his leadership the church grew rapidly. In 1866 he became pastor of the Chalmers Memorial Church in Edinburgh.

Bonar was influenced by Edward Irving to take an interest in prophecy and though he did not follow Irving into his excesses, he soon became a premillennialist and an ardent student of prophecy. He supported the D.L. Moody evangelistic campaigns and for these two reasons was suspect by some of his fellow ministers. But his Calvinism and orthodoxy were never in doubt.

Bonar was devoted to preaching the Bible as clearly and as evangelically as possible. His sermons glisten with the gospel. He was just as quick to reject, write and preach against the preparationism that was accepted by many of his fellow Presbyterians as he was to counter the aberrations of those premillennial brethren who were uncritically adopting strange views of man and sanctification. Anything that obscured the gospel or smacked of human merit was utterly abhorrent to Bonar.

In all of his works, Bonar proclaimed a salvation that was totally free from human merit. The line in the first verse of his hymn, *I Heard the Voice of Jesus Say*, gives clear evidence of this fact: "I came to Jesus just as I was ...." There is no room for preparationism in that! And consider this line from *Not What My Hands Have Done*: " ... Not all my prayers and sighs and tears ...." He refers here to the works of contrition that some taught merited regeneration.

In his sermons, you may look not only for the gospel and for a clear defense of what he believed to be Bible truth, but you will also find careful, clear exposition presented with a simplicity that is both disarming and convincing. His sermon on I John 5:16,17, for instance, which is included in this textbook, is a lucid piece of careful exposition.

In studying Bonar, look for his warm evangelicalism, the Biblical tone that pervades all that he preached, and the clarity and simplicity with which he said it. The clarity and imagery of a hymn writer who can say what he wants to say movingly, plainly and memorably because he has worked long and hard at learning how to do so, is everywhere evident. Study Bonar's preaching for these elements.

THE SIN UNTO DEATH

"If any man see his brother sin a sin which is not unto death, he shall ask, and he shall give him life for them that sin not unto death. There is a sin unto death: I do not say that he shall pray for it. All unrighteousness is sin: and there is a sin not unto death." (1 John 5:16,17)

The sin mentioned here is not the same as the "sin against the Holy Ghost." The persons spoken of, as respectively guilty, are very different from each other. In the latter sin, it is the Scribes and Pharisees, the malignant enemies of Christ, that are the criminals; in the former, that is, the case before us, it is a *Christian brother* that is the offender: "If any man see *his brother* sin." We must beware of confounding the two sins and the two parties. The sin unto death is spoken of as that which a believer could commit; but no believer could possibly be guilty of the blasphemy against the Holy Ghost.

This clears the way so far, or at least it narrows the ground, and so facilitates our inquiry.

But while removing one difficulty, does it not introduce another? Does it not assume the possibility of falling from grace, and deny the "perseverance of the saints?" We think not. But, as much depends on the meaning of the expression, "a sin unto death," we must first take up this.

Death may mean either temporal or eternal death; either the death of the soul, or that of the body. In the passage before us, it seems to me to mean the latter. The sin unto death, would mean a sin involving temporal death; such a sin as God would chastise with disease and death, though he would not exclude the doer of it from his kingdom. The difference between these two kinds of sins may be illustrated by the case of Israel in the desert. The generation that came out of Egypt died in the wilderness, because of their murmurings; yet many of these were believing men and women, who, though thus chastised, by the infliction of temporal death, and deprivation of the earthly Canaan, were not delivered over to eternal death. Moses himself (we might add, Aaron and Miriam) is an example of the same thing. In him we see a believing man suffering temporal death for his sin, yet still a child of God, and an heir of the heavenly Canaan.

But have we any cases of this kind in the New Testament? If we have, they will tend greatly to confirm our interpretation of the passage before us, and shew that, in all ages, God's way of dealing with his saints has been the same; and that, while in some instances there was chastisement, in the shape of pain, or disease, or loss of property, or loss of friends, in others there was chastisement in the shape of death. In the case of Moses, we have this paternal chastisement, involving death; in the case of Job, we see it involving loss of substance, loss of family, loss of health, but stopping short of death; but in the New Testament, we shall see it in the infliction of *death* upon the saint.

The most remarkable instance of the kind is in the Corinthian church. That church was in many respects noble and Christ-like, "coming behind in no gift." Yet there was much sin in it, and many of its members were not walking "as becometh saints." Specially in reference to the Lord's Supper, there was grievous sin, as the latter part of the eleventh chapter of the First Epistle to that church intimates. God could not suffer such sin in his saints. They are not indeed to be cast away, nor condemned with the unbelieving world; but they are not to be permitted to go on in evil, unrebuked. Accordingly, God interposes. He sends disease on some of these transgressing members, and death on others. "For this cause," says the apostle, "many are weak and sickly among you, and many sleep" (1 Cor. 11:30). Weakness, sickliness, and death, were the three forms of chastisement with which the Corinthian church was visited. Some were sinning sins which required to be visited with weakness; others were sinning sins which required to be punished with sickness; while others were sinning sins which needed to be chastised with "death;" for this the word "sleep" evidently means (1 Cor. 7:39—15:18). Against these sins unto disease, these "sins unto death," the apostle warns these Corinthians, when he says, "If we would judge ourselves, *we should not be judged*;" that is, we might have been spared these chastisements. If we had judged ourselves, and condemned our own sin, we should not have been thus judged by God. And then he adds, that even this judgment was in love, not in wrath: "When we are thus judged, it is the Lord chastising us, in order that we may not be condemned with the world."

We find the same solemn truth in the Epistle of James (5:14,15): "The prayer of faith shall save the sick, and the Lord shall raise him up; and if he have committed sins, they shall be forgiven him." Here sickness is spoken of as the consequence of sin,—sin in a saint. The sick and sinning one is to be prayed for; and if his sin and sickness be not unto death, God will have mercy on him. The sin shall be forgiven, and the sickness taken away.

We find the same truth in 1 Cor. 8:11, "Through thy knowledge shall the weak brother perish, for whom Christ died" where the "perishing" is the infliction of temporal death.

These passages shew the true meaning of our text. The sin unto death is a sin such as God chastises by the infliction of disease and death.

What this sin is, we do not know. It was not the same sin in all, but different in each. In the case of the Corinthian Church, unworthy communicating was "the sin unto death;" but what it was in others, is not recorded.

Thus the passage in John and that in James correspond strikingly, the one illustrating the other. In the case of the sick brother, spoken of by James, we have the very thing referred to in the first clause of our text: "If any man see his brother sin a sin which is not unto death, he shall ask, and he (*i.e.,* God) shall give him life for them that sin not unto death." Thus the prayer of faith was to save the sick man from death, to raise him up, and to secure for him forgiveness of the sin which had produced the sickness.

But then the question would arise, How are we to know when a sin is unto death, and when it is not unto death, so that we may pray in faith? The last clause of the 16th verse answers this question. It admits that there is a sin unto death; which admission is thus put in the 17th verse: "All unrighteousness is sin; but all sin is not unto death." But what does the apostle mean by saying, in the end of the 16th verse, "I do not say that he shall pray for it?" If we cannot know when a sin is unto death, and when not, what is the use of saying, "I do not say that he shall pray for it?"

The word translated "pray" means also "inquire," and is elsewhere translated so: John 1:19, "The Jews sent priests and Levites from Jerusalem to *ask* him, Who art thou?" (See also John 1:21,25, 5:12, 9:2, 19:21.) If thus rendered, the meaning would be, "I say he is to ask no questions about that." That is to say, if he sees a brother sick and ready to die, he is not to say, Has he committed a sin unto death, or has he not? He is just to pray, letting alone all such inquiries, and leaving the matter in the hands of God, who, in answer to prayer, will raise him up, if he have not committed the sin unto death.

The passage now becomes plain; and while it remains as an unspeakably solemn warning, it does not teach us that there is some one mysterious sin which infers eternal damnation; still less, that a saint of God can commit such a sin. It may be thus paraphrased: "If any one see his brother in Christ sin a sin, and see him also laid upon a sickbed in consequence of this, he shall pray for the sick brother; and if his sin be one of which the punishment is disease, not death, the sick man shall be raised up; for all sins that lead to sickness do not necessarily lead to death. And as to the difficulty, How shall we know when the sin is one which merely infers sickness, and when it is one which infers death? I say this, Ask no questions on this point, but pray, and leave the case to God."

Let us now come to the lessons of our text.

1. *Don't puzzle yourself with hard questions about the particular kind of sins committed.*—Be satisfied that it is sin, and deal with it as such. There are sins unto death, and there are sins not unto death. Do not trouble yourself or others with questions on this point, which no man can answer. Remember that all unrighteousness is sin; and that it is simply with sin, as sin, as a breach of the perfect law of righteousness, that you have to do. It is not the nature or the measure of its punishment that you have to consider, but its own exceeding sinfulness.

2. *Be concerned about a brother's welfare.*— "Look not every man on his own things, but look also every man on the things of others," as said the apostle. If any of you see a brother sin, do not let him alone, as if it did not concern you. Do not say, "Am I my brother's keeper?" Desire the spiritual prosperity of all

the saints. Seek, too, the salvation of the unsaved. They need your pity and your effort. Leave them not.

3. *Don't trifle with sin.* — Count no sin trivial, either in yourself or another. Do not dally with temptation. Do not extenuate guilt. Do not say, May I not keep my beloved sin a little longer? Part with it, or it will cost you dear. In what way it may do so I know not; but I can say this, that sooner or later it will cost you dear, both in soul and body.

4. *Take it at once to God.* — Don't puzzle yourself with useless questions as to its nature, but take it straight to God. In the case of a brother, do not raise evil reports against him because of it, but go and tell God about it. In your own case do the same. Do not let it remain unconfessed a moment after it is discovered. It is unrighteousness; it is sin; it is breach of law. God hates it; you must hate it too. You must bring it to that God who hates it; and who, just because he hates it, wants you to bring it to him. Give it at once to him. He knows how to keep it, and to deal with it. If you want to keep it to yourself, it will be your ruin. It will be poison in your veins. It will eat as doth a canker. It is not too great for him to deal with or to cover. The blood of his only-begotten Son will cover it. Let that blood prove its divine efficacy by the cleansing which it can administer to *your* soul. Rest not without forgiveness through the great propitiation. An unforgiven man is an unhappy man. Blessedness is the portion only of the forgiven. If you have not yet found the pardon, this blessedness cannot be yours. And if you but felt the misery of the unpardoned, and the joy of the pardoned, you would not rest till you had *made sure* of the forgiveness that there is with God, and tasted the reconciliation that they only know, who have settled the great question for eternity, at the foot of the cross.

There is such a thing as THE SECOND DEATH. And who shall deliver the doomed one from it? Who shall pray him up out of hell? The second death! Ah, when it has come to that, all is over! No Christ will do then; no blood; no cross! Oh, wait not till your sins have landed you in that! Take the proffered pardon. God gives it to you in his Son. Take it, and live for ever. He who died and lives presents to you the gift of the everlasting life, — life that no second death can touch, — life in Himself, — life beyond the valley of the shadow of death, in the city of the Living One, from which no life departs, and into which no death can enter.

BELIEVE JUST NOW

You are in earnest now; but I fear you are making your earnestness your Christ, and actually using it as a reason for not trusting Christ *immediately*. You think your earnestness will lead on to faith, if it be but sufficiently intense, and long enough persisted in.

But there is such a thing as earnestness in the wrong direction: earnestness in unbelief, and a substitution of earnestness for simple faith in Jesus. You must not soothe the alarms of conscience by this earnestness of yours. It is unbelieving earnestness; and that will not do. What God demands is simple faith in the record which He has given you of His Son. You say, I can't offer Him faith, but I can bring Him earnestness; and by giving Him earnestness, I hope to persuade Him to give me faith. This is self-righteousness. It shews that you regard both faith and earnestness as something to be done in order to please God, and secure His good-will. You say, Faith is the gift of God, but earnestness is not; it is in my own power; therefore I will earnestly labour, and struggle, and pray, hoping that before long God will take pity on my earnest struggles. You even feel secretly that it would be hardly fair in Him to disregard such earnestness.

Now, if God has anywhere said that unbelieving earnestness or the unbelieving use of means is the way of procuring faith, I cannot object to such proceedings on your part. But I do not find that He has said so, or that the apostles, in dealing with inquirers, set them upon this preliminary process for acquiring faith. I find that the apostles shut up their hearers to *immediate faith and repentance*, bringing them face to face with the great object of faith, and commanding them in the name of the living God to believe, *just as Jesus commanded the man with the withered hand to stretch it out*. The Lord did not give him any directions as to a preliminary work, or preparatory efforts, and struggles, and using of means.

These are man's attempts to bridge over the great gulf of human appliances; man's way of evading the awful question of his own *utter impotence*, man's unscriptural devices for sliding out of inability into ability, out of unbelief into faith; man's plan for helping God to save him; man's self-made ladder for climbing up a little way out of the horrible pit, in the hope that God will so commiserate his earnest struggles, as to do all the rest that is needed.

Now God has commanded all men everywhere to repent; but He has nowhere given us any directions for obtaining repentance. God has commanded sinners to believe, but He has not prescribed for them any preparatory process, the undergoing of which will induce Him to give them something which He is not from the first most willing to do. It is thus that He shuts them up to faith, by "concluding them in unbelief". It is thus that He brings them to feel both the greatness and the guilt of their inability; and so constrains them to give up every hope of doing anything to save themselves; driving them out of every

_____
_____
_____
_____
_____
_____
_____
_____
_____
_____
_____
_____
_____
_____
_____
_____
_____
_____
_____
_____
_____
_____
_____
_____
_____
_____
_____
_____

refuge of lies, and shewing them that these prolonged efforts of theirs are hindrances, not helps, and are just so many rejections of His own immediate help; so many distrustful attempts to persuade Him to do what He is already most willing to do in their behalf.

The great manifestation of self-righteousness is this struggle to believe. Believing is not a *work*, but a ceasing from work; and this struggle to believe is just the sinner's attempt to make a work out of that which is no work at all; to make a labour out of that which is a resting from labour. Sinners will not let go their hold of their former confidences and drop into Christ's arms. Why? Because they still trust these confidences, and do not trust Him who speaks to them in the gospel. Instead, therefore, of encouraging you to exert more and more earnestly these preliminary efforts, I tell you they are all the sad indications of self-righteousness. They take for granted that Christ has not done His work sufficiently, and that God is not willing to give you faith, till you have plied Him with the arguments and importunities of months or years.

God is at this moment willing to bless you; and these struggles of yours are not, as you fancy, humble attempts on your part to take the blessing, but proud attempts either to put it from you, or to get hold of it in some way of your own. You cannot, with all your struggles, make the Holy Spirit more willing to give you faith than He is at this moment. But your self-righteousness rejects this precious truth; and if I were to encourage you in these "efforts", I should be fostering your self-righteousness and your rejection of this grace of the Spirit.

You say you cannot change your heart or do any good thing. So say I. But I say more. I say that you are not at all aware of the extent of your helplessness and of your guilt. These are far greater and far worse than you suppose. And it is your imperfect view of these that leads you to resort to these endeavours. You are not yet sensible of your weakness, in spite of all you say. It is this that is keeping you from God and God from you.

God commands you to believe and to repent. It is at your peril that you attempt to alter this imperative and immediate obligation, by the substitution of something preliminary, the performance of which may perhaps soothe your terrors, and lull your conscience to sleep, but will not avail either to propitiate God or to lift you into a safer or more salvable condition, as you imagine. For we are saved by *faith*, not by efforts to induce "an unwilling God" to give us faith. In going to God, we are to take for granted that He will fulfil His Word, and act according to His character. Our appeals are to be made, not to an unwilling, but to a willing God. We are not to try by our prayers or earnestness to persuade God to be gracious, to exhort salvation from the hand of a grudging and austere giver. God is pressing His salvation upon us, and declaring His infinite willingness to bless at this moment.

God *commands* you to believe; and so long as you do not believe, you are making Him a liar, you are rejecting the truth, you are believing a lie; for unbelief is, in reality, the belief of a lie. Yes, God commands you to believe; and your not believing is your worst sin; and it is by exhibiting it as your worst sin, that God shuts you up to faith. Now, if you try to extenuate this sin—if you flatter your soul, that, by making all these earnest and laborious efforts to believe, you are lessening this awful sin, and rendering your unbelieving state a less guilty one—then you are deluding your conscience, and thrusting away from you that divine hand which, by this conviction of unbelief, is shutting you up to faith.

I do not remember having seen this better stated than in Fuller's *Gospel Worthy of All Acceptation*.

I give just a few sentences: "It is the duty of ministers not only to exhort their carnal hearers to believe in Jesus Christ for the salvation of their souls; but it is at our peril to exhort them to anything short of it, or which does not involve or imply it. We have sunk into such a compromising way of dealing with the unconverted, as to have well nigh lost sight of the spirit of the primitive preachers; and hence it is that sinners of every description can sit so quietly as they do in our places of worship. Christ and his apostles, without any hesitation, called on sinners to repent and believe the gospel: but we, considering them as poor, impotent, and depraved creatures, have been disposed to drop this part of the Christian ministry. Considering such things as beyond the power of their hearers, they seem to have contented themselves with pressing on them the things they *could* perform, still continuing enemies of Christ; such as behaving decently in society, reading the Scriptures, and attending the means of grace.

"Thus it is that hearers of this description sit at ease in our congregations. But as this implies no *guilt* on their part, they sit unconcerned, conceiving that all that is required of them is to lie in the way and wait the Lord's time. But is this the religion of the Scriptures? Where does it appear that the prophets or apostles treated that kind of inability, which is merely the effect of reigning aversion, as affording any excuse? And where have they descended in their exhortations to things which might be done, and the parties still continue the enemies of God? Instead of leaving out everything of a spiritual nature, because their hearers could not find it in their hearts to comply with it, it may be safely affirmed that they exhorted to nothing else, treating such inability not only as of no account with regard to the lessening of obligation, but as rendering the subjects of it worthy of the severest rebuke . . . .

"Repentance toward God, and faith towards our Lord Jesus Christ, are allowed to be duties, but not *immediate* duties. The sinner is considered as unable to comply with them, and therefore they are not urged upon him; but instead of them, he is directed to pray for the Holy Spirit to enable him to repent and believe. This, it seems, he *can* do, notwithstanding the aversion of his heart from everything of the kind! But if any man be required to pray for the Holy Spirit, it must be either sincerely and in the name of Jesus, or insincerely and in some other way. The latter, I suppose, will be allowed to be an abomination in the sight of God; he cannot, therefore, be required to do this; and as to the former, it is just as difficult and as opposite to the carnal heart as repentance and faith themselves. Indeed, it amounts to the same thing; for a sincere desire after a spiritual blessing, presented in the name of Jesus, is no other than the prayer of faith."

The great thing which I would press upon your conscience is *the awful guilt* that there is in unbelief. Continuance in unbelief is continuance in the very worst of sins; and continuance in it, because (as you say) you cannot help it, is the worst aggravation of your sin. The habitual drunkard says he "cannot help it"; the habitual swearer says he "cannot help it"; the habitual unbeliever says he "cannot help it". Do you admit the drunkard's excuse? Or do you not tell him that it is the worst feature of his case, and that he ought to be utterly ashamed of himself for using such a plea? Do you say, I know you can't give up your drunken habits, but you can go and pray to God to enable you to give up these habits, and perhaps God will hear you and enable you to do so? What would this be but to tell him to go on drinking and praying alternately; and that, possibly, God may hear his drunken prayers, and give him sobriety? You would not thus deal with drunkenness, ought you to deal so with unbelief? Ought you not to press home its guilt; and to shew a sinner that, when he says, "I can't help my unbelief", he is uttering his worst condemnation, and saying, I can't help distrusting God, I can't help hating God, I can't help making God a liar; and that he might just as well say, I can't help stealing, and lying, and swearing.

Never let unbelief be spoken of as a *misfortune*. It is awfully sinful. Its root is the desperate wickedness of the heart. How evil must that heart be, when it will not even believe! If our helplessness and hardness of heart lessened our guilt then the more wicked we became, we should be the less responsible and the less guilty. The sinner who loves sin so much that he "cannot" part with it, is the most guilty. He who says, I "cannot" love God, is proclaiming himself one of the worst of sinners; but he who says, I "cannot" even believe, is taking to himself a guilt which we may truly call the darkest and most damnable of all.

Oh, the unutterable guilt involved even in one moment's unbelief; one single act of an unbelieving soul! How much more is the continuous unbelief of twenty or sixty years! To steal once is bad enough, how much more to be a thief by habit and repute! We think it bad enough when a man is overtaken with drunkenness, how much more when we have to say of him, he is never sober. Such is our charge against the man who has not yet known Christ. He is a *continuous* unbeliever. His life is one unbroken course of unbelief, and hence of false worship, if he worships at all. Every new moment is a new act of unbelief; a new commission of the worst of sins; a sin in comparison with which all other sins both of heart and life, awful as they are, seem to lose their enormity.

Let the thought of this guilt cut your conscience to the quick! Oh, tremble as you think of what it is to be, not for a day or an hour, but for a whole lifetime, *an unbelieving man*!

ROBERTSON
(1816 - 1853)

A Sketch of His Life

Frederick William Robertson was 37 years of age when he died of an abcess on the brain and heart trouble in August 1853. He had preached for only six years in the Brighton, Sussex church on the English channel, his first and only church. At his death he was scarcely known beyond his own congregation. Only one or two of his sermons had been published. His fame is entirely posthumous. Yet, he has become one of the outstanding preachers of the English speaking world.

Robertson was born in London in 1816 into a military family of several generations. He was a soldier at heart, "rocked and cradled to the roar of artillery." Yet, though he desired and sought it, he failed to receive a military appointment. So he applied for training in ministerial studies leading to ordination in the Anglican church. Belatedly, just five days after being accepted at Oxford, he received his military commission. But, having decided for the ministry, he stuck by his guns. From youth, he was a man of principle. He graduated in 1841. After traveling for awhile in Germany, he served six unhappy years as a curate in Cheltenham.

In 1847 he became the minister of the Brighton church. He knew the English poets and had direct influence on Tennyson. He committed the Bible to memory while shaving. He could recite the entire New Testament in English (and much of it in Greek) as well as most of the Old Testament.

Content

Robertson preached topical sermons in the morning and expository sermons in the afternoon. In the six years at Brighton he went through I and II Samuel, Genesis, Acts and the Corinthian letters expositorially. The sermons on Samuel and the Acts are not available. He preached from principles abstracted from the Bible. Studying the aspects of this method will yield fruit to the serious student of Robertson's sermons.

There is an undercurrent of sorrow in his sermons. Often, what he had to say came from the depths of his own experiences and from the hidden lives of men. It was his belief that one should preach truth suggestively, not exhaustively; positively, not negatively. He was alone, doctrinally, standing between the tractarians and the evangelicals. He often preached about human problems and needs.

He began preaching as a Calvinist, but drifted toward broader church views. He could conduct a high church service, then toss aside his garments and go out and do street preaching. As he aged, he became more liberal in his theology. It is these more liberal sermons that are available in print.

Organization

Most of his sermons have two points corresponding to the structure of Biblical writing and thinking from which he learned to exploit the method of antithesis. This is worth study; Brooks also excelled in the use of antithesis. Robertson's sermons are never very long. Usually, they were deductive, theory leading to practice, with strong outlines.

Style

The style was colloquial; there are few oratorical sentences in Robertson's printed sermons. He held attention by thought rather than by other means. He declared that eloquence cheapened the preacher. He was always clear, exhibiting great skill in applying truth. His sermons are full of people in action.

Delivery

Robertson was not graceful in the pulpit. His voice was somewhat affected at first. His sermons were written out, in abridged form, after he preached them. They have been fitted for publication and probably, when delivered, were a good bit looser in wording. He preached from a skeleton, which he crumbled while preaching. There are 93 sermons extant.

Effects

Crowds of workingmen came to hear him and held him in high regard. His preaching techniques also affected many later preachers such as Harry Emerson Fosdick. His last recorded words were:

> I have grown worse and worse every day for a fortnight. From intensity of suffering in the brain and utter powerlessness and prostration too dreadful to describe, and the acknowledged anxiety of medical men, I think now that I shall not get over this. I write in torture.

THE LONELINESS OF CHRIST

"Jesus answered them, Do ye now believe? Behold the hour cometh, yea, is now come, that ye shall be scattered, every man to his own, and shall leave me alone; and yet I am not alone, because the Father is with me." (John 16:31-32)

There are two kinds of solitude: the first consisting of insulation in space, the other of isolation in spirit. The first is simply separation by distance. When we are seen, touched, heard by none, we are said to be alone. And all hearts respond to the truth of that saying, This is not solitude; for sympathy can people our solitude with a crowd. The fisherman on the ocean alone at night is not alone when he remembers the earnest longings which are arising up to heaven at home for his safety; the traveller is not alone when the faces which will greet him on his arrival seem to beam upon him as he trudges on; the solitary student is not alone when he feels that human hearts will respond to the truths which he is preparing to address to them.

The other is loneliness of the soul. There are times when hands touch ours, but only send an icy chill of unsympathetic indifference to the heart: when eyes gaze into ours, but with a glazed look which cannot read into the bottom of our souls: when words pass from our lips, but only come back as an echo reverberated without reply through a dreary solitude: when the multitude throng and press us, and we cannot say, as Christ said, "Somebody hath *touched* me:" for the contact has been not between soul and soul, but only between form and form.

And there are two kinds of men who feel this last solitude in different ways. The first are men of self-reliance: self-dependent: who ask no counsel, and crave no sympathy: who act and resolve alone—who can go sternly through duty, and scarcely shrink let what will be crushed in them. Such men command respect: for whoever respects himself, constrains the reverence of others. They are invaluable in all those professions of life in which sensitive feelings would be a superfluity; they make iron commanders: surgeons who do not shrink; and statesmen who do not flinch from their purpose for the dread of unpopularity. But mere self-dependence is weakness: and the conflict is terrible when a human sense of weakness is felt by such men.

Jacob was alone when he slept in his way to Padan-aram, the first night that he was away from his father's roof, with the world before him, and all the old associations broken up: and Elijah was alone in the wilderness when the court had deserted him, and he said, "They have digged down Thine altars, and slain Thy prophets with the sword: and I, even I, only am left, and they seek my life to take it away." But the loneliness of the tender Jacob was very different from that of the stern Elijah. To Jacob the sympathy he yearned for was realized in the form of a simple dream. A ladder raised from earth to heaven figured the possibility of communion between the spirit of man and the Spirit of God. In Elijah's case, the storm, and the earthquake, and the fire, did their convulsing work in the soul, before a still, small voice told him that he was not alone. In such a spirit the sense of weakness comes with a burst of agony, and the dreadful conviction of being alone manifests itself with a rending of the heart of rock. It is only so that such souls can be taught that the Father is with them, and that they are not alone.

There is another class of men who live in sympathy. These are affectionate minds which tremble at the thought of being alone: not from want of courage, nor from weakness of intellect comes their dependence upon others, but from the intensity of their affections. It is the trembling spirit of Humanity in them. They want not aid, nor even countenance: but only sympathy. And the trial comes to them not in the shape of fierce struggle, but of chill and utter loneliness, when they are called upon to perform a duty on which the world looks coldly, or to embrace a truth which has not found lodgment yet in the breasts of others.

It is to this latter and not to the former class that we must look if we would understand the spirit in which the words of the text were pronounced. The deep Humanity of the Soul of Christ was gifted with those finer sensibilities of affectionate nature which stand in need of sympathy. He not only gave sympathy, but wanted it too, from others. He who selected the gentle John to be his friend—who found solace in female sympathy, attended by the women who ministered to him out of their substance—who in the trial-hour could not bear even to pray without the human presence, which is the pledge and reminder of God's presence, had nothing in Him of the hard, merely self-dependent character. Even this verse testifies to the same fact. A stern spirit never could have said, "I am not alone: the Father is with me"—never would have felt the loneliness which needed the balancing truth. These words tell of a struggle: an inward reasoning: a difficulty and a reply: a sense of solitude—"I shall be alone;" and an immediate correction of that, "not alone—the Father is with Me."

There is no thought connected with the Life of Christ more touching, none that seems so peculiarly to characterize His spirit than the solitariness in which He lived. Those who understood Him best only half understood Him. Those who knew Him best scarcely could be said to *know* Him. On this occasion the disciples thought—Now we do understand—now we believe. The lonely spirit answered, "Do ye now believe? Behold the hour cometh that ye shall be scattered, every man to his own, and shall leave Me alone."

Very impressive was that trait in His history. He was in the world alone.

I. First then we meditate on the loneliness of Christ.
II. On the temper of His solitude.

1. The Loneliness of Christ was caused by the Divine elevation of His character. His infinite superiority severed Him from sympathy—His exquisite affectionateness made that want of sympathy a keen trial.

There is a second-rate greatness which the world can comprehend. If we take two who are brought into direct contrast by Christ Himself, the one the type of human, the other that of Divine excellence, the Son of Man and John the Baptist, this becomes clearly manifest. John's life had a certain rude, rugged goodness, on which was written, in characters that needed no magnifying-glass to read, spiritual excellence. The world on the whole accepted him. Pharisees and Sadducees went to his baptism. The people idolized him as a prophet. And if he had not chanced to cross the path of a weak prince and a revengeful woman, we can see no reason why John might not have finished his course with joy, recognized as irreproachable. If we inquire why it was that the world accepted John and rejected Christ, one reply appears to be that the life of the one was finitely simple and one-sided, that of the Other divinely complex.

In physical nature, the naturalist finds no difficulty in comprehending the simple structure of the lowest organization of animal life, where one uniform texture, and one organ performing the office of brain and heart and lungs, at once, leave little to perplex. But when he comes to study the complex anatomy of man, he has the labour of a lifetime before him. It is not difficult to master the constitution of a single country; but when you try to understand the entire universe, you find infinite appearances of contradiction: law opposed to law: motion balanced by motion: happiness blended with misery: and the power to elicit a divine order and unity out of this complex variety is given to only a few of the gifted of the race. That which the structure of man is to the structure of the limpet: that which the universe is to a single country, the complex and boundless soul of Christ was to the souls of other men.

Therefore, to the superficial observer, His life was a mass of inconsistencies and contradictions. All thought themselves qualified to point out the discrepancies. The Pharisees could not comprehend how a holy Teacher could eat with publicans and sinners. His own brethren could not reconcile His assumption of a public office with the privacy which He aimed at keeping. "If thou doest these things, show thyself to the world." Some thought He was "a good man,"—others said, "Nay—but He deceiveth the people." And hence it was that He lived to see all that acceptance which had marked the earlier stage of His career, as, for instance, at Capernaum, melt away. First the Pharisees took the alarm: then the Sadducees: then the political party of the Herodians: then the people. That was the most terrible of all: for the enmity of the upper classes is impotent; but when the cry of brute force is stirred from the deeps of society, as deaf to the voice of reason as the ocean in its strength churned into raving foam by the winds, the heart of mere earthly oak quails before that. The apostles, at all events, did quail. One denied: another betrayed: all deserted. They "were scattered, each to his own:" and the Truth Himself was left alone in Pilate's judgment-hall.

Now we learn from this a very important distinction. To feel solitary is no uncommon thing. To complain of being alone, without sympathy and misunderstood, is general enough. In every place, in many a family, these victims of diseased sensibility are to be found, and they might find a weakening satisfaction in observing a parallel between their feelings and those of Jesus. But before that parallel is assumed, be very sure that it is, as in His case, the elevation of your character which severs you from your species. The world has small sympathy for Divine goodness: but it also has little for a great many other qualities which are disagreeable to it. You meet with no response—you are passed by—find yourself unpopular—meet with little communion—Well? Is that because you are *above* the world, nobler, devising and executing grand plans which they cannot comprehend: vindicating the wronged, proclaiming the living on great principles: offending it by the saintliness of your purity, and the unworldliness of your aspirations? Then yours is the loneliness of Christ. Or is it that you are wrapped up in self—cold, disobliging, sentimental, indifferent about the welfare of others, and very much astonished that they are not deeply interested in you? *You* must not use these words of Christ. They have nothing to do with you.

Let us look at one or two of the occasions on which this loneliness was felt.

The first time was when He was but twelve years old, when His parents found Him in the temple, hearing the doctors and asking them questions. High thoughts were in the Child's soul: expanding views of life: larger views of duty and His own destiny.

There is a moment in every true life—to some it comes very early—when the old routine of duty is not large enough—when the paternal roof seems too low, because the Infinite above is arching over the soul—when the old formulas, in creeds, catechisms, and articles, seem to be narrow, and they must either be thrown aside, or else transformed into living and breathing realities—when the earthly father's authority is being superseded by the claims of a Father in heaven.

That is a lonely, lonely moment, when the young soul first feels God—when this earth is recognised as an "awful place, yea, the very gate of heaven." When the dream ladder is seen planted against the skies, and we wake, the dream haunts us as a sublime reality.

You may detect the approach of that moment in the young man or the young woman by the awakened spirit of inquiry: by a certain restlessness of look, and an eager earnestness of tone: by the devouring study of all kinds of books: by the waning of your own influence, while the inquirer is asking the truth of the doctors and teachers in the vast temple of the world: by a certain opinionativeness, which is austere and disagreeable enough: but the austerest moment of the fruit's taste is that in which it is passing from greenness into ripeness. If you wait in patience, the sour will become sweet. Rightly looked at, that opinionativeness is more truly anguish: the fearful solitude of feeling the insecurity of all that is human; the discovery that life is real, and many forms of social and religious existence hollow. The old moorings are torn away, and the soul is drifting, drifting, drifting, very often without compass, except the guidance of an unseen hand, into the vast infinite of God. Then come the lonely words, and no wonder, "How is it that ye sought me? Wist ye not that I must be about my Father's business?"

That solitude was felt by Christ in trial. In the desert, in Pilate's judgment-hall, in the garden, He was alone—and alone must every son of man meet his trial-hour. The individuality of the soul necessitates that. Each man is a new soul in this world: untried, with a boundless possible before him. No one can predict what he may become, prescribe his duties, or mark out his obligations. Each man's own nature has its own peculiar rules: and he must take up his life-plan alone, and persevere in it in a perfect privacy with which no stranger intermeddleth. Each man's temptations are made up of a host of peculiarities, internal and external, which no other mind can measure. You are tried alone—alone you pass into the desert—alone you must bear and conquer in the agony—alone you must be sifted by the world. There are moments known only to a man's own self, when he must sit by the poisoned springs of existence, "yearning for a morrow which shall free him from the strife." And there are trials more terrible than that. Not when vicious inclinations are opposed to holy, but when virtue conflicts with virtue, is the real rending of the soul in twain. A temptation, in which the lower nature struggles for mastery, can be met by the whole united force of the spirit. But it is when obedience to a heavenly Father can be only paid by disobedience to an earthly one: or fidelity to duty can be only kept by infidelity to some entangling engagement: or the straight path must be taken over the misery of others: or the counsel of the affectionate friend must be met with a "Get thee behind me, Satan,"—Oh! it is then, when human advice is unavailable, that the soul feels what it is to be alone.

Once more—the Redeemer's soul was alone in dying. The hour had come—they were all gone, and He was, as He predicted, left alone. All that is human drops from us in that hour. Human faces flit and fade, and the sounds of the world become confused. "I shall die alone"—yes, and alone you live. The philosopher tells us that no atom in creation touches another atom—they only approach within a certain distance; then the attraction ceases, and an invisible something repels—they only *seem* to touch. No soul touches another soul except at one or two points; and those chiefly external,—a fearful and a lonely thought; but one of the truest of life. Death only realizes that which has been the fact all along. In the central deeps of our being we are all alone.

II. The spirit or temper of that solitude.
1. Observe its grandeur. I am alone, yet not alone.

There is a feeble and sentimental way in which we speak of the Man of Sorrows. We turn to the Cross, and the agony, and the loneliness, to touch the softer feelings, to arouse compassion. You degrade *that* loneliness by your compassion. Compassion! Compassion for Him? Adore if you will—respect and reverence that sublime solitariness with which none but the Father was—but no pity: let it draw out the firmer and manlier graces of the soul. Even tender sympathy seems out of place.

For even in human things, the strength that is in a man can be only learnt when he is thrown upon his own resources and left alone. What a man can do in conjunction with others does not test the man. Tell us what he can do alone. It is one thing to defend the truth when you know that your audience are already prepossessed, and that every argument will meet a willing response: and it is another thing to hold the truth when truth must be supported, if at all, alone—met by cold looks and unsympathizing suspicion. It is one thing to rush on to danger with the shouts and the sympathy of numbers: it is another thing when the lonely chieftain of the sinking ship sees the last boatful disengage itself, and folds his arms to go down into the majesty of darkness, but not subdued.

Such and greater far was the strength and majesty of the Saviour's solitariness. It was not the trial of the lonely hermit. There is a certain gentle and pleasing melancholy in the life which is lived alone. But there are the forms of nature to speak to him, and he has not the positive opposition of mankind if he has the absence of actual sympathy. It is a solemn thing doubtless, to be apart from men, and to feel eternity rushing by like an arrowy river. But the solitude of Christ was the solitude of a crowd. In that single human bosom dwelt the thought which was to be the germ of the world's life: a thought unshared, misunderstood, or rejected. Can you not feel the grandeur of those words, when the Man reposing on His solitary strength, felt the last shadow of perfect isolation pass across His soul: "My God, my God, why hast *Thou* forsaken me?"

Next, learn from these words self-reliance. "Ye shall leave me alone." Alone then the Son of man was content to be. He threw Himself on His own solitary thought: did not go down to meet the world; but waited, though it might be for ages, till the world should come round to Him. He appealed to the future, did not aim at seeming consistent: left His contradictions unexplained. "I came from the Father, I leave the world, and go to the Father." "Now," said they, "thou speakest no proverb:" that is, enigma. But many a hard and enigmatical saying before He had spoken, and He left them all. A thread runs through all true acts, stringing them together into one harmonious chain: but it is not for the Son of God to be anxious to prove their consistency with each other.

This is self-reliance—to repose calmly on the thought which is deepest in our bosoms, and be unmoved if the world will not accept it yet. To live on your own convictions against the world, is to overcome the world—to believe that what is truest in you is true for all: to abide by that, and not be over-anxious to be heard or understood, or sympathized with, certain that at last all must acknowledge the same, and that while you stand firm, the world will come round to you: that is independence. It is not difficult to get away into retirement, and there live upon your own convictions: nor is it difficult to mix with men, and follow their convictions: but to enter into the world, and there live out firmly and fearlessly according to your own conscience, that is Christian greatness.

There is a cowardice in this age which is not Christian. We shrink from the consequences of truth. We look round and cling dependently. We ask what men will think—what others will say—whether they will not stare in astonishment. Perhaps they will; but he who is calculating that, will accomplish nothing in this life. The Father—the Father who is with us and in us—what does He think? God's work cannot be done without a spirit of independence. A man is got some way in the Christian life when he has learned to say humbly and yet majestically, "I dare to be alone."

Lastly,—I remark the humility of this loneliness. Had the Son of Man simply said, I can be alone, He would have said no more than any proud, self-relying man can say. But when He added "because the Father is with me," that independence assumed another character, and self-reliance became only another form of reliance upon God. Distinguish between genuine and spurious humility. There is a false humility which says, "It is my own poor thought, and I must not trust it. I must distrust my own reason and judgment, because they are my own. I must not accept the dictates of my own conscience, for it is not my own, and it is not in self the great fault of our fallen nature?"

Very well. Now remember something else. There is a Spirit which beareth witness with our spirits—there is a God who "is not far from any one of us"—there is a "Light which lighteth every man which cometh into the world." Do not be unnaturally humble. The thought of your mind perchance is the thought of God. To refuse to follow *that* may be to disown God. To take the judgment and conscience of other men to live by,—where is the humility of that? From whence did their conscience and judgment come? Was the fountain from which they drew exhausted for you? If they refuse like you to rely on their own conscience, and you rely upon it, how are you sure that it is more the mind of God, than your own which you have refused to hear?

Look at it another way. The charm of the words of great men, those grand sayings which are recognised as true as soon as heard, is this, that you recognise them as wisdom which has passed across your own mind. You feel that they are your own thoughts come back to you, else you would not at once admit them: "All that floated across me before, only I could not say it, and did not feel confident enough to assert it: or had not conviction enough to put it into words." Yes, God spoke to you what He did to them: only they believed it, said it, trusted the Word within them, and you did not. Be sure that often when you say, "It is only my own poor thought, and I am alone,"—the real correcting thought is this, "alone, but the Father is with me,"—therefore I can live that lonely conviction.

There is no danger in this, whatever tender minds may think—no danger of mistake, if the character be a true one. For we are not left in uncertainty in this matter. It is given us to know our base from our noble hours: to distinguish between the voice which is from above, and that which speaks from below, out of the abyss of our animal and selfish nature. Samuel could distinguish between the impulse, quite a human one, which would have made him select Eliab out of Jesse's sons, and the deeper judgment by which "the Lord said, Look not on his countenance, nor on the height of his stature, for I have refused him." Doubtless deep truth of character is required for this: for the whispering voices get mixed together, and we dare not abide by our own thoughts, because we think them our own, and not God's: and this because we only now and then endeavour to know in earnest. It is only given to the habitually true to know the difference. He knew it, because all His blessed life long He could say, "My judgment is just, *because* I seek not my own will, but the will of Him which sent me."

The practical result and inference of all this is a very simple, but a very deep one: the deepest of existence. Let life be a life of faith. Do not go timorously about, inquiring what others think, what others believe, and what others say. It seems the easiest, it is the most difficult thing in life to do this—believe in God. God is near you. Throw yourself fearlessly upon Him. Trembling mortal, there is an unknown might within your soul which will wake when you command it. The day may come when all that is human, man and woman, will fall off from you, as they did from Him. Let His strength be yours. Be independent of them all now. The Father is with you. Look to Him, and He will save you.

INSPIRATION

"We then that are strong ought to bear the infirmities of the weak, and not to please ourselves. Let every one of us please his neighbor for his good to edification. For even Christ pleased not himself; but, as it is written, The reproaches of them that reproached thee fell on me. For whatsoever things were written aforetime were written for our learning, that we through patience and comfort of the Scriptures might have hope." (Rom. 15:1-4)

We will endeavor, brethren, to search the connection between the different parts of these verses.

First, the apostle lays down a Christian's duty—"Let every one of us please his neighbor for his good to edification." After that he brings forward as the sanction of that duty, the spirit of the life of Christ—"For even Christ pleased not Himself." Next, he adds an illustration of that principle by a quotation from Psalm 69: "It is written, The reproaches of them that reproached thee fell on me." Lastly, he explains and defends that application of the psalm, as if he had said, "I am perfectly justified in applying that passage to Christ, for 'whatsoever things were written aforetime were written for our learning.'"

So that in this quotation, and the defense of it as contained in these verses, we have the principle of apostolical interpretation; we have the principle upon which the apostles used the Old Testament Scriptures, and we are enabled to understand their view of inspiration. This is one of the most important considerations upon which we can be at this moment engaged. It is the deepest question of our day: the one which lies beneath all others, and in comparison of which the questions just now agitating the popular mind—whether the Papal jurisdiction or varieties of Church doctrine in our own communion—are but superficial: it is this grand question of inspiration which is given to this age to solve.

Our subject will break itself up into questions such as these: What the Bible is, and what the Bible is not? What is meant by inspiration? Whether inspiration is the same thing as infallibility? When God inspired the minds, did He dictate the words? Does the inspiration of men mean the infallibility of their words? Is inspiration the same as dictation? Whether, granting that we have the Word of God, we have also the words of God? Are the operations of the Holy Spirit, inspiring men, compatible with partial error, as His operations in sanctifying them are compatible with partial evil? How are we to interpret and apply the Scriptures? Is Scripture, as the Romanists say, so unintelligible and obscure that we can not understand it without having the guidance of an infallible Church? Or is it, as some fanciful Protestants will tell us, a book upon which all ingenuity may be used to find Christ in every sentence? Upon these things there are many views, some of them false, some superstitious; but it is not our business now to deal with these; our way is rather to teach positively than negatively: we will try to set up the truth, and error may fall before it.

The collect for this day leads us to the special consideration of Holy Scripture; We shall therefore take this for our subject, and endeavor to understand what was the apostolical principle of interpretation.

In the text we find two principles: first, that Scripture is of universal application;

And second, that all the lines of Scripture converge towards Jesus Christ.

First, then, there is here a universal application of Scripture. This passage quoted by the apostle is from the sixty-ninth Psalm. That was evidently spoken by David of himself. From first to last, no unprejudiced mind can detect a conception in the writer's mind of an application to Christ, or to any other person after him; the psalmist is there full of himself and his own sorrows. It is a natural and touching exposition of human grief and a good man's trust. Nevertheless, you will observe that St. Paul extends the use of these words, and applies them to Jesus Christ. Nay, more than that, he uses them as belonging to all Christians; for, he says, "Whatsoever things were written aforetime, were written for our learning." Now this principle will be more evident if we state it in the words of Scripture, "Knowing that no prophecy of Scripture is of any private interpretation:" those holy men spake not their own limited individual feelings, but as feeling that they were inspired by the Spirit of God. Their words belonged to the whole of our common humanity. No prophecy of the Scriptures is of any private interpretation. Bear in mind that the word prophecy does not mean what we now understand by it—merely prediction of future events—in the Scriptures it signifies inspired teaching. The teaching of the prophets was by no means always prediction. Bearing this in mind, let us remember that the apostle says it is of no private interpretation. Had the Psalm applied only to David, then it would have been of private interpretation—it would have been special, limited, particular; it would have belonged to an individual; instead of which, it belongs to humanity. Take again the subject of which we spoke last Sunday—the prophecy of the destruction of Jerusalem. Manifestly that was spoken originally at Jerusalem; in a manner it seemed limited to Jerusalem, for its very name was mentioned; and besides, as we read this morning, our Saviour says, "This generation shall not pass until all be fulfilled."

But had the prophecy ended there, then you would still have had prophecy, but it would have been of private—that is, peculiar, limited—interpretation; whereas our Redeemer's principle was this: that this doom pronounced on Jerusalem was universally applicable, that it was but a style and specimen of God's judgments. The judgment-coming of the Son of Man takes place wherever there is evil grown ripe, whenever corruption is complete. And the gathering of the Roman eagles is but a specimen of the way in which judgment at last overtakes every city, every country and every man in whom evil has reached the point where there is no possibility of cure.

So that the prophecy belongs to all ages, from the

destruction of Jerusalem to the end of the world. The words of St. Matthew are universally applicable. For Scripture deals with principles; not with individuals, but rather with states of humanity. Promises and threatenings are made to individuals, because they are in a particular state of character; but they belong to all who are in that state, for "God is no respecter of persons."

First, we will take an instance of the state of blessing.

There was blessing pronounced to Abraham, in which it will be seen how large a grasp on humanity this view of Scripture gave to St. Paul. The whole argument in the Epistle to the Romans is, that the promises made to Abraham were not to his person, but to his faith; and thus the apostle says, "They who are of faith, are blessed with faithful Abraham."

We will now take the case of curse or threatening. Jonah, by Divine command, went through Nineveh, proclaiming its destruction; but that prophecy belonged to the state in which Nineveh was; it was true only while it remained in that state; and therefore, as they repented, and their state was thus changed, the prophecy was left unfulfilled. From this we perceive the largeness and grandeur of Scripture interpretation. In the Epistle to the Corinthians, we find the apostle telling of the state of the Jews in their passage towards the promised land, their state of idolatry and gluttony, and then he proceeds to pronounce the judgments that fell upon them, adding that he tells us this not merely as a matter of history, but rather as an illustration of a principle. They are specimens of eternal, unalterable law. So that whosoever shall be in the state of these Jews, whosoever shall imitate them, the same judgments must fall upon them, the same satiety and weariness, the same creeping of the inward serpent polluting all their feelings; and therefore he says, "All these things happened unto them for ensamples." Again, he uses the same principle, not as a private, but a general application; for he says, "There hath no temptation taken you but such as is common to man."

We will take now another case, applied not to nations, but to individuals. In Hebrews 13 we find these words from the Old Testament, "I will never leave thee nor forsake thee;" and there the apostle's inference is that we may boldly say, "The Lord is my helper, I will not fear what men shall do unto me." Now, when we refer to Scripture, we shall find that this was a promise originally made to Jacob. The apostle does not hesitate to take that promise and appropriate it to all Christians; for it was made, not to Jacob as a person, but to the state in which Jacob was; it was made to all who, like Jacob, are wanderers and pilgrims in the world; it was made to all whom sin has rendered outcasts and who are longing to return. The promises made to the meek belong to meekness; the promises made to the humble belong to humility.

And this it is which makes this Bible, not only a blessed book, but *our* book. It is this universal applicability of Scripture which has made the influence of the Bible universal: this book has held

_____
_____
_____
_____
_____
_____
_____
_____
_____
_____
_____
_____
_____
_____
_____
_____
_____
_____
_____
_____
_____
_____
_____
_____
_____
_____

spell-bound the hearts of nations, in a way in which no single book has ever held men before. Remember, too, in order to enhance the marvellousness of this, that the nation from which it emanated was a despised people. For the last eighteen hundred years the Jews have been proverbially a by-word and a reproach. But that contempt for Israel is nothing new to the world, for before even the Roman despised them, the Assyrian and Egyptian regarded them with scorn. Yet the words which came from Israel's prophets have been the life-blood of the world's devotions. And the teachers, the psalmists, the prophets, and the lawgivers of this despised nation spoke out truths that have struck the key-note of the heart of man: and this, not because they were of Jewish, but just because they were of universal application.

This collection of books has been to the world what no other book has ever been to a nation. States have been founded on its principles. Kings rule by a compact based on it. Men hold the Bible in their hands when they prepare to give solemn evidence affecting life, death, or property; the sick man is almost afraid to die unless the book be within reach of his hands; the battle-ship goes into action with one on board whose office is to expound it; its prayers, its psalms are the language which we use when we speak to God; eighteen centuries have found no holier, no diviner language. If ever there has been a prayer or a hymn enshrined in the heart of a nation, you are sure to find its basis in the Bible. There is no new religious idea given to the world, but it is merely the development of something given in the Bible. The very translation of it has fixed language and settled the idioms of speech. Germany and England speak as they speak because the Bible was translated. It has made the most illiterate peasant more familiar with the history, customs, and geography of ancient Palestine than with the localities of his own country. Men who know nothing of the Grampians, of Snowden, or of Skiddaw, are at home in Zion, the Lake of Gennesareth, or among the rills of Carmel. People who know little about London, know by heart the places in Jerusalem where those blessed feet trod which were nailed to the cross. Men who know nothing of the architecture of a Christian cathedral, can yet tell you all about the pattern of the holy temple. Even this shows us the influence of the Bible. The orator holds a thousand men for half an hour breathless—a thousand men as one, listening to his single word. But this Word of God has held a thousand nations for thrice a thousand years spell-bound; held them by an abiding power, even the universality of its truth; and we feel it to be no more a collection of books, but _the_ book.

We pass on now to consider the second principle contained in these words, which is, that all Scripture bears towards Jesus Christ. St. Paul quotes these Jewish words as fulfilled in Christ. Jesus of Nazareth is the central point in which all the converging lines of Scripture meet. Again we state this principle in Scripture language: in the book of Revelation we find it written, "The testimony of Jesus is the spirit of prophecy," that is, the sum and substance of prophecy, the very spirit of Scripture is to bear testimony to Jesus Christ. We must often have been surprised and perplexed at the way in which the apostles quote passages in reference to Christ which originally had no reference to Him. In our text, for instance, David speaks only of himself, and yet St. Paul refers it to Christ. Let us understand this. We have already said that Scripture deals not with individuals, but with states and principles. Promises belong to persons only so far as they are what they are taken to be; and consequently all unlimited promises made to individuals, so far as they are referred merely to those individuals, are necessarily exaggerated and hyperbolical. They can only be true of One in whom that is fulfilled which was unfulfilled in them.

We will take an instance. We are all familiar with the well-known prophecy of Balaam. We all remember the magnificent destinies he promised to the people whom he was called to curse. Those promises have never been fulfilled, neither from the whole appearance of things does it seem likely that they ever will be fulfilled in their literal sense. To whom, then, are they made? To Israel? Yes; so far as they developed God's own conception. Balaam says, "God hath not beheld iniquity in Jacob, neither hath He seen perverseness in Israel." Is this the character of Israel, an idolatrous and rebellious nation? Spoken of the literal Israel, this prophecy is false; but it was not false of that spotlessness and purity of which Israel was the temporal and imperfect type. If one can be found of whom that description is true, of whom we can say, the Lord hath not beheld iniquity in him, to him then that prophecy belongs.

Brethren, Jesus of Nazareth is that pure and spotless One. Christ is perfectly, all that every saint was partially. To Him belongs all: all that description of a perfect character, which would be exaggeration if spoken of others, and to this character the blessing belongs; hence it is that all the fragmentary representations of character collect and centre in Him alone. Therefore, the apostle says, "It was added until the seed should come to whom the promise was made." Consequently St. Paul would not read the Psalm as spoken only of David. Were the lofty aspirations, the purity and humbleness expressed in the text, true of him, poor, sinful, erring David? These were the expressions of the Christ within his heart—the longing of the Spirit of God within Him; but they were no proper representation of the spirit of his life, for there is a marvellous difference between a man's ideal and his actual—between the man and the book he writes—a difference between the aspirations within the man and the character which is realized by his daily life. The promises are to the Christ within David; therefore they are applied to the Christ when He comes. Now, let us extract from that this application.

Brethren, Scripture is full of Christ. From Genesis to Revelation every thing breathes of Him, not every letter of every sentence, but the spirit of every chapter. It is full of Christ, but not in the way that some suppose;

for there is nothing more miserable, as specimens of perverted ingenuity, than the attempts of certain commentators and preachers to find remote, and recondite, and intended allusions to Christ everywhere. For example, they chance to find in the construction of the temple the fusion of two metals, and this they conceive is meant to show the union of Divinity with Humanity in Christ. If they read of coverings to the tabernacle, they find implied the doctrine of imputed righteousness. If it chance that one of the curtains of the tabernacle be red, they see in that the prophecy of the blood of Christ. If they are told that the kingdom of heaven is a pearl of great price, they will see it in the allusion—that, as a pearl is the production of animal suffering, so the kingdom of heaven is produced by the sufferings of the Redeemer. I mention this perverted mode of comment, because it is not merely harmless, idle, and useless; it is positively dangerous. This is to make the Holy Spirit speak riddles and conundrums, and the interpretation of Scripture but clever riddle-guessing. Putting aside all this childishness, we say that the Bible is full of Christ. Every unfulfilled aspiration of humanity in the past; all partial representation of perfect character; all sacrifices, nay even those of idolatry, point to the fulfillment of what we want, the answer to every longing—the type of perfect humanity, the Lord Jesus Christ.

Get the habit—a glorious one—of referring all to Christ. How did He feel?—think?—act? So then must I feel, and think, and act. Observe how Christ was a living reality in St. Paul's mind. "Should I please myself?" "For even Christ pleased not Himself;" "It is more blessed to give than to receive."

BROOKS
(1835 - 1893)

Brief Sketch of His Life

Phillips Brooks was born in Boston in 1835. He was baptized in a Congregational church. When it gradually became Unitarian, his family withdrew and united with Saint Paul's Episcopal church. As a boy he kept a "Sabbath Notebook" in which he recorded the texts of the morning and evening sermons, the Scripture lessons and the hymns. He attended the Boston Latin School, Harvard University (where he majored in Classics and the Church Fathers) and The Episcopal Theological Seminary in Alexandria, Virginia from which he graduated in 1859.

From 1859-1862 he ministered at the Church of the Advent in Philadelphia and at Trinity Church from 1862-1869. From 1869-1891 he pastored the Trinity Episcopal Church of Boston. During this time he was made a bishop.

Brooks held low church beliefs. His theology, though basically orthodox, was open to certain emphases of liberalism. At the age of 30 he was offered the presidency of the Episcopal Theological Seminary of Cambridge but declined it. In Boston he became so famous that the city erected a statue of him preaching. His *Lectures on Preaching* are the best known and loved of the Yale lecture series. In these lectures he set forth his famous definition of preaching: "Truth through personality."

Content

Brooks, like Robertson, preached a principle abstracted from the Bible and applied to life now. The method is worth study. While the principle abstracted was not always taught in the passage Brooks chose, and he cannot be followed very closely in his exegesis (of which there is often far too little), the method itself is useful when preaching from the book of Proverbs or from some of the general, summary principles that occasionally appear in the epistles. It is interesting that after demonstrating the truth of the principle in various areas of life, in one way or another Brooks nearly always shows how, *par excellence*, the principle is exemplified in the life and work of Christ.

In Philadelphia Brooks's aim was to address social problems of the day. But in Boston, he concentrated on pastoral work, and the themes of his sermons were evangelism and doctrine. Here Brooks grew doctrinally. He preached the Trinity in Unitarian Boston in such a way that he neither compromised his beliefs nor made too many enemies. Indeed, in spite of his outspoken advocacy of the doctrine of the Trinity, Brooks was invited to be the college preacher for Unitarian Harvard University! He declined the position, but preached there often and became the most popular preacher in the history of Harvard. About half of his sermons are evangelistic. Because the sermons show a deep, accurate understanding of sinful human nature, Brooks should be studied for his ability to analyze and describe man. Brooks makes the listener think. In sermon after sermon, at some point or other, he addressed and challenged young men.

Organization

Behind every sermon there was careful planning. Brooks preached from a strong outline that is always apparent but does not protrude. Climactically, his sermons usually move from the lesser to the greater, from man to Christ, from explanation to application. Within the early section, he frequently moved from the general to the specific, from the abstract to the concrete, from the principle to the practice. Taking the time to outline a number of his sermons could be an instructive lesson in outlining. However, the outlines need to be translated out of their essentially lecture format into a preaching form. (For more on this, see my books, *Preaching with Purpose* and *Truth Apparent.*)

Style

Brooks knew the poets well and was himself a poet. It was he who wrote the Christmas carol, "O Little Town of Bethlehem." The key word in his sermons was "light," an image word. He most often selected texts with a central figure in them. "Out of 119 texts" studied, says Andrew W. Blackwood, "111 had a striking figure, an interesting person in action or something else to appeal to the eye." This feature of Brooks's preaching is well worth studying. Brooks's illustrative materials and his descriptive language are also outstanding and profitable for analysis. Brooks did not use the second person throughout his sermons, but when he did, he used it fearlessly. Try turning some of his first and third person language into second person language at other appropriate points and note the powerful difference that it makes.

Delivery

Brooks wrote out and read his sermons. But he developed an effective oral style and his reading was not noticeable. He spoke very rapidly— 200 words per minute. He appealed primarily to men, indeed, his preaching neglects women.

THE FIRE AND THE CALF

"So they gave it me: then I cast it into the fire, and there came out this calf." (Exod. 32:24)

In the story from which these words are taken we see Moses go up into the mountain to hold communion with God. While he is gone the Israelites begin to murmur and complain. They want other gods, gods of their own. Aaron, the brother of Moses, was their priest. He yielded to the people, and when they brought him their golden earrings he made out of them a golden calf for them to worship. When Moses came down from the mountain he found the people deep in their idolatry. He was indignant. First he destroyed the idol, "He burnt it in the fire, and ground it to powder, and strawed it upon the water, and made the children of Israel drink of it." Then he turned to Aaron: "What did this people unto thee that thou hast brought so great sin upon them?" And Aaron meanly answered: "Let not the anger of my Lord wax hot: thou knowest the people, that they are set on mischief. For they said unto me, Make us gods which shall go before us...And I said unto them, Whosoever hath any gold, let them break it off. So they gave it me: then I cast it into the fire, and there came out this calf." That was his mean reply. The real story of what happened had been written earlier in the chapter. When the people brought Aaron their golden earrings "he received them at their hand, and fashioned it with a graving tool, after he had made it a molten calf: and they said, These be thy gods, O Israel, which brought thee up out of the land of Egypt." That was what really happened, and this is the description which Aaron gave of it to Moses: "So they gave it me: then I cast it into the fire, and there came out this calf."

Aaron was frightened at what he had done. He was afraid of the act itself, and of what Moses would say. Like all timid men, he trembled before the storm which he had raised. And so he tried to persuade Moses, and perhaps in some degree even to persuade himself, that it was not he that had done this thing. He lays the blame upon the furnace. "The fire did it," he declares. He will not blankly face his sin, and yet he will not tell a lie in words. He tells what is literally true. He had cast the earrings into the fire, and this calf had come out. But he leaves out the one important point, his own personal agency in it all; the fact that he had moulded the earrings into the calf's shape, and that he had taken it out and set it on its pedestal for the people to adore. He tells it so that it shall all look automatic. It is a curious, ingenious, but transparent lie.

Let us look at Aaron's speech a little while this morning and see what it represents, for it does represent something. There never was a speech more true to our human nature. We are all ready to lay the blame upon the furnaces. "The fire did it," we are all of us ready to say. Here is a man all gross and sensual, a man still young, who has lost the freshness and the glory and the purity of youth. He is profane; he is cruel;

he is licentious; all his brightness has grown lurid; all his wit is ribaldry. You know the man. As far as a man can be, he is a brute. Suppose you question him about his life. You expect him to be ashamed, repentant. There is not a sign of anything like that! He says, "I am the victim of circumstances. What a corrupt, licentious, profane age is this in which we live! When I was in college I got into a bad set. When I went into business I was surrounded by bad influences. When I grew rich, men flattered me. When I grew poor, men bullied me. The world has made me what I am, this fiery, passionate, wicked world. I had in my hands the gold of my boyhood which God gave me. Then I cast it into the fire, and there came out this calf." So the poor wronged miserable creature looks into your face with his bleared eyes and asks your pity. Another man is not a profligate, but a miser, or a mere business machine. "What can you ask of me?" he says. "This is a mercantile community. The business man who does not attend to his business goes to the wall. I am what this intense commercial life has made me. I put my life in there, and it came out this." And he gazes fondly at his golden calf and his knees bend under him with the old habit of worshipping it, and he loves it still even while he abuses and disowns it. And so with the woman of society. "The fire made me this," she says of her frivolity and pride. And so of the politician and his selfishness and partisanship. "I put my principles into the furnace and this came out." And so of the bigot and his bigotry, the one-sided conservative with his stubborn resistance to all progress, the one-sided radical with his ruthless iconoclasm. So of all partial and fanatical men. "The furnace made us," they are ready to declare. "These things compel us to be this. In better times we might have been better, broader men; but, now behold, God put us into the fire, and we came out this." It is what one is perpetually hearing about disbelief. "The times have made me sceptical. How is it possible for a man to live in days like these and yet believe in God and Jesus and the Resurrection? You ask me how I, who was brought up in the faith and in the Church, became a disbeliever. Oh, you remember that I lived five years here," or "three years there." "You know I have been very much thrown with this set or with that. You know the temper of our town. I cast myself into the fire, and I came out this." One is all ready to understand, my friends, how the true soul, struggling for truth, seems often to be worsted in the struggle. One is ready to have tolerance, respect, and hope for any man who, reaching after God, is awed by God's immensity and his own littleness, and falls back crushed and doubtful. His is a doubt which is born in the secret chambers of his own personal conscientiousness. It is independent of his circumstances and surroundings. The soul which has truly come to a personal doubt finds it hard to conceive of any ages of the most implicit faith in which it could have lived in which that doubt would not have been in it. It faces its doubt in a solitude where there is none but it and God. All that one understands, and the more he understands it the more unintelligible does it seem to him, that any earnest soul can really lay its doubt upon the age, the set, or the society it lives in. No; our age, our society is what, with this figure taken out of the old story of Exodus, we have been calling it. It is the furnace. Its fire can set and fix and fasten what the man puts into it. But, properly speaking, it can create no character. It can make no truly faithful soul a doubter. It never did. It never can.

Remember that the subtlety and attractiveness of this excuse, this plausible attributing of power to inanimate things and exterior conditions to create what only man can make, extends not only to the results which we see coming forth in ourselves; it covers also the fortunes of those for whom we are responsible. The father says of his profligate son whom he has never done one wise or vigorous thing to make a noble and pure-minded man: "I cannot tell how it has come. It has not been my fault. I put him into the world and this came out." The father whose faith has been mean and selfish says the same of his boy who is a sceptic. Everywhere there is this cowardly casting off of responsibilities upon the dead circumstances around us. It is a very hard treatment of the poor, dumb, helpless world which cannot answer to defend itself. It takes us as we give ourselves to it. It is our minister fulfilling our commissions for us upon our own souls. If we say to it, "Make us noble," it does make us noble. If we say to it, "Make us mean," it does make us mean. And then we take the nobility and say, "Behold, how noble I have made myself." And we take the meanness and say, "See how mean the world has made me."

You see, I am sure, how perpetual a thing the temper of Aaron is, how his excuse is heard everywhere and always. I need not multiply illustrations. But now, if all the world is full of it, the next question is, What does it mean? Is it mere pure deception, or is there also delusion, self-deception in it? Take Aaron's case. Was he simply telling a lie to Moses and trying to hide the truth from his brother whom he dreaded, when he said, "I cast the earrings into the fire, and this calf came out"? Or was he in some dim degree, in some half-conscious way, deceiving himself? Was he allowing himself to attribute some power to the furnace in the making of the calf? Perhaps as we read the verse above in which it is so distinctly said that Aaron fashioned the idol with a graving tool, any such supposition seems incredible. But yet I cannot but think that some degree, however dim, of such self-deception was in Aaron's heart. The fire was mysterious. He was a priest. Who could say that some strange creative power had not been at work in the heart of the furnace which had done for him what he seemed to do for himself. There was a human heart under that ancient ephod, and it is hard to think that Aaron did not succeed in bringing himself to be somewhat imposed upon by his own words, and hiding his responsibility in the heart of the hot furnace. But however it may have been with Aaron, there can be no doubt that in almost all cases this is so. Very rarely indeed does a man excuse himself to other men and yet remain absolutely unexcused in his own eyes. When Pilate stands washing the responsibility of Christ's murder from his hands before the people, was he not feeling himself as if his hands grew cleaner while he washed? When Shakespeare paints Macbeth with the guilty ambition which was to be his ruin first rising in his heart, you remember how he makes him hide his new-born purpose to the king even from himself, and pretend that he is willing to accept the kingdom only if it shall come to him out of the working of things, for which he is not responsible, without an effort of his own.

> If chance will have me king, why, chance
> may crown me, Without my stir.

That was the first stage of the growing crime which finally was murder. Often it takes this form. Often the very way to help ourselves most to a result which we have set before ourselves is just to put ourselves into a current which is sweeping on that way, and then lie still and let the current do the rest; and in all such cases it is so easy to ignore or to forget the first step, which was that we chose that current for our resting place, and so to say that it is only the drift of the current which is to blame for the dreary shore on which at last our lives are cast up by the stream. Suppose you are today a scornful man, a man case-hardened in conceit and full of disbelief in anything generous or supernatural, destitute of all enthusiasm, contemptuous, supercilious. You say the time you live in has made you so. You point to one large tendency in the community which always sets that way. You parade the specimens of enthusiastic people whom you have known who have been fanatical and silly. You tell me what your favorite journal has been saying in your ears every week for years. You bid me catch the tone of the brightest people whom you live among, and then you turn to me and say, "How could one live in such an atmosphere and not grow cynical? Behold, my times have made me what I am." What does that mean? Are you merely trying to hide from me, or are you also hiding from yourself, the certain fact that you have chosen that special current to launch your boat upon, that you have given your whole attention to certain kinds of facts and shut your eyes to certain others, that you have constantly valued the brightness which went to the depreciation of humanity and despised the urgency with which a healthier spirit has argued for the good in man and for his everlasting hope? Is it not evident that you yourself have been able to half forget all this, and so when the stream on which you launched your boat at last drives it upon the beach to which it has been flowing all the time, there is a certain lurking genuineness in the innocent surprise with which you look around upon the desolate shore on which you land, and say to yourself, "How unhappy I am that I should have fallen upon these evil days, in which it is impossible that a man should genuinely respect or love his fellowmen"?

For there are currents flowing always in all bad directions. There is a perpetual river flowing towards sensuality and vice. There is a river flowing perpetually towards hypocrisy and religious pretence. There is a river always running towards skepticism and infidelity. And when you once have given yourself up to either of these rivers, then there is quite enough in the continual pressure, in that great movement like a fate beneath your keel, to make you lose the sense and remembrance that it is by your own will that you are there, and only think of the resistless flow of the river which is always in your eyes and ears. This is the mysterious, bewildering mixture of the consciousness of guilt and the consciousness of misery in all our sin. We live in a perpetual confusion of self-pity and self-blame. We go up to the scaffolds where we are to suffer, half like culprits crawling to the gallows and half like martyrs proudly striding to their stakes. When we think of what sort of reception is to meet us in the other world as the sum and judgment of the life we have been living here, we find ourselves ready, according to the moment's mood, either for the bitterest denunciation, as of souls who have lived in deliberate sin; or for tender petting and refreshment, as of souls who have been buffeted and knocked about by all the storms of time, and for whom now there ought to be soft beds in eternity. The confusion of men's minds about the judgments of the eternal world is only the echo of their confusion about the responsibilities of the life which they are living now.

Suppose there is a man here this morning who committed a fraud in business yesterday. He did it in a hurry. He did not stop to think about it then. But now, in this quiet church, with everything calm and peaceful round him, with the words of prayer which have taken God for granted sinking into his ears, he has been thinking it over. How does it look to him? Is he not certainly sitting in the mixture of self-pity and self-reproach of which I spoke? He did the sin, and he is sorry as a sinner. The sin did itself, and he is sorry as a victim. Nay, perhaps in the next pew to him, or perhaps in the same pew, or perhaps in the same body there is sitting a man who means to do a fraud tomorrow. In him too is there not the same confusion? One moment he looks it right in the face, and says, "Tomorrow night I shall despise myself." The next moment he is quietly thinking that the sin will do itself and give him all its advantage, and he need not interfere. "If chance will make me cheat, why chance may crown me, without my stir." Both thoughts are in his mind, and if he has listened to our service, it is likely enough that he has found something in it—even in the words of the Bible—for each thought to feed upon.

I own this freely, and yet I do believe, and I call you to bear me witness, that such self-deception almost never is absolutely complete. We feel its incompleteness the moment that anyone else attempts to excuse us with the same excuse with which we have excused ourselves. Suppose that some one of the Israelites who stood by had spoken up in Aaron's behalf and said to Moses: "Oh, he did not do it. It was not his act. He only cast the gold into the fire, and there came out this calf." Must not Aaron as he listened have felt the wretchedness of such a telling of the story, and been ashamed, and even cried out and claimed his responsibility and his sin? Very often it is good for us to imagine someone saying aloud in our behalf what we are silently saying to ourselves in self-apology. We see its thinness when another hand holds it up against the sun, and we stand off and look at it. If I might turn again to Shakespeare and his wonderful treasury of human character, there is a scene in Hamlet which exactly illustrates what I mean. The king has determined that Hamlet must die, and is just sending him off upon the voyage from which he means that he is never to return. And the king has fully explained the act of his own conscience, and accepted the crime as a necessity. And then he meets the courtiers, Rosencrantz and Guildenstern, who are to have the execution of the base commission. And they, like courtiers, try to repeat to the king the arguments with which he has convinced himself. One says—

> Most holy and religious fear it is
> To keep those many many bodies safe
> That live and feed upon your majesty.

And the other takes up the strain and says—

> The single and peculiar life is bound,
> With all the strength and armour of the mind,
> To keep itself from 'noyance; but much more
> That spirit upon whose weal depend and rest
> The lives of many."

They are the king's own arguments. With them he has persuaded his own soul to tolerate the murder. But when they come to him from these other lips, he will none of them. He cuts them short. He cannot hear from others what he has said over and over to himself.

> Arm you, I pray you, to this speedy voyage.

So he cries out and interrupts them. Let the deed be done, but let not these echoes of his self-excuse parade before him the way in which he is trifling with his own soul.

So it is always. I think of the mysterious judgment-day, and sometimes it appears to me as if our souls would need no more than merely that voices outside ourselves should utter in our ears the very selfsame pleas and apologies with which we, here upon the earth, have extenuated our own wickedness. They of themselves, heard in the open air of eternity, would let us see how weak they were, and so we should be judged. Is not that partly the reason why we hate the scene of some old sin? The room in which we did it seems to ring forever with the sophistries by which we persuaded ourselves that it was right, and will not let us live in comfortable delusion. Our life there is an anticipated judgment day.

I doubt not that this tendency to self-deception and apology with reference to the sins which they commit differs exceedingly with different men. Men differ, perhaps, nowhere else more than in their disposition to face the acts of their lives and to recognize their own personal part and responsibility for the things they do. Look, for instance, at this Aaron and his brother Moses. The two men are characterized by their own sins. The sin of Aaron was a denial or concealment of his own personal agency: "I cast it into the fire, and there came out this calf." The sin of Moses, you remember, was just the opposite. As he stood with his thirsty people in front of the rock of Horeb, he intruded his personal agency where it had no right. "Hear now, ye rebels; must we fetch water out of this rock?" To be sure, in the case of Moses it was a good act of mercy to which he put in his claim, while in Aaron's case it was a wicked act whose responsibility he desired to avoid. And men are always ready to claim the good deeds in which they have the slightest share, even when they try to disown the sins which are entirely their own. But still the actions seem to mark the men. Moses is the franker, manlier, braver man. In Aaron the priest there is something of that oversubtle, artificial, complicated character, that power of being morally confused even in the midst of pious feeling, that lack of simplicity, and of the disposition to look things frankly in the eye; in a word, that vague and defective sense of personality and its responsibilities which has often in the history of religion made the very name of priestcraft a reproach. Moses is the prophet. His distinct mission is the utterance of truth. He is always simple; never more simple than when he is most profound; never more sure of the fundamental principles of right and wrong, of honesty and truth, than when he is deepest in the mystery of God; never more conscious of himself and his responsibilities than when he is most conscious of God and His power.

And this brings me to my last point, which I must not longer delay to reach. If the world is thus full of the Aaron spirit, of the disposition to throw the blame of wrong-doing upon other things and other people, to represent to others, and to our own souls, that our sins do themselves, what is the spiritual source of such a tendency, and where are we to look to find its cure? I have just intimated what seems to me to be its source. It is a vague and defective sense of personality. Anything which makes less clear to a man the fact that he, standing here on his few inches of earth, is a distinct separate being, in whom is lodged a unit of life, with his own soul, his own character, his own chances, his own responsibilities, distinct and separate from any other man's in all the world; anything that makes all that less clear demoralizes a man, and opens the door to endless self-excuses. And you know, surely, how many tendencies there are today which are doing just that for men. Every man's personality, in his clear sense of himself, seems to be standing where almost all the live forces of the time are making their attacks upon it. It is like a tree in the open field from which every bird carries away some fruit. The enlargement of our knowledge of the world, the growing tendency of men to work in large companies, the increased despotism of social life, the interesting studies of hereditation, the externality of a large part of our action, the rush and competition for the prizes which represent the most material sort of success, the spread of knowledge by which at once all men are seen to know much, and, at the same time, no man is seen to know everything; all these causes enfeeble the sense of personality. The very prominence of the truth of a universal humanity, in which our philanthropy justly glories, obscures the clearness of the individual human life. Once it was hard to conceive of man, because the personalities of men were so distinct. Once people found it hard, as the old saying was, to see the forest for the trees. Now it is the opposite. To hundreds of people it is almost impossible to see the trees for the forest. Man is so clear that men become obscure. As the Laureate of the century sings of the time which he so well knows: "The individual withers and the race is more and more." These are the special causes, working in our time, of that which has its general causes in our human nature working everywhere and always.

And if this is the trouble, where, then, is the help? If this is the disease, where is the cure? I cannot look for it anywhere short of that great assertion of the human personality which is made when a man personally enters into the power of Jesus Christ. Think of it! Here is some Aaron of our modern life trying to cover up some sin which he has done. The fact of the sin is clear enough. It stands out wholly undisputed. It is not by denying that the thing was done but by beclouding the fact that he did it with his own hands, with his own will; thus it is that the man would cover up his sin. He has been nothing but an agent, nothing but a victim; so he assures his fellowmen, so he assures himself. And now suppose that while he is doing that, the great change comes to that man by which he is made a disciple and servant of Jesus Christ. It becomes known to him as a certain fact that God loves him individually, and is educating him with a separate personal education which is all his own. The clear individuality of Jesus stands distinctly out and says to him, "Follow me!" Jesus stops in front of where he is working just as evidently as He stopped in front of the booth where Matthew was sitting collecting taxes, and says, "Follow me." He is called separately, and separately he does give himself to Christ. Remember all that is essential to a Christian faith. You cannot blur it all into indistinctness and generality. In the true light of the redeeming Incarnation, every man in the multitude stands out as every blade of grass on the hillside stands distinct from every other when the sun has risen. In this sense, as in many another, this is the true light which lighteneth every man that cometh into the world.

The Bible calls it a new birth, and in that name too there are many meanings. And among other meanings in it must there not be this—the separateness and personality of every soul in Christ? Birth is the moment of distinctness. The meanest child in the poorest hovel of the city, who by and by is to be lost in the great whirlpool of human life, here at the outset where his being comes, a new fact, into the crowded world, is felt in his distinctness, has his own personal tending, excites his own personal emotion. When he is born and when he dies, but perhaps most of all when he is born, the commonest, the most commonplace and undistinguished of mankind asserts the fact of privilege of his separateness. And so when the possession of the soul by Christ is called the "New Birth," one of the meanings of that name is this, that then there is a reassertion of personality, and the soul which had lost itself in the slavery of the multitude finds itself again in the obedience of Christ.

And now what will be the attitude of this man, with his newly-awakened selfhood, towards that sin which he has been telling himself that his hands did, but that he did not do? May he not almost say that he will need that sin for his self-identification? Who is he? A being whom Christ has forgiven, and then in virtue of that forgiveness made His servant. All his new life dates from and begins with his sin. He cannot afford to find his consciousness of himself only in the noble parts of his life, which it makes him proud and happy to remember. There is not enough of that to make for him a complete and continuous personality. It will have great gaps if he disowns the wicked demonstrations of his selfhood and says, "It was not I," wherever he has done wrong. No! Out of his sin, out of the bad, base, cowardly acts which are truly his, out of the weak and wretched passages of his life which it makes him ashamed to remember, but which he forces himself to recollect and own, out of these he gathers the consciousness of a self all astray with self-will, which he then brings to Christ and offers in submission and obedience to His perfect will.

You try to tell some soul rejoicing in the Lord's salvation that the sins over whose forgiveness by its Lord it is gratefully rejoicing, were not truly its; and see what strange thing comes. The soul seems to draw back from your assurance as if, if it were true, it would be robbed of all its surest confidence and brightest hope. You meant to comfort the poor penitent, and he looks into your face as if you were striking him a blow. And you can see what such a strange sight means. It is not that the poor creature loves those sins or is glad that he did them, or dreams for an instant of ever doing them again. It is only that through those sins, which are all the real experience he has had, he has found himself, and finding himself has found his Saviour and the new life.

So the only hope for any of us is in a perfectly honest manliness to claim our sins. "I did it! I did it," let me say of all my wickedness. Let me refuse to listen for one moment to any voice which would make my sins less mine. It is the only honest and the only hopeful way, the only way to know and be ourselves. When we have done that, then we are ready for the Gospel, ready for all that Christ wants to show us that we may become, and for all the powerful grace by which He wants to make us be it perfectly.

THE CANDLE OF THE LORD

"The spirit of man is the candle of the Lord." (Prov. 20:27)

The essential connection between the life of God and the life of man is the great truth of the world; and that is the truth which Solomon sets forth in the striking words which I have chosen for my text this morning. The picture which the words suggest is very simple. An unlighted candle is standing in the darkness and some one comes to light it. A blazing bit of paper holds the fire at first, but it is vague and fitful. It flares and wavers and at any moment may go out. But the vague, uncertain, flaring blaze touches the candle, and the candle catches fire and at once you have a steady flame. It burns straight and clear and constant. The candle gives the fire a manifestation-point for all the room which is illuminated by it. The candle is glorified by the fire and the fire is manifested by the candle. The two bear witness that they were made for one another by the way in which they fulfil each other's life. That fulfilment comes by the way in which the inferior substance renders obedience to its superior. The candle obeys the fire. The docile wax acknowledges that the subtle flame is its master and it yields to his power; and so, like every faithful servant of a noble master, it at once gives its master's nobility the chance to utter itself, and its own substance is clothed with a glory which is not its own. The disobedient granite, if you try to burn it, neither gives the fire a chance to show its brightness nor gathers any splendor to itself. It only glows with sullen resistance, and, as the heat increases, splits and breaks but will not yield. But the candle obeys, and so in it the scattered fire finds a point of permanent and clear expression.

Can we not see, with such a picture clear before us, what must be meant when it is said that one being is the candle of another being? There is in a community a man of large, rich character, whose influence runs everywhere. You cannot talk with any man in all the city but you get, shown in that man's own way, the thought, the feeling of that central man who teaches all the community to think, to feel. The very boys catch something of his power, and have something about them that would not be there if he were not living in the town. What better description could you give of all that, than to say that that man's life was fire and that all these men's lives were candles which he lighted, which gave to the rich, warm, live, fertile nature that was in him multiplied points of steady exhibition, so that he lighted the town through them? Or, not to look so widely, I pity you if in the circle of your home there is not some warm and living nature which is your fire. Your cold, dark candle-nature, touched by that fire, burns bright and clear. Wherever you are carried, perhaps into regions where that nature cannot go, you carry its fire and set it up in some new place. Nay, the fire itself may have disappeared, the nature may have vanished from the earth and gone to heaven;

and yet still your candle-life, which was lighted at it, keeps that fire still in the world, as the fire of the lightning lives in the tree that it has struck, long after the quick lightning itself has finished its short, hot life and died. So the man in the countingroom is the candle of the woman who stays at home, making her soft influence felt in the rough places of trade where her feet never go; and so a man who lives like an inspiration in the city for honesty and purity and charity may be only the candle in whose obedient life burns still the fire of another strong, true man who was his father, and who passed out of men's sight a score of years ago. Men call the father dead, but he is no more dead than the torch has gone out which lighted the beacon that is blazing on the hill.

And now, regarding all this lighting of life from life, two things are evident, the same two which appeared in the story of the candle and its flame: First, there must be a correspondency of nature between the two; and second, there must be a cordial obedience of the less to the greater. The nature which cannot feel the other nature's warmth, even if it is held close to it; and the nature which refuses to be held where the other nature's flame can reach it,—both of these must go unlighted, no matter how hotly the fire of the higher life may burn.

I think that we are ready now to turn to Solomon and read his words again and understand them. "The spirit of man is the candle of the Lord," he says. God is the fire of this world, its vital principle, a warm pervading presence everywhere. What thing of outward nature can so picture to us the mysterious, the subtle, the quick, live, productive and destructive thought, which has always lifted men's hearts and solemnized their faces when they have said the word GOD, as this strange thing,—so heavenly, so earthly, so terrible, and yet so gracious; so full of creativeness, and yet so quick and fierce to sweep whatever opposes it out of its path,—this marvel, this beauty and glory and mystery of fire? Men have always felt the fitness of the figure; and the fire has always crowded, closest of all earthly elements, about the throne on which their conception of Deity was seated. And now of this fire the spirit of man is the candle. What does it mean? If, because man is of a nature which corresponds to the nature of God, and just so far as man is obedient to God, the life of God, which is spread throughout the universe, gathers itself into utterance; and men, aye, and all other beings, if such beings there are, capable of watching our humanity, see what God is, in gazing at the man whom He has kindled,—then is not the figure plain? It is a wondrous thought, but it is clear enough. Here is the universe, full of the diffused fire of divinity. Men feel it in the air, as they feel an intense heat which has not broken into a blaze. That is the meaning of a great deal of the unexplained, mysterious awfulness of life, of which they who are very much in its power are often only half aware. It is the sense of God, felt but unseen, like an atmosphere burdened with heat that does not burst out into fire. Now in the midst of this solemn, burdened world there stands up a man, pure, God-like, and perfectly obedient to God. In an instant it is as if the heated room had found some sensitive, inflammable point where it could kindle to a blaze. The vague oppressiveness of God's felt presence becomes clear and definite. The fitfulness of the impression of divinity is steadied into permanence. The mystery changes its character, and is a mystery of light and not of darkness. The fire of the Lord has found the candle of the Lord, and burns clear and steady, guiding and cheering instead of bewildering and frightening us, just so soon as a man who is obedient to God has begun to catch and manifest His nature.

I hope that we shall find that this truth comes very close to our personal, separate lives; but, before we come to that, let me remind you first with what a central dignity it clothes the life of man in the great world. Certain philosophies, which belong to our time, would depreciate the importance of man in the world, and rob him of his centralness. Man's instinct and man's pride rebel against them, but he is puzzled by their speciousness. Is it indeed true, as it seems, that the world is made for man, and that from man, standing in the centre, all things besides which the world contains get their true value and receive the verdict of their destiny? That was the old story that the Bible told. The book of Genesis with its Garden of Eden, and its obedient beasts waiting until the man should tell them what they should be called, struck firmly, at the beginning of the anthem of the world's history, the great note of the centralness of man. And the Garden of Eden, in this its first idea, repeats itself in every cabin of the western forests or the southern jungles, where a new Adam and a new Eve, a solitary settler and his wife, begin as it were the human history anew. There once again the note of Genesis is struck, and man asserts his centralness. The forest waits to catch the color of his life. The beasts hesitate in fear or anger till he shall tame them to his service or bid them depart. The earth under his feet holds its fertility at his command, and answers the summons of his grain or flower-seeds. The very sky over his head regards him, and what he does upon the earth is echoed in the changes of the climate and the haste or slowness of the storms. This is the great impression which all the simplest life of man is ever creating, and with which the philosophies, which would make little of the separateness and centralness of the life of man, must always have to fight. And this is the impression which is taken up and strengthened and made clear, and turned from a petty pride to a lofty dignity and a solemn responsibility, when there comes such a message as this of Solomon's. He says that the true separateness and superiority and centralness of man is in that likeness of nature to God, and that capacity of spiritual obedience to Him, in virtue of which man may be the declaration and manifestation of God to all the world. So long as that truth stands, the centralness of man is sure. "The spirit of man is the candle of the Lord."

This is the truth of which I wish to speak to you to-day, the perpetual revelation of God by human life. You must ask yourself first, what God is. You must see how at the very bottom of His existence, as you conceive of it, lie these two thoughts—purpose and righteousness; how absolutely impossible it is to give God any personality except as the fulfilment of these two qualities—the intelligence that plans in love, and the righteousness that lives in duty. Then ask yourself how any knowledge of these qualities—of what they are, of what kind of being they will make in their perfect combination—could exist upon the earth if there were not a human nature here in which they could be uttered, from which they could shine. Only a person can truly utter a person. Only from a character can a character be echoed. You might write it all over the skies that God was just, but it would not burn there. It would be, at best, only a bit of knowledge; never a Gospel; never something which it would gladden the hearts of men to know. That comes only when a human life, capable of a justice like God's, made just by God, glows with His justice in the eyes of men, a candle of the Lord.

I have just intimated one thing which we need to observe. Man's utterance of God is purely an utterance of quality. It can tell me nothing of the quantities which make up His perfect life. That God is just, and what it is to be just—those things I can learn from the just lives of the just men about me; but how just God is, to what unconceived perfection, to what unexpected developments of itself, that majestic quality of justice may extend to Him,—of that I can form no judgment, that is worth anything, from the justice that I see in fellow-man. This seems to me to widen at once the range of the truth which I am stating. If it be the quality of God which man is capable of uttering, then it must be the quality of manhood that is necessary for the utterance; the quality of manhood, but not any specific quantity, not any assignable degree of human greatness. Whoever has in him the human quality, whoever really has the spirit of man, may be a candle of the Lord. A larger measure of that spirit may make a brighter light; but there must be a light wherever any human being, in virtue of his humanness, by obedience becomes luminous with God. There are the men of lofty spiritual genius, the leaders of our race. How they stand out through history! How all men feel as they pass into their presence that they are passing into the light of God! They are puzzled when they try to explain it. There is nothing more instructive and suggestive than the bewilderment which men feel when they try to tell what inspiration is,—how men become inspired. The lines which they draw through the continual communication between God and man are always becoming unsteady and confused. But in general, he who comes into the presence of any powerful nature, whose power is at all of a spiritual sort, feels sure that in some way he is coming into the presence of God. But it would be melancholy if only the great men could give us this conviction. The world would be darker than it is if every human spirit, so soon as it became obedient, did not become the Lord's candle. A poor, meagre, starved, bruised life, if only it keeps the true human quality and does not become inhuman, and if it is obedient to God in its blind, dull, half-conscious way, becomes a light. Lives yet more dark than it is, become dimly aware of God through it. A mere child, in his pure humanity, and with his easy and instinctive turning of his life toward the God from whom he came,—it is one of the commonplaces of your homes how often he may burn with some suggestion of divinity, and cast illumination upon problems and mysteries whose difficulty he himself has never felt. There are great lamps and little lamps burning everywhere. The world is bright with them. You shut your book in which you have been holding communion with one of the great souls of all time; and while you are standing in the light which he has shed about him, your child beside you says some simple, childlike thing, and a new thread of shining wisdom runs through the sweet and subtle thoughts that the great thinker gave you, as the light of a little taper sends its special needle of brightness through the pervasive splendor of a sunlit world. It is not strange. The fire is the same, whatever be the human lamp that gives it its expression. There is no life so humble that, if it be true and genuinely human and obedient to God, it may not hope to shed some of His light. There is no life so meagre that the greatest and wisest of us can afford to despise it. We cannot know at all what sudden moment it may flash forth with the life of God.

And in this truth of ours we have certainly the key to another mystery which sometimes puzzles us. What shall we make of some man rich in attainments and in generous desires, well educated, well behaved, who has trained himself to be a light and help to other men, and who, now that his training is complete, stands in the midst of his fellow-men completely dark and helpless? There are plenty of such men. We have all known them who have seen how men grow up. Their brethren stand around them expecting light from them, but no light comes. They themselves are full of amazement at themselves. They built themselves for influence, but no one feels them. They kindled themselves to give light, but no one shines a grateful answer back to them. Perhaps they blame their fellow-men, who are too dull to see their radiance. Perhaps they only wonder what is the matter, and wait, with a hope that never quite dies out into despair, for the long-delayed recognition and gratitude. At last they die, and the men who stand about their graves feel that the saddest thing about their death is that the world is not perceptibly the darker for their dying. What does it mean? If we let the truth of Solomon's figure play upon it, is not the meaning of the familiar failure simply this: These men are unlighted candles; they are the spirit of man, elaborated, cultivated, finished to its very finest, but lacking the last touch of God. As dark as a row of silver lamps, all chased and wrought with wondrous skill, all filled with rarest oil, but all untouched with fire,—so dark in this world is a long row of cultivated men, set up along the corridors of some age of history, around the halls of some wise university or in the pulpits of some stately church, to whom there has come no fire of devotion, who stand in awe and reverence before no wisdom greater than their own, who are proud and selfish, who do not know what it is to obey. There is the explanation of your wonder when you cling close to some man whom the world calls bright, and find that you get no brightness from him. There is the explanation of yourself, O puzzled man, who never can make out why the world does not turn to you for help. The poor blind world cannot tell its need, nor analyze its instinct, nor say why it seeks one man and leaves another; but through its blind eyes it knows when the fire of God has fallen on a human life. This is the meaning of the strange helpfulness which comes into a man when he truly is converted. It is not new truth that he knows, not new wonders that he can do, but it is that the unlighted nature, in the utter obedience and self-surrender of that great hour, has been lifted up and lighted at the life of God, and now burns with Him.

But it is not the worst thing in life for a man to be powerless or uninfluential. There are men enough for whom we would thank God if they did no harm, even if they did no good. I will not stop now to question whether there be such a thing possible as a life totally without influence of any kind, whether perhaps the men of whom I have been speaking do not also belong to the class of whom I want next to speak. However that may be, I am sure you will recognize the fact that there is a multitude of men whose lamps are certainly not dark, and yet who certainly are not the candles of the Lord. A nature furnished richly to the very brim, a man of knowledge, of wit, of skill, of thought, with the very graces of the body perfect, and yet profane, impure, worldly, and scattering scepticism of all good and truth about him wherever he may go. His is no unlighted candle. He burns so bright and lurid that often the purer lights grow dim in the glare. But if it be possible for the human candle, when it is all made, when the subtle components of a human nature are all mingled most carefully,—if it be possible that then, instead of being lifted up to heaven and kindled at the pure being of Him who is eternally and absolutely good, it should be plunged down into hell and lighted at the yellow flames that burn out of the dreadful brimstone of the pit, then we can understand the sight of a man who is rich in every brilliant human quality, cursing the world with the continual exhibition of the devilish instead of the godlike in his life. When the power of pure love appears as a capacity of brutal lust; when the holy ingenuity with which man may search the character of a fellow-man, that he may help him to be his best, is turned into the unholy skill with which the bad man studies his victim, that he may know how to make his damnation most complete; when the almost divine magnetism, which is given to a man in order that he may instil his faith and hope into some soul that trusts him, is used to breathe doubt and despair through all the substance of a friend's reliant soul; when wit, which ought to make truth beautiful, is deliberately prostituted to the service of a lie; when earnestness is degraded to be the slave of blasphemy, and the slave's reputation is made the cloak for the master's shame,—in all these cases, and how frequent they are no man among us fails to know, you have simply the spirit of man kindled from below, not from above, the candle of the Lord burning with the fire of the devil. Still it will burn; still the native inflammableness of humanity will show itself. There will be light; there will be power; and men who want nothing but light and power will come to it. It is wonderful how mere power, or mere brightness, apart altogether from the work that the power is doing and the story that the brightness has to tell, will win the confidence and admiration of men from whom we might have expected better things. A bright book or a bright play will draw the crowd, although its meaning be detestable. A clever man will make a host of boys and men stand like charmed birds while he draws their principles quietly out of them and leaves them moral idiots. A whole great majority of a community will rush like foolish sheep to the polls and vote for a man who they know is false and brutal, because they have learned to say that he is strong. All this is true enough; and yet while men do these wild and foolish things, they know the difference between the illumination of a human life that is kindled from above and that which is kindled from below. They know the pure flames of one and the lurid glare of the other; and however they may praise and follow wit and power, as if to be witty or powerful were an end sufficient in itself, they will always keep their sacredest respect and confidence for that power or wit which is inspired by God, and works for righteousness.

There is still another way, more subtle and sometimes more dangerous than these, in which the spirit of man may fail of its completest function as the candle of the Lord. The lamp may be lighted, and the fire at which it is lighted may be indeed the fire of God, and yet it may not be God alone who shines forth upon the world. I can picture to myself a candle which should in some way mingle a peculiarity of its own substance with the light it shed, giving to that light a hue which did not belong essentially to the fire at which it was lighted. Men who saw it would see not only the brightness of the fire. They would see also the tone and color of the lamp. And so it is, I think, with the way in which some good men manifest God. They have really kindled their lives at Him. It is His fire that burns in them. They are obedient, and so He can make them His points of exhibition; but they cannot get rid of themselves. They are mixed with the God they show. They show themselves as well as Him. It is as when a mirror mingles its own shape with the reflections of the things that are reflected from it, and gives them a curious convexity because it is itself convex. This is the secret of all pious bigotry, of all holy prejudice. It is the candle, putting its own color into the flame which it has borrowed from the fire of God. The violent man makes God seem violent. The feeble man makes God seem feeble. The speculative man makes God look like a beautiful dream. The legal man makes God look like a hard and steel-like law. Here is where all the harsh and narrow part of sectarianism comes from. The narrow Presbyterian or Methodist, or Episcopalian or Quaker, full of devoutness, really afire with God,—what is he but a candle which is always giving the flame its color and which, by a disposition which many men have to value the little parts of their life more than the greater, makes less of the essential brightness of the flame than of the special color which it lends to it? It seems, perhaps, as if, in saying this, I threw some slight or doubt upon that individual and separate element in every man's religion, on which, upon the contrary, I place the very highest value. Every man who is a Christian must live a Christian life that is peculiarly his own. Every candle of the Lord must utter its peculiar light; only the true individuality of faith is marked by these characteristics which rescue it from bigotry: first, that it does not add something to the universal light, but only brings out most strongly some aspect of it which is specially its own; second, that it always cares more about the essential light than about the peculiar way in which it utters it; and third, that it easily blends with other special utterances of the universal light, in cordial sympathy and recognition of the value which it finds in them. Let these characteristics be in every man's religion, and then the individuality of faith is an inestimable gain. Then the different candles of the Lord burn in long rows down His great palace-halls of the world; and all together, each complementing all the rest, they light the whole vast space with Him.

I have tried to depict some of the difficulties which beset the full exhibition in the world of this great truth of Solomon, that "the spirit of man is the candle of the Lord." Man is selfish and disobedient, and will not let his life burn at all. Man is wilful and passionate, and kindles his life with ungodly fire. Man is narrow and bigoted, and makes the light of God shine with his own special color. But all these are accidents. All these are distortions of the true idea of man. How can we know that? Here is the perfect man. Christ Jesus! What a man He is! How nobly, beautifully, perfectly human! What hands, what feet, what an eye, what a heart! How genuinely, unmistakably a man! I bring the men of my experience or of my imagination into His presence, and behold, just when the worst or best of them falls short of Him, my human consciousness assures me that they fall short also of the best idea of what it is to be a man. Here is the spirit of man in its perfection. And what then? Is it not also the candle of the Lord? "I am come a light into the world," said Jesus. "He that hath seen Me hath seen the Father." "In Him was life and the life was the light of men." So wrote the man of all men who knew Him best. And in Him where are the difficulties that we saw? Where for one moment is the dimness of selfishness? O, it seems to me a wonderful thing that the supremely rich human nature of Jesus never for an instant turned with self-indulgence in on its own richness, or was beguiled by that besetting danger of all opulent souls, the wish, in the deepest sense, just to enjoy himself. How fascinating that desire is. How it keeps many and many of the most abundant natures in the world from usefulness. Just to handle over and over their hidden treasures, and with a spiritual miserliness to think their thought for the pure joy of thinking, and turn emotion into the soft atmosphere of a life of gardened selfishness. Not one instant of that in Jesus. All the vast richness of His human nature only meant for Him more power to utter God to man.

And yet how pure His rich life was. How it abhorred to burn with any fire that was not divine. Such abundant life, and yet such utter incapacity of any living but the holiest; such power of burning, and yet such utter incapacity of being kindled by any torch but God's; such fulness with such purity was never seen besides upon the earth; and yet we know as we behold it that it is no monster, but only the type of what all men must be, although all men but Him as yet have failed to be it.

And yet again there was intense personality in Him without a moment's bigotry. A special life, a life that stands distinct and self-defined among all the lives of men, and yet a life making the universal God all the more universally manifest by its distinctness, appealing to all lives just in proportion to the intensity of the individuality that filled His own. O, I think I need only bid you look at Him, and you must see what it is to which our feeble lights are struggling. There is the true spiritual man who is the candle of the Lord, the light that lighteth every man.

It is distinctly a new idea of life, new to the standards of all our ordinary living, which this truth reveals. All our ordinary appeals to men to be up and doing, and make themselves shining lights, fade away and become insignificant before this higher message which comes in the words of Solomon and in the life of Jesus. What does the higher message say? "You are a part of God! You have no place or meaning in this world but in relationship to Him. The full relationship can only be realized by obedience. Be obedient to Him, and you shall shine by His light, not your own. Then you cannot be dark, for He shall kindle you. Then you shall be as incapable of burning with false passion as you shall be quick to answer with the true. Then the devil may hold his torch to you, as he held it to the heart of Jesus in the desert, and your heart shall be as uninflammable as His. But as soon as God touches you, you shall burn with a light so truly your own that you shall reverence your own mysterious life, and yet so truly His that pride shall be impossible." What a philosophy of human life is that. "O, to be nothing, nothing!" cries the mystic singer in his revival hymn, desiring to lose himself in God. "Nay not that; O to be something, something," remonstrates the unmystical man, longing for work, ardent for personal life and character. Where is the meeting of the two? How shall self-surrender meet that high self-value without which no man can justify his living and honor himself in his humanity? Where can they meet but in this truth? Man must be something that he may be nothing. The something which he must be must consist in simple fitness to utter the divine life which is the only original power in the universe. And then man must be nothing that he may be something. He must submit himself in obedience to God, that so God may use him, in some way in which his special nature only could be used, to illuminate and help the world. Tell me, do not the two cries meet in that one aspiration of the Christian man to find his life by losing it in God, to be himself by being not his own but Christ's?

In certain lands, for certain holy ceremonies, they prepare the candles with most anxious care. The very bees which distil the wax are sacred. They range in gardens planted with sweet flowers for their use alone. The wax is gathered by consecrated hands; and then the shaping of the candles is a holy task, performed in holy places, to the sound of hymns, and in the atmosphere of prayers. All this is done because the candles are to burn in the most lofty ceremonies on most sacred days. With what care must the man be made whose spirit is to be the candle of the Lord! It is his spirit which God is to kindle with Himself. Therefore the spirit must be the precious part of him. The body must be valued only for the protection and the education which the soul may gain by it. And the power by which his spirit shall become a candle is obedience. Therefore obedience must be the struggle and desire of his life; obedience, not hard and forced, but ready, loving, and spontaneous; the obedience of the child to the father, of the candle to the flame; the doing of duty not merely that the duty may be done, but that the soul in doing it may become capable of receiving and uttering God; the bearing of pain not merely because the pain must be borne, but that the bearing of it may make the soul able to burn with the divine fire which found it in the furnace; the repentance of sin and acceptance of forgiveness, not merely that the soul may be saved from the fire of hell but that it may be touched with the fire of heaven, and shine with the love of God, as the stars, forever.

Above all the pictures of life,—of what it means, of what may be made out of it,—there stands out this picture of a human spirit burning with the light of the God whom it obeys, and showing Him to other men. O, my young friends, the old men will tell you that the lower pictures of life and its purposes turn out to be cheats and mistakes. But this picture can never cheat the soul that tries to realize it. The man whose life is a struggle after such obedience, when at last his earthly task is over, may look forward from the borders of this life into the other, and humbly say, as his history of the life that is ended, and his prayer for the life that is to come, the words that Jesus said—"I have glorified Thee on the earth; now, O Father, glorify Me with Thyself forever."

(When this sermon was preached in Westminster Abbey, on the evening of Sunday, the Fourth of July, 1880, the following sentences were added:—)

My friends,—may I ask you to linger while I say to you a few words more, which shall not be unsuited to what I have been saying, and which shall, for just a moment, recall to you the sacredness which this day—the Fourth of July, the anniversary of American Independence—has in the hearts of us Americans. If I dare—generously permitted as I am to stand this evening in the venerable Abbey, so full of our history as well as yours—to claim that our festival shall have some sacredness for you as well as us, my claim rests on the simple truth that to all true men the birthday of a nation must always be a sacred thing. For in our modern thought the nation is the making-place of men. Not by the traditions of its history, nor by the splendor of its corporate achievements, nor by the abstract excellencies of its constitution, but by its fitness to make men, to beget and educate human character, to contribute to the complete humanity, the "perfect man" that is to be,—by this alone each nation must be judged to-day. The nations are the golden candlesticks which hold aloft the candles of the Lord. No candlestick can be so rich or venerable that men shall honor it if it holds no candle. "Show us your man," land cries to land.

In such days any nation, out of the midst of which God has led another nation as He led ours out of the midst of yours, must surely watch with anxiety and prayer the peculiar development of our common humanity of which that new nation is made the home, the special burning of the human candle in that new candlestick; and if she sees a hope and promise that God means to build in that new land some strong and free and characteristic manhood which shall help the world to its completeness, the mother-land will surely lose the thought and memory of whatever anguish accompanied the birth, for gratitude over the gain which humanity has made, "for joy that a man is born into the world."

It is not for me to glorify to-night the country which I love with all my heart and soul. I may not **ask** **y**our praise for anything admirable which the United States has been or done. But on my country's birthday I may do something far more solemn and more worthy of the hour. I may ask for your prayer in her behalf. That on the manifold and wondrous chance which God is giving her,—on her freedom (for she is free, since the old stain of slavery was washed out in blood); on her unconstrained religious life; on her passion for education, and her eager search for truth; on her jealous care for the poor man's rights and opportunities; on her countless quiet homes where the future generations of her men are growing; on her manufacturers and her commerce; on her wide gates open to the east and to the west; on her strange meetings of the races out of which a new race is slowly being born; on her vast enterprise and her illimitable hopefulness,—on all these materials and machineries of manhood, on all that the life of my country must mean for humanity, I may ask you to pray that the blessing of God the Father of man, and Christ the Son of man, may rest forever.

Because you are Englishmen and I am an American; also because here, under this high and hospitable roof of God, we are all more than Englishmen and more than Americans; because we are all men, children of God, waiting for the full coming of our Father's kingdom, I ask you for that prayer.

SPURGEON
(1834 - 1892)

Life and Ministry

The "Prince of Preachers," as Charles Haddon Spurgeon was called, was born in Kelvedon, Essex in 1834. His family was of Flemish Huguenot stock who had emigrated to England to escape persecution. His grandfather was a Congregational preacher and his father a lay preacher in the Congregational church.

He was converted in 1850 at the age of 16 in a Primitive Methodist church in Colchester when a lay preacher preached on Isaiah 45:22. Here is his own account:

> *I remember the hour when I stepped into a little place of worship and saw a tall, thin man step into the pulpit... He opened his Bible and read, with a feeble voice, "Look unto Me and be saved all the ends of the earth." ... "Ah," thought I, "I am one of the ends of the earth." Then, turning around, and fixing his gaze on me, as if he knew me, the minister said, "Look, look, look."*

In another account, he adds:

> *... he said "Young man, you are in trouble." Well I was sure enough.*

And in a third:

> *O, I looked until I could have almost looked my eyes away. And in heaven I will look on still in my joy unutterable.*

From that time forward, he began to read the Bible and the Puritan writers he found in his grandfather's library—which he ultimately inherited. (Spurgeon's entire library is now located at William Jewell College, in Liberty, Missouri.) He received his education in Colchester and at an agricultural college in Maidstone, Kent.

In 1851 Spurgeon became a Baptist. His first sermon was preached just before his seventeenth birthday in a cottage in Teversham, outside Cambridge. It was a spur-of-the-moment affair, but very successful. He was asked to preach again and again.

In 1851 while he was still 16, he became the pastor of a small church at Waterbeach, near Cambridge. It met in a barn. At the age of 19, Spurgeon was asked to supply the New Park Street Chapel for six months. This was a famous, two hundred year old congregation in a changing neighborhood. The building then seated 1200, but scarcely 200 were attending. The first Sunday they heard him, the people were amazed; they gathered in groups talking about the new pastor. They decided to call him, and he accepted the call in April 1854. It was not long until all of London had heard of him. The church was packed out in no time. One night Spurgeon pointed to the back wall and declared, "By faith the walls of Jericho fell down, and by faith we shall have this wall down, too." Soon the church was enlarged to seat 1800.

After that the congregation moved to Exeter Hall, then to the Royal Music Hall in Surrey Gardens. The Great Metropolitan Tabernacle was opened in 1861. Here he preached for over 30 years. The normal Sunday attendance at two services was over 10,000.

Spurgeon began to teach theological students as early as 1855, first at home, then in the tabernacle. In time, this ministry developed into The Pastor's College and he trained over 700 students. In 1874 separate facilities were built for it in the south of London. In 1867 he founded the Stockwell orphanage which grew to 500 children, housed in twelve buildings. He also organized a Bible society with 90 colporteurs and edited a paper called *The Sword and the Trowel.*

Spurgeon devoted one day a week to carefully revising his sermons. So, what we have are the sermons the way that Spurgeon wished he had preached them. Millions of copies of his sermons were printed and distributed. His sermons filled almost forty printed volumes before his death.

Three preaching periods may be distinguished in his life.

1. The Early Period (1854-1859)

2. The Middle Period (1860-1867). This was the building period and not his best.

3. The Late Period (1868-1891). The best. Astounding high quality persisted throughout these three periods. Spurgeon's preaching began strong and remained strong throughout his entire ministry.

Spurgeon was a short, stocky man, heavy-set and homely. But he was also good humored, witty and had a strong, clear voice that he fortified with swigs of chili vinegar which he kept on the pulpit. For a husky throat he called this "a sovereign remedy"! Over 100,000 people attended various funeral and memorial services in the Metropolitan Tabernacle at his death. Business in London was suspended during his funeral.

Content

Spurgeon was concerned about Biblical Christianity. His sermons are filled with doctrinal teaching. *The Forgotten Spurgeon*, by Ian Murray, tells of his uncompromising fight for truth and his separation from unbelief. He was also concerned about Calvinistic Christianity.

His library in William Jewell College not only includes the Puritan authors that his grandfather left to him, and the many other theological acquisitions that he made, but also a great number of scientific volumes and other books on a large variety of subjects. There are many non-theological works in this 7,000 volume library.

Spurgeon was not always exegetical. A keynote of his preaching was assurance; he knew the Puritans well, but clearly avoided the preparationist error into which so many of them fell. (Compare comments on preparationism under Edwards.) In a book on Spurgeon entitled *Sense Appeal in the Sermons of Charles Haddon Spurgeon*, the importance of this matter in his preaching is shown. I commend sense appeal in Spurgeon's sermons as a very valuable study.

Organization

There was some variety in the organization of his sermons, though the organization was always sturdy and usually protruded. Largely, it was of a teaching type.

Style

Here was Spurgeon's forte. His style was lively, musical and often poetic. He used vivid imagery. He appealed to all of the senses and was strong on the use of examples. See his comments on illustrating sermons in his *Lectures to my Students*. Also note his comments in *The Art of Illustration*. In the preface to *Illustrations and Meditations*, Spurgeon tells how he studied other preachers. One example is his book, *Flowers from a Puritan's Garden*, which is an enlargement of illustrations found in the writings of Thomas Manton. He believed in clarity, simplicity and homey, rustic ways. (Compare *John Ploughman's Talk*.)

Delivery

Spurgeon had an excellent voice. His chapter on the voice in *Lectures*, and especially his comments on ministerial affectations, is priceless. He was a master of gesture, and it is worth reading what he has to say about gestures in his *Lectures*. He preached without notes.

What was the real secret of his success? His brother wrote, "I think it lies in the fact that he loves Jesus of Nazareth and Jesus of Nazareth loves him."

THE LAW WRITTEN ON THE HEART

"After those days, saith the Lord, I will put my law in their inward parts, and write it in their hearts." (Jeremiah 30:33)

Last Lord's-day morning we spoke of the first great blessing of the covenant of grace, namely, the full forgiveness of sins. Then we dilated with delight upon that wonderful promise, "Their sins and their iniquities will I remember no more." I hope our consciences were pacified and our hearts filled with wonder as we thought of God's casting behind his back all the sins of his people; so that we could sing with David, "Bless the Lord, O my soul: and all that is within me, bless his holy name. Bless the Lord, O my soul, and forget not all his benefits: who forgiveth all thine iniquities." This great blessing of pardoned sin is always connected with the renewal of the heart. It is not given because of the change of heart, but it is always given with the change of heart. If God takes away the guilt of sin, he is sure at the same time to remove the power of sin. If he puts away our offences against his law, he also makes us desire in the future to obey the law.

In our text we observe the excellence and dignity of the law of God. The gospel has not come into the world to set aside the law. Salvation by grace does not erase a single precept of the law, nor lower the standard of justice in the smallest degree; on the contrary, as Paul says, we do not make void the law through faith, but we establish the law. The law is never honoured by fallen man till he comes from under its condemning rule, and walks by faith, and lives under the covenant of grace. When we were under the covenant of works we dishonoured the law, but now we venerate it as a perfect display of moral rectitude. Our Lord Jesus has shown to an assembled universe that the law is not to be trifled with, and that every transgression and disobedience must receive a just recompense of reward, since the sin which he bore on our account brought upon him, as our innocent substitute, the doom of suffering and death. Our Lord Jesus has testified by his death that, even if sin be pardoned, yet it is not put away without an expiatory sacrifice. The death of Christ rendered more honour to the law than all the obedience of all who were ever under it could have rendered; and it was a more forcible vindication of eternal justice than if all the redeemed had been cast into hell. When the Holy One smites his own Son, his wrath against sin is evident to all. But this is not enough. The law is in the gospel not only vindicated by the sacrifice of Christ, but it is honoured by the work of the Spirit of God upon the hearts of men. Whereas under the old covenant the commands of the law excited our evil natures to rebellion, under the covenant of grace we consent unto the law that it is good, and our prayer is, "Teach me to do thy will, O Lord." What the law could not do because of the weakness of the flesh, the gospel has done through the Spirit of God. Thus the law is had in honour among believers, and though they are no more under it as a covenant of works, they are in a measure conformed to it as they see it in the life of Christ Jesus, and they delight in it after the inward man. Things required by the law are bestowed by the gospel. God demands obedience under the law: God works obedience under the gospel. Holiness is asked of us by the law: holiness is wrought in us by the gospel; so that the difference between the economies of law and gospel is not to be found in any diminution of the demands of the law, but in the actual giving unto the redeemed that which the law exacted of them, and in the working in them that which the law required.

Notice, beloved friends, that under the old covenant the law of God was given in a most awe-inspiring manner, and yet it did not secure loyal obedience. God came to Sinai, and the mountain was altogether on a smoke, because the Lord descended upon it in fire; and the smoke thereof ascended as the smoke of a furnace, and the whole mount quaked greatly. So terrible was the sight of God manifesting himself on Sinai that even Moses said, "I exceedingly fear and quake." Out of the thick darkness which covered the sublime summit there came forth the sound of a trumpet, waxing exceeding loud and long, and a voice proclaimed one by one the ten great statutes and ordinances of the moral law. I think I see the people at a distance, with bounds set about the mount, crouching with abject fear, and at last entreating that these words might not be spoken to them any more. So terrible was the sound of Jehovah's voice, even when he was not declaring vengeance, but simply expounding righteousness, that the people could not endure it any longer: and yet no permanent impression was left upon their minds, no obedience was shown in their lives. Men may be cowed by power, but they can only be converted by love. The sword of justice hath less power over human hearts than the sceptre of mercy.

Further to preserve that law, God himself inscribed it upon two tables of stone, and he gave these tablets into the hands of Moses. What a treasure! Surely no particles of matter had hitherto been so honoured as these slabs, which had been touched by the finger of God, and bore on them the legible impress of his mind. But these laws on stone were not kept: neither the stones nor the laws were reverenced. Moses had not long gone up into the mount before the once awe-struck people were bowing before the golden calf, forgetful of Sinai and its solemn voice, and making to themselves the likeness of an ox that eateth grass, and bowing before it as the symbol of the godhead. When Moses came down from the hill with those priceless tablets in his hands, he saw the people wholly given up to base idolatry, and in his indignation he dashed the tablets to the ground and broke them in pieces, as well he might when he saw how the people had spiritually broken them and violated every word of the Most High. From all which I gather that the law is never really obeyed as the result of servile fear. You may preach up the anger of God, and the terrors of the world to come, but these do not melt the heart to loyal obedience. It is needful for other ends that man should know of God's resolve to punish sin, but the heart is not by that fact won to virtue. Man revolts yet more and more; so stubborn is he that the more he is commanded the more he rebels. The decalogue upon your Church walls and in your daily service has its ends, but it can never be operative upon men's lives until it is also written on their hearts. Tables of stone are hard, and men count obedience to God's law to be a hard thing: the commands are judged to be stony while the heart is stony, and men harden themselves because the way of the precept is hard to their evil minds. Stones are proverbially cold, and the law seems a cold, chill thing, for which we have no love as long as the appeal is to our fears. Tablets of stone, though apparently durable, can readily enough be broken, and so can God's commands; so are they indeed broken every day by us, and those who have the clearest knowledge of the will of God nevertheless offend against him. As long as they have nothing to keep them in check but a servile dread of punishment, or a selfish hope of reward, they yield no loyal homage to the statutes of the Lord.

At this time I have to show you the way in which God secures to himself obedience to his law in quite another fashion; not by thundering it out from Sinai, nor by engraving it upon tablets of stone, but by coming in gentleness and infinite compassion into the hearts of men, and there, upon fleshy tables, inscribing the commands of his law in such a manner that they are joyfully obeyed, and men become the willing servants of God.

This is the second great privilege of the covenant: not second in value, but in order—"who forgiveth all thine iniquities; who healeth all thy diseases." It is thus described by Ezekiel: "And I will put my spirit within you, and cause you to walk in my statutes, and ye shall keep my judgments, and do them." In the Epistle to the Hebrews we have it in another form, and we read it thus: "Behold, the days come, saith the Lord, when I will make a new covenant with the house of Israel and with the house of Judah: not according to the covenant that I made with their fathers in the day when I took them by the hand to lead them out of the land of Egypt; because they continued not in my covenant, and I regarded them not, saith the Lord. For this is the covenant that I will make with the house of Israel after those days, saith the Lord; I will put my laws into their mind, and write them in their hearts: and I will be to them a God, and they shall be to me a people." This is so inestimably precious that you who know the Lord are longing for it, and it is your great delight that it is to be wrought in you by the sovereign grace of God.

We shall, first of all, look at *the tablets*,—"I will put my law in their inward parts, and write it in their hearts"; secondly, at *the writing*; thirdly, at *the writer*; and, fourthly, at *the results* which come of this wondrous writing. O that the Spirit who is promised to lead us into all truth may illuminate us now.

I. First, I invite your attention to THE TABLETS upon

which God writes his law,—"I will put my law in their inward parts." Just as once he put the two tables into the ark of gopher wood, so he will put his holy law into our inward nature, and enclose it in our thoughts and minds and memories and affections, as a jewel in a casket. Then he adds, "And I will write it in their hearts." Just as the holy words were engraven upon stone, so shall they now be written in the heart, in the handwriting of the Lord himself. Mark that the law is written not *on* the heart, but *in* the heart, in the very texture and constitution of it, so that into the centre and core of the soul obedience shall be infused as a vital principle.

Thus, you see, the Lord has selected for his tablets *that which is the seat of life.* It is in the heart that life is to be found, a wound there is fatal: where the seat of life is there the seat of obedience shall be. In the heart life has its permanent palace and perpetual abode: and God saith that, instead of writing his holy law on stones which may be left at a distance, he will write it on the heart, which must always be within us. Instead of placing the law upon phylacteries which can be bound between the eyes but may easily be taken off, he will write it in the heart, where it must always remain. He has bidden his people write his laws upon the posts of their doors and upon their gates; but in those conspicuous places they might become so familiar as to be unnoticed; the Lord now himself writes them where they must always be noted and always produce effect. If men have the precepts written in the abode of their life, they live with the law, and cannot live without it. It is a wonderful thing that God should do this. It displays infinitely greater wisdom than if the law had been inscribed on slabs of granite or engraven on plates of gold. What wisdom is this which operates upon the original spring of life, so that all that flows forth from man shall come from a sanctified fountain-head!

Observe next, that not only is the heart the seat of life, but it is *the governing power.* It is from the heart, as from a royal metropolis, that the imperial commands of the man are issued by which hand and foot, and eye and tongue, and all the members are ordered. If the heart be right, then the other powers must yield submission to its sway, and become right too. If God writes his law upon the heart, then the eye will purify its glances, and the tongue will speak according to rule, and the hand will move and the foot will travel as God ordains. When the heart is fully influenced by God's Spirit, then the will and the intellect, the memory and the imagination, and everything else which makes up the inward man, comes under cheerful allegiance to the King of kings. God himself saith, "Give me thine heart," for the heart is the key of the entire position. Hence the supreme wisdom of the Lord in setting up his law where it becomes operative upon the entire man.

But before God can write upon man's heart *it must be prepared.* It is most unfit to be a writing-table for the Lord until it is renewed. The heart must first of all undergo erasures. What is written on the heart already, some of us know to our deep regret. Original sin has cut deep lines, Satan has scored his horrible handwriting in black letters, and our evil habits have left their impressions. How can the Lord write there? No one would expect the holy God to inscribe his holy law upon an unholy mind. The former things must be taken away, that there may be clear space upon which new and better things may be engraven. But who can erase these lines? "Can the Ethiopian change his skin, or the leopard his spots? then may ye also do good, that are accustomed to do evil." The God who can take away the spots from the leopard, and the blackness from the Ethiopian, can also remove the evil lines which now deface the heart.

As the heart must undergo erasure, it must also experience a thorough cleansing, not of the surface only, but of its entire fabric. Truly, brethren, it was far easier for Hercules to purge the Augean stables than for our hearts to be purged; for the sin that lies within us is not an accumulation of external defilement, but an inward, all-pervading corruption. The taint of secret and spiritual evil is in man's natural life, every pulse of his soul is disordered by it. The eggs of all crimes are within our being: the accursed virus, from whose deadly venom every foul design will come, is present in the soul. Not only tendency to sin, but sin itself hath taken possession of the soul, and blackened and polluted it through and through, till there is not a fibre of the heart untinged with iniquity. God cannot write his law in our inward parts till with water and with blood he has purged us. Tables on which the Lord shall write must be clean, therefore the heart on which God is to engrave his law must be a cleansed heart; and it is a great joy to perceive that from the person of our Lord heart-cleansing blood and water flowed, so that the provision is equal to the necessity. Blessed be the name of our gracious God, he knows how to erase the evil and to cleanse the soul through his Holy Spirit's applying the work of Jesus to us.

In addition to this, the heart needs to be softened, for the heart is naturally hard, and in some men it has become harder than an adamant stone. They have resisted God's love till they are impervious to it: they have stood out obstinately against God's will till they have become desperately set on mischief, and nothing can affect them. God must melt the heart, must transform it from granite into flesh; and he has the power to do it. Blessed be his name, according to the covenant of grace he has promised to work this wonder, and he will.

Nor would the softening be enough, for there are some who have a tenderness of the most deceiving kind. They receive the word with joy: they feel every expression of it, but they speedily go their way and forget what manner of men they are. They are as impressible as the water, but the impression is as soon removed; so that another change is needed, namely, to make them retentive of that which is good: else might you engrave and re-engrave, but, like an inscription upon wax, it would be gone in a moment if exposed to heat. The devil, the world, and the temptations of life, would soon erase out of the heart all that God had written there if he did not create it anew with the faculty of holding fast that which is good.

In a word, the heart of man needs to be totally changed, even as Jesus said to Nicodemus, "Ye must be born again." Dear hearers, we preach to you that whosoever believeth in Christ hath everlasting life, and we speak neither more nor less than the truth of God when we say so; but yet, believe us, there must be as great a change in the heart as if a man were slain and made alive again. There must be a new creation, a resurrection from the dead; old things must pass away, and all things must become new. God's law can never be written upon the old natural heart: there must be a new and spiritual nature given, and then upon the centre of that new life, upon the throne of that new power within our life, God will set up the proclamation of his blessed will, and what he commands shall be done. So, then, you see these tablets are not so easily written upon as perhaps at the first we thought. If God is to write the law upon the heart, the heart must be prepared, and in order to being prepared, it must be entirely renewed by a miracle of mercy, such as can only be wrought by that omnipotent hand which made both heaven and earth.

II. Secondly, let us pass on to notice THE WRITING. "I will put my law in their inward parts, and write it in their hearts." What is this writing? First, *the matter of it is the law of God.* God writes upon the hearts of his people that which is already revealed; he inscribes there nothing novel and unrevealed, but his own will which he has already given us in the book of the law. He writes upon the heart by gracious operation that which he has already written in the Bible by gracious revelation. He writes: not philosophy, nor imagination, nor superstition, nor fanaticism, nor idle fancies. If any man says to me, "God has written such and such a thing on my heart," I reply, "Show me it in the Book," for if it be not according to the other Scriptures it is not a scripture of God. A fancy as to a man's being a prophet, or a prince, or an angel, may be on a man's heart, but God did not write it there, for his own declaration is, "I will write my law in their hearts," and he speaks not of anything beyond. The nonsense of modern pretenders to prophecy is no writing of God; it would be a dishonour to a sane man to ascribe it to him: how can it be of the Lord? He here promises to write his own law on the heart, but nothing else. Be you content to have the law written on your soul, and wander not into vain imaginings lest you receive a strong delusion to believe a lie.

Observe, however, that God says he will write his whole law on the heart,—this is included in the words, "my law." God's work is complete in all its parts, and beautifully harmonious. He will not write one command and leave out the rest as so many do in their reforms. They become indignant in their virtue against a particular sin, but they riot in other evils. Drunkenness is to them the most damnable of all transgressions, but covetousness and uncleanness they wink at. They denounce theft, and yet defraud; cry out against pride, and yet indulge envy: thus they are partial, and do the work of the Lord deceitfully. It must not be so. God does not set before us a partial holiness, but the whole moral law. "I will write my law in their hearts." Human reforms are generally lopsided, but the Lord's work of grace is balanced and proportionate. The Lord writes the perfect law in the hearts of men because he intends to produce perfect men.

Mark, again, that on the heart there is written not the law toned down and altered, but "my law,"—that very same law which was at first written on the heart of man unfallen. Paul says of natural men, that "they show the work of the law written in their hearts." There is enough of light left on the conscience to condemn men for most of their iniquities. The original record of the law upon man's heart at his creation has been injured and almost obliterated by man's fall and his subsequent transgressions, but the Lord, in renewing the heart, makes the writing fresh and vivid, even the writing of the first principles of righteousness and truth.

But to come a little closer to the matter: what does the Scripture mean by writing the law of God in the heart? *The writing itself includes a great many things.* A man who has the law of God written on his heart, first of all, knows it. He is instructed in the ordinances and statutes of the Lord. He is an illuminated person, and no longer one of those who know not the law and are cursed. God's Spirit has taught him what is right and what is wrong: he knows this by heart, and therefore can no longer put darkness for light, and light for darkness.

This law, next, abides upon his memory. When he had it only upon a tablet he must needs go into his house to look at it, but now he carries it about with him in his heart, and knows at once what will be right and what will be wrong. God has given him a touchstone by which he tries things. He finds that "all is not gold that glitters," and all is not holy which pretends to that character. He separates the precious from the vile, and does this habitually; for his knowledge of God's law and his memory of it are attended by a discernment of spirit which God has wrought in him, so that he quickly discerns what is according to the mind of God and what is not. Now this is a great point, for some things are commonly done by men which they will even defend, and say that there is no wrong in them; but according to the divine rule they are utterly unjust. God's people judge these things, and take no pleasure in them. A sacred instinct warns the believer of the approach of sin. Long before public sentiment has proclaimed a hue and cry against questionable practices, the Christian man, even if deluded for a while by current custom, yet feels a trembling and an uneasiness. Even if he consents outwardly, being overborne by general opinion, a something within protests, and leads him to consider whether the matter can be defended. As soon as he detects the evil, he shrinks from it. It is a grand thing to possess a universal detector, so that, go where you may, you are not dependent upon the judgment of others, and therefore are not deceived as multitudes are.

This, however, is only a part of the matter, and a very

small part comparatively. The law is written on a man's heart further than this: when he consents unto the law that it is good; when his conscience, being restored, cries, "Yes, that is so, and ought to be so. That command by which God has forbidden a certain course is a proper and prudent command: it ought to be enjoined." It is a hopeful sign when a man no longer wishes that the divine commands were other than they are, but confirms them by the verdict of his judgment. Are there not men who in their anger wish that killing were no murder? Are there not others who do not steal, and yet wish they might take their neighbors' goods? Are there not many who wish that fornication and adultery were not vices? This proves that their hearts are depraved; but it is not so with the regenerate, they would not have the law altered on any account. Their vote is with the law, they regard it as the guardian of society, the basis on which the peace of the universe can alone be built, for only by righteousness can any order of things be established. If we could possess the wisdom of God, we should make just that law which God has made, for the law is holy, and just, and good, and promotes man's highest advantage. It is a great thing when a man gets as far as that.

But, furthermore, there is wrought in the heart by God a love to the law as well as a consent to it, such a love that the man thanks God that he has given him such a fair and lovely representation of what perfect holiness would be; that he has given such measuring lines, by which he knows how a house is to be builded in which God can dwell. Thus thanking the Lord, his prayer, desire, longing, hungering, and thirsting, are after righteousness, that he may in all things be according to the mind of God. It is a glorious thing when the heart delights itself in the law of the Lord, and finds therein its solace and pleasure. The law is fully written on the heart when a man takes pleasure in holiness, and feels a deep pain whenever sin approaches him. Oh, my dear friend, the Lord has done great things for you when every evil thing is obnoxious to you. Even though you fall into sin through the infirmity of your flesh, yet if it causes you intense agony and sorrow it is because God has written his law in your heart. Even though you cannot be as holy as you want to be, yet if the ways of holiness are your pleasure, if they are the very element in which you live as much as the fish lives in the sea, then you are the subject of a very wonderful change of heart. It is not so much what you do as what you delight to do, which becomes the clearest test of your character. Many strictly religious people who go to and fro to church and chapel would be uncommonly glad if they did not feel bound to do so. Is not their public worship a dead formality? A great many people have family-prayers and private prayers who wish they could be rid of the nuisance. Is there any religion in bodily exercises which are burdensome to the heart? Nothing is acceptable to God until it is acceptable to yourself: God will not receive your sacrifice unless you offer it willingly. How contrary this is to the notion of many, for they say, "You see I deny myself by going so many times to a place of worship and by private prayer, therefore I must be truly religious." The very reverse far nearer the truth. When it becomes a misery to serve God, then indeed the heart is far away from spiritual health; for when the heart is renewed, it delights to worship and serve the Lord. Instead of saying, "I would omit prayer if I could," the regenerate mind cries, "I wish I could be always praying." Instead of saying, "I would keep away from the assembly of God's people if I could," the newborn nature wishes like David to dwell in the house of the Lord for ever. This is a great evidence of the writing of the law upon the heart, when holiness becomes a pleasure, and sin becomes a sorrow. When this is done, what great things God has done for us!

The main point of the whole is this, that whereas our nature was once contrary to the law of God, so that whatever God forbade we at once desired, and whatever God commanded we therefore began to dislike, the Holy Spirit comes and changes our nature, and makes it congruous to the law, so that now whatsoever God forbids we forbid, whatsoever God commands, our will commands. How much better to have the law written upon the heart than upon tables of stone!

If anybody should enquire *how the Lord keeps the writing upon the heart legible*, I should like to spend a minute or two in showing the process. How the Holy Ghost first writes the law on the heart I cannot tell. The outward means are the preaching of the word and the reading of it; but how the Holy Ghost directly operates on the soul we do not know; it is one of the great mysteries of grace. This much we know within ourselves, that whereas we were blind now we see, and whereas we abhorred the law of God we now feel an intense delight in it: that the Holy Ghost wrought this change we also know, but how he did it remains unknown. That part of his holy office which we can discern is done according to the usual laws of mental operation. He enlightens by knowledge, convinces by argument, leads by persuasion, strengthens by instruction, and so forth. So far also we know that one way by which the law is kept written upon a Christian's heart is this,—a sense of God's presence. The believer feels that he could not sin with God looking on. It would need a brazen face for a man to play the traitor in the presence of a king; such things are done "under the rose," as men word it, but not before the monarch's face. So the Christian feels that he dwells in God's sight, and this forbids him to disobey. The eye of the heavenly Father is the best monitor of the child of God.

Next, the Christian has a lively sense within him of the degradation which sin once brought upon him. If there is one thing I never can forget personally, it is the horror of my heart while I was yet under sin, God revealed my state to me. Ah, friends, the old proverb that a burnt child dreads the fire has an intensity of truth about it in the case of one who has ever been burnt by sin so as to be driven to despair by it; he hates it with a perfect hatred, and by that means God writes the law upon his heart.

But a sense of love is a yet more powerful factor. Let

a man know that God loves him, let him feel sure that God always did love him from before the foundations of the world, and he must try to please God. Let him be assured that the Father loved him so much as to give his only-begotten Son to die that he might live through him, and he must love God and hate evil. A sense of pardon, of adoption, and of God's sweet favour both in providence and in grace, must sanctify man. He cannot wilfully offend against such love; on the contrary, he feels himself bound to obey God in return for such unsearchable grace; and thus by a sense of love doth God write his law upon the hearts of his people.

Another very powerful pen with which the Lord writes is to be found in the sufferings of our Lord Jesus Christ. When we see Jesus spit upon, and scourged, and crucified, we feel that we must hate sin with all the intensity of our nature. Can you count the purple drops of his redeeming blood and then go back to live in the iniquity which cost the Lord so dear? Impossible! The death of Christ writes the law of God very deeply upon the central heart of man. The cross is the crucifier of sin.

Besides that, God actually establishes his holy law in the throne of the heart by giving to us a new and heavenly life. There is within a Christian an immortal principle which cannot sin because it is born of God, and cannot die, for it is the living and incorruptible seed which liveth and abideth forever. In regeneration there is imparted to us a something altogether foreign to our corrupt nature; a divine principle is dropped into the soul which can neither be corrupted nor made to die, and by this means the law is written on the heart. I do not pretend to explain the process of regeneration, but for certain it involves a divine life, implanted of the Holy Spirit.

Once more, the Holy Ghost himself dwells in believers. I pray you, never forget this marvellous doctrine, that as truly as ever God dwelt in human flesh in the person of the God-man Mediator, so truly doth the Holy Ghost dwell in the bodies of all redeemed men and women who have been born again; and by the force of that indwelling he keeps the mind for ever permeated with holiness, for ever subservient to the will of the Most High.

III. Now we turn for just a minute to think of THE WRITER. Who is it that writes the law upon the heart? It is God himself. "I will do it," saith he.

Note, first, that *he has a right* to indite his law on the heart. He made the heart; it is his tablet: let him write there whatever he wills. As clay in the hands of the potter so are we in his hands.

Note, next, that *he alone can write* the law on the heart. It will never be written there by any other hand. The law of God is not to be written on the heart by human power. Alas, how often have I expounded the law of God and the gospel of God, but I have got no further than the ear: only the living God can write upon the living heart. This is noble work, angels themselves cannot attain to it. "This is the finger of God." As God alone can write there and must write there, so he alone shall have the glory of that writing when once it is perfected.

When God writes *he writes perfectly.* You and I make blots and errors: there needs to be a list of errata at the end of every human piece of writing, but when God writes, blots or mistakes are out of the question. No holiness can excel the holiness produced by the Holy Spirit when his inward work is fully completed.

Moreover, *he writes indelibly.* I defy the devil to get a single letter of the law of God out of a man's heart when God has written it there. When the Holy Ghost has come with all the power of his divinity and rested on our nature, and stamped into it the life of holiness, then the devil may come with his black wings and all his unhallowed craftiness, but he can never erase the eternal lines. We bear in our hearts the marks of the Lord God eternal, and we shall bear them eternally. Written rocks bear their inscriptions long, but written hearts bear them for ever and ever. Does not the Lord say, "I will put my fear in their hearts that they shall not depart from me"? Blessed be God for those immortal principles which forbid the child of God to sin.

IV. I wish to finish by noticing THE RESULTS of the law being thus written in the heart. I hope while I have been preaching about it many of you have been saying, "I hope that the law will be written in my heart." Remember that this is a gift and privilege of the covenant of grace, and not a work of man. Dear friends, if any of you have said, "I do not find anything good in me, therefore I cannot come to Christ," you talk foolishly. The absence of good is the reason why you should come to Christ to have your needs supplied. "Oh, but if I could write God's law on my heart I would come to Christ." Would you? What would you want Christ for? But if the law is not written on your heart, then come to Jesus to have it so written. The new covenant says, "I will put my law in their inward parts, and will write my law in their hearts." Come then to have the law thus inscribed within. Come just as you are, before a single line has been inscribed. The Lord Jesus loves to prepare his own tablets, and write every letter of his own epistles: come to him just as you are, that he may do all things for you.

What are the results of the law being written on the hearts of men? Frequently the first result is great sorrow. If I have God's law written on my heart, then I say to myself, "Ah me, that I should have lived a law-breaker so long! This blessed law, this lovely law, why I have not even thought of it, or if I have thought of it, it has provoked me to disobedience. Sin revived, and I died when the commandment came." We wring our hands and cry, "How could we be so wicked as to break so just a law? How could we be so wilful as to go against our own interests? Knew we not that a breach of the commandment is an injury to ourselves?" Thus we are in bitterness as one that is in bitterness for the death of his first-born. I do not believe God has ever written his law on your hearts if you have not mourned over sin. One of the earliest signs of grace is a dew upon the eyes because of sin.

The next effect of it is, there comes upon the man a strong and stern resolve that he will not break that law again, but will keep it with all his might. He cries out with David, "I have sworn and I will perform it, that I will keep thy righteous judgments." His whole heart says, when reading the precepts of the Lord,—"Yes, that is what I ought to be, that is what I wish to be, and that is what I will be, according to the will of God."

That strong resolve soon leads to a fierce conflict; for another law lifts up its head, a law in our members; and that other law cries, "Not so quick there; your new law which has come into your soul to rule you shall not be obeyed: I will be master." He who is born within us to be our king finds the old Herod ready to slay the young child. The lust of the eye, and the lust of the flesh, and the pride of life, each one of these swears warfare against the new monarch and the fresh power that is come into the heart. Some of you know what this struggle means. It is a very hard fight with some to keep from actual sin. Have you not when troubled with a quick temper had to put your hand to your mouth to stop yourself from saying what you used to say, but what you never wish to say again? Have you not often gone upstairs to get alone, feeling that you would soon slip if the Lord did not hold you up? How wise to get alone with God and cry to him for help! How prudent to watch day and night against evil! Certain braggers talk about having got beyond all that. I should be glad to think that there are such brethren: but I should want to keep them in a glass-case to show them round, or in an iron safe where thieves could not get at them. I conceive it to be a snare of the devil to imagine that you are beyond the need of daily watchfulness. For my own part, I have not passed beyond conflict and struggle: I bear testimony that the battle grows more stern every day. Those of God's people with whom I associate I find fighting and wrestling still. Sometimes I know the devil does not roar, but I am more afraid of him when he is quiet than when he rages. I would sooner he would roar of the two, for a roaring devil is better than a sleeping devil. Whenever he gives way he only gives an inch to take an ell; and whenever you begin to say to yourself, "My corruptions are all dead; I have no tendencies to sin now," you are in awful peril. Poor soul, you do not know what you are talking about. God send you to school, and give you a little light, and you will sing to another tune, I am sure, before long. These are the incidental results—when the Lord writes the law in the heart, strifes and struggles are common within the man, for holiness strives for the mastery.

But does not something better than this come of the divine heartwriting? Oh, yes. There comes actual obedience. The man not only consents to the law that it is good, but he obeys it; and if there be anything which Christ commands, no matter what it is, the man seeks to do it,—not only wishes to do it, but actually does it; and if there be aught that is wrong, he not only wishes to abstain from it, but he does abstain from it. God helping him, he becomes upright, and righteous, and sober, and godly, and loving, and Christlike, for this it is which the Spirit of God works in him. He would be perfect were it not for the old lusts of the flesh which linger even in the hearts of the regenerate. Now the believer feels intense pleasure in everything that is good. If there be anything right and true in the world, he is on the side of it: if there be defeats to truth, he is defeated; but if truth marches on conquering and to conquer he conquers, and takes and divides the spoil with joy. Now he is on God's side, now he is on Christ's side, now he is on truth's side, now he is on holiness' side; and a man cannot be that without being a happy man. With all his strugglings, and all his weepings, and all his confessions, he is a happy man because he is on the happy side. God is with him, and he is with God, and he must be blessed.

As this proceeds, the man becomes more and more prepared to dwell in heaven. He is changed into God's image from glory to glory even as by the Spirit of the Lord. Our fitness for heaven is not a thing that will be clapped upon us in the last few minutes of our life, just as we are going to die; but the children of God have a meetness for heaven as soon as ever they are saved, and that meetness grows and increases till they are ripe, and then, like ripe fruit, they drop from the tree and find themselves in the bosom of their Father God. God will never keep a soul out of heaven half a minute after it is fully prepared to go there; and so, when God has fitted us to be partakers of the inheritance of the saints in light, we shall enter at once into the joy of our Lord.

My brethren, I feel I have talked feebly and prosily about one of the most blessed subjects that ever occupied the thoughts of man—how God's law shall be kept, how it shall be honoured, how holiness shall come into the world, and we shall no longer be rebellious. Herein let us trust in our Lord Jesus, who is to us the surety of that covenant of which this is one great promise—"I will put my law in their inward parts, and in their hearts will I write it." God do so to us, for Christ's sake. Amen.

SALVATION TO THE UTTERMOST

"Wherefore he is able also to save them to the uttermost that come unto God by him, seeing he ever liveth to make intercession for them." (Hebrews 7:25)

Salvation is a doctrine peculiar to revelation. Revelation affords us a complete history of it, but nowhere else can we find any trace thereof. God has written many books, but only one book has had for its aim the teaching of the ways of mercy. He has written the great book of creation, which it is our duty and our pleasure to read. It is a volume embellished on its surface with starry gems and rainbow colours, and containing in its inner leaves marvels at which the wise may wonder for ages, and yet find a fresh theme for their conjectures. Nature is the spelling-book of man, in which he may learn his Maker's name, he hath studded it with embroidery, with gold, with gems. There are doctrines of truth in the mighty stars, and there are lessons written on the green earth and in the flowers upspringing from the sod. We read the books of God when we see the storm and tempest, for all things speak as God would have them; and if our ears are open we may hear the voice of God in the rippling of every rill, in the roll of every thunder, in the brightness of every lightning, in the twinkling of every star, in the budding of every flower. God has written the great book of creation, to teach us what he is—how great, how mighty. But I read nothing of salvation in creation. The rocks tell one, "Salvation is not in us;" the winds howl, but they howl not salvation: the waves rush upon the shore, but among the wrecks which they wash up, they reveal no trace of salvation; the fathomless caves of the ocean bear pearls, but they bear no pearls of grace; the starry heavens heave their flashing meteors, but they have no voices of salvation. I find salvation written nowhere, till in this volume of my Father's grace I find his blessed love unfolded towards the great human family, teaching them that they are lost, but that he can save them, and that in saving them he can be "just, and yet the justifier of the ungodly." Salvation, then, is to be found in the Scriptures, and in the Scriptures only; for we can read nothing of it elsewhere. And while it is to be found only in Scripture, I hold that the peculiar doctrine of revelation is salvation. I believe that the Bible was sent not to teach me history, but to teach me grace—not to give me a system of philosophy, but to give me a system of divinity—not to teach worldly wisdom, but spiritual wisdom. Hence I hold all preaching of philosophy and science in the pulpit to be altogether out of place. I would check no man's liberty in this matter, for God only is the Judge of man's conscience; but it is my firm opinion that if we profess to be Christians, we are bound to keep to Christianity; if we profess to be Christian ministers, we drivel away the Sabbath-day, we mock our hearers, we insult God, if we deliver lectures upon botany, or geology, instead of delivering sermons on salvation. He who does not always preach the gospel, ought not to be accounted a true-called minister of God.

Well, then it is salvation I desire to preach to you. We have, in our text, two or three things. In the first place, we are told *who they are who will be saved*, "them that come unto God by Jesus Christ;" in the second place we are told *the extent of the Saviour's ability to save*, "he is able to save to the uttermost;" and in the third place, we have *the reason given why he can save*, "seeing he ever liveth to make intercession for them."

I. First, we are told THE PEOPLE WHO ARE TO BE SAVED. And the people who are to be saved are "those who come unto God by Jesus Christ." There is no limitation here of sect or denomination: it does not say, the Baptist, the Independent, or the Episcopalian that comes unto God by Jesus Christ, but it simply says, "*them*," by which I understand men of all creeds, men of all ranks, men of all classes, who do but come to Jesus Christ. They shall be saved, whatever their apparent position before men, or whatever may be the denomination to which they have linked themselves.

1. Now, I must have you notice, in the first place, *where these people come to*. They "come unto God." By coming to God we are not to understand the mere formality of devotion, since this may be but a solemn means of sinning. What a splendid general confession is that in the Church of England Prayer Book: "We have erred and strayed from thy ways like lost sheep; we have done those things which we ought not to have done, and we have left undone those things which we ought to have done, and there is no health in us." There is not to be found a finer confession in the English language. And yet how often, my dear friends, have the best of us mocked God by repeating such expressions verbally, and thinking we have done our duty! How many of you go to chapel, and must confess your own absence of mind while you have bowed your knee in prayer, or uttered a song of praise! My friends, it is one thing to go to church or chapel; it is quite another thing to go *to God*. There are many people who can pray right eloquently, and who do so; who have learned a form of prayer by heart, or, perhaps, use an extemporary form of words of their own composing: but who, instead of going to God, are all the while going from God. Let me persuade you all not to be content with mere formality. There will be many damned who never broke the Sabbath, as they thought, but who, all their lives were Sabbath-breakers. It is as much possible to break the Sabbath in a church as it is to break the Sabbath in the park; it is as easy to break it here in this solemn assembly as in your own houses. Every one of you virtually break the Sabbath when you merely go through a round of duties, having done which, you retire to your chambers, fully content with yourselves, and fancy that all is over—that you have done your day's work—whereas, you have never come to God at all, but have merely come to the outward ordinance and to the visible means, which is quite another thing from coming to God himself.

And let me tell you, again, that coming *to God is not what some of you suppose—now and then sincerely performing an act of devotion, but giving to the world the greater part of your life.* You think that if sometimes you are sincere, if now and then you put up an earnest cry to heaven, God will accept you; and though your life may be still worldly, and your desires still carnal, you suppose that for the sake of this occasional devotion God will be pleased, in his infinite mercy, to blot out your sins. I tell you, sinners, there is no such thing as bringing half of yourselves to God, and leaving the other half away. If a man has come here, I suppose he has brought his whole self with him; and so if a man comes to God, he cannot come, half of him, and half of him stay away. Our whole being must be surrendered to the service of our Maker. We must come to him with an entire dedication of ourselves, giving up all we are, and all we ever shall be, to be thoroughly devoted to his service, otherwise we have never come to God aright. I am astonished to see how people in these days try to love the world and love Christ too; according to the old proverb, they "hold with the hare and run with the hounds." They are real good Christians sometimes, when they think they ought to be religious; but they are right bad fellows at other seasons, when they think that religion would be a little loss to them. Let me warn you all. It is of no earthly use for you to pretend to be on two sides of the question. "If God be God, serve him; If Baal be God, serve him." I like an out-and-out man of any sort. Give me a man that is a sinner: I have some hope for him when I see him sincere in his vices, and open in acknowledging his own character; but if you give me a man who is half-hearted, who is not quite bold enough to be all for the devil, nor quite sincere enough to be all for Christ, I tell you, I despair of such a man as that. The man who wants to link the two together is in an extremely hopeless case. Do you think, sinners, you will be able to serve two masters, when Christ has said you cannot? Do you fancy you can walk with God and walk with mammon too? Will you take God on one arm, and the devil on the other? Do you suppose you can be allowed to drink the cup of the Lord, and the cup of Satan at the same time? I tell you, ye shall depart, as cursed and miserable hypocrites, if so you come to God. God will have the whole of you come, or else you shall not come at all. The whole man must seek after the Lord; the whole soul must be poured out before him; otherwise it is no acceptable coming to God at all. Oh, halters between two opinions, remember this and tremble.

I think I hear one say, "Well, then, tell us what it is to come to God." I answer, coming to God implies, *leaving something else.* If a man comes to God, he must leave his sins; he must leave his righteousness; he must leave both his bad works and his good ones, and come to God, leaving them entirely.

Again, coming to God implies, *that there is no aversion towards him;* for a man will not come to God while he hates God; he will be sure to keep away. Coming to God signifies having *some love to God.* Again: coming to God signifies *desiring God,* desiring to be near to him. And, above all, it signifies *praying to God and putting faith in him.* That is coming to God; and those that have come to God in that fashion are among the saved. They come *to God:* that is the place to which their eager spirits hasten.

2. But notice, next, *how they come.* They "come unto God *by Jesus Christ.*" We have known many persons who call themselves natural religionists. They worship the God of nature, and they think that they can approach God apart from Jesus Christ. There be some men we wot of who despise the mediation of the Saviour, and, who, if they were in an hour of peril, would put up their prayer at once to God, without faith in the Mediator. Do such of you fancy that you will be heard and saved by the great God your Creator, apart from the merits of his Son? Let me solemnly assure you, in God's most holy name, there never was a prayer answered for salvation, by God the Creator, since Adam fell, without Jesus Christ the Mediator. "No man can come unto God but by Jesus Christ;" and if any one of you deny the Divinity of Christ, and if any soul among you do not come to God through the merits of a Saviour, bold fidelity obliges me to pronounce you condemned persons; for however amiable you may be, you cannot be right in the rest, unless you think rightly of him. I tell you, ye may offer all the prayers that ever may be prayed, but ye shall be damned, unless ye put them up through Christ. It is all in vain for you to take your prayers and carry them yourself to the throne. "Get thee hence, sinner; get thee hence," says God; "I never knew thee. Why didst not thou put thy prayer into the hands of a Mediator? It would have been sure of an answer. But as thou presentest it thyself, see what I will do with it!" And he reads your petition, and casts it to the four winds of heaven; and thou goest away unheard, unsaved. The Father will never save a man apart from Christ; there is not one soul now in heaven who was not saved by Jesus Christ; there is not one who ever came to God aright, who did not come through Jesus Christ. If you would be at peace with God, you must come to him through Christ, as the way, the truth, and the life, making mention of his righteousness, and of his only.

3. But when these people come, *what do they come for?* There are some who think they come to God, who do not come for the right thing. Many a young student cries to God to help him in his studies; many a merchant comes to God that he may be guided through a dilemma in his business. They are accustomed, in any difficulty, to put up some kind of prayer, which, if they knew its value, they might cease from offering, for "the sacrifice of the wicked is an abomination to the Lord." But the poor sinner, in coming to Christ, has only one object. If all the world were offered to him, he would not think it worth his acceptance if he could not have Jesus Christ. There is a poor man, condemned to die, locked up in the condemned cell: the bell is tolling: he will soon be taken off to die on the gallows. There, man, I have brought you a fine robe. What! not smile at it? Look! it is stiff with silver! Mark you not how it is bedizened with jewels? Such a robe as that cost many and many a pound, and much fine workmanship was expended

on it. Contemptuously he smiles at it! See here, man, I present thee something else: here is a glorious estate for thee, with broad acres, fine mansions, parks and lawns; take that title deed, 'tis thine. What! not smile, sir? Had I given that estate to any man who walked the street, less poor than thou art, he would have danced for very joy. And wilt not thou afford a smile, when I make thee rich and clothe thee with gold? Then let me try once more. There is Caesar's purple for thee; put it on thy shoulders—there is his crown; it shall sit on no other head but thine. It is the crown of empires that know no limit. I'll make thee a king; thou shalt have a kingdom upon which the sun shall never set; thou shalt reign from pole to pole. Stand up; call thyself Caesar. Thou art emperor. What! no smile? What dost thou want? "Take away that bauble," says he of the crown; "rend up that worthless parchment; take away that robe; ay, cast it to the winds. Give it to the kings of the earth who live; but I have to die, and of what use are these to me? Give me a pardon, and I will not care to be a Caesar. Let me live a beggar, rather than die a prince." So is it with the sinner when he comes to God: he comes for salvation. He says—

> "Wealth and honor I disdain;
> Earthly comforts, Lord, are vain,
> These will never satisfy,
> Give me Christ, or else I die."

Mercy is his sole request. O my friends, if you have ever come to God, crying out for salvation, and for salvation only, then you have come unto God aright. It were useless then to mock you. You cry for bread: should I give you stones? You would but hurl them at me. Should I offer you wealth? It would be little. We must preach to the sinner who comes to Christ, the gift for which he asks—the gift of salvation by Jesus Christ the Lord—as being his own by faith.

4. One more thought upon this coming to Christ. *In what style do these persons come?* I will try and give you a description of certain persons, all coming to the gate of mercy, as they think, for salvation. There comes one, a fine fellow in a coach and six! See how hard he drives, and how rapidly he travels; he is a fine fellow: he has men in livery, and his horses are richly caparisoned; he is rich, exceeding rich. He drives up to the gate, and says, "Knock at that gate for me; I am rich enough, but still I dare say it would be as well to be on the safe side; I am a very respectable gentleman; I have enough of my own good works and my own merits, and this chariot, I dare say would carry me across the river death, and land me safe on the other side; but still, it is fashionable to be religious, so I will approach the gate. Porter! undo the gates, and let me in; see what an honorable man I am." You will never find the gates undone for that man; he does not approach in the right manner. There comes another; he has not quite so much merit, but still he has some; he comes walking along, and having leisurely marched up, he cries, "Angel! open the gate to me; I am come to Christ: I think I should like to be saved. I do not feel that I very much require salvation; I have always been a very honest, upright, moral man; I do not know myself to have been much of a sinner; I

have robes of my own; but I would not mind putting Christ's robes on; it would not hurt me. I may as well have the wedding garment; then I can have mine own too." Ah! the gates are still hard and fast, and there is no opening of them. But let me show you the right man. There he comes, sighing and groaning, crying and weeping all the way. He has a rope on his neck, for he thinks he deserves to be condemned. He has rags on him, he comes to the heavenly throne; and when he approaches mercy's gate he is almost afraid to knock. He lifts up his eyes and he sees it written, "Knock, and it shall be opened to you;" but he fears lest he should profane the gate by his poor touch; he gives at first a gentle rap, and if mercy's gate open not, he is a poor dying creature; so he gives another rap, then another and another; and although he raps times without number, and no answer comes, still he is a sinful man, and he knows himself to be unworthy; so he keeps rapping still; and at last the good angel smiling from the gate, says, "Ah! this gate was built for beggars, not for princes; heaven's gate was made for spiritual paupers, not for rich men. Christ died for sinners, not for those who are good and excellent. He came into the world to save the vile.

Not the righteous,—
Sinners, Jesus came to call.

Come in, poor man! Come in. Thrice welcome!" And the angels sing, "Thrice welcome!" How many of you, dear friends, have come to God by Jesus Christ in that fashion? Not with the pompous pride of the Pharisee, not with the cant of the good man who thinks he deserves salvation, but with the sincere cry of a penitent, with the earnest desire of a thirsty soul after living water, panting as the thirsty hart in the wilderness after the water-brooks, desiring Christ as they that look for the morning; I say, more than they that look for the morning. As my God who sits in heaven liveth, if you have not come to God in this fashion, you have not come to God at all; but if you have thus come to God, here is the glorious word for you—"He is able to save to the uttermost them that come unto God by him."

II. Thus we have disposed of the first point, the coming to God; and now, secondly, WHAT IS THE MEASURE OF THE SAVIOUR'S ABILITY? This is a question as important as if it were for life or death—a question as to the ability of Jesus Christ. How far can salvation go? What are its limits and its boundaries? Christ is a Saviour: how far is he able to save? He is a Physician: to what extent will his skill reach to heal diseases? What a noble answer the text gives! "He is able to save to the uttermost." Now, I will certainly affirm, and no one can deny it, that no one here knows how far the uttermost is. David said, if he took the wings of the morning, to fly to the uttermost parts of the sea, even there should God reach him. But who knoweth where the uttermost is? Borrow the angel's wing, and fly far, far beyond the most remote star: go where wing has never flapped before, and where the undisturbed ether is as serene and quiet as the breast of Deity itself: you will not come to the uttermost. Go on still; mounted on a morning ray, fly on still, beyond the bounds of creation, where space itself fails, and where chaos takes up its reign: you will not come to the uttermost. It is too far for mortal intellect to conceive of; it is beyond the range of reason or of thought. Now, our text tells us that Christ is "able to save to the uttermost."

1. Sinner, I shall address thee first; and saints of God, I shall address you afterwards. Sinner, Christ is "able to save to the uttermost;" by which we understand that *the uttermost extent of guilt* is not beyond the power of the Saviour. Can any one tell what is the uttermost amount to which a man might sin? Some of us conceive that Palmer has gone almost to the uttermost of human depravity; we fancy that no heart could be much more vile than that which conceived a murder so deliberate, and contemplated a crime so protracted; but I can conceive it possible that there might be even worse men than he, and that if his life were spared, and he were set at large, he might become even a worse man than he is now. Yea, supposing he were to commit another murder, and then another, and another, would he have gone to the uttermost? Could not a man be yet more guilty? As long as ever he lives, he may become more guilty than he was the day before. But yet my text says, Christ is "able to save to the uttermost." I may imagine a person has crept in here, who thinks himself to be the most loathsome of all beings, the most condemned of all creatures. "Surely," says he, "I have gone to the utmost extremity of sin; none could outstrip me in vice." My dear friend, suppose you had gone to the uttermost, remember that even then you would not have gone beyond the reach of divine mercy; for he is "able to save to the uttermost," and it is possible that you yourself might go a little further, and therefore you have not gone to the uttermost yet. However far you may have gone—if you have gone to the very arctic regions of vice, where the sun of mercy seems to scatter but a few oblique rays, there can the light of salvation reach you. If I should see a sinner staggering on in his progress to hell, I would not give him up, even when he had advanced to the last stage of iniquity. Though his foot hung trembling over the very verge of perdition, I would not cease to pray for him; and though he should in his poor drunken wickedness go staggering on till one foot were over hell, and he were ready to perish, I would not despair of him. Till the pit had shut her mouth upon him I would believe it still possible that divine grace might save him. See there! he is just upon the edge of the pit, ready to fall; but ere he falls, free grace bids, "Arrest that man!" Down mercy comes, catches him on her broad wings, and he is saved, a trophy of redeeming love. If there be any such in this vast assembly—if there be any here of the outcast of society, the vilest of the vile, the scum, the draff of this poor world,—oh! ye chief of sinners! Christ is "able to save to the uttermost." Tell that everywhere, in every garret, in every cellar, in every haunt of vice, in every kennel of sin; tell it everywhere! "To the uttermost!" "He is able also to save them to the uttermost."

2. Yet again: not only to the uttermost of crime, but *to the uttermost of rejection.* I must explain what I mean by this. There are many of you here who have heard the gospel from your youth up. I see some here, who like myself are children of pious parents. There are some of you upon whose infant forehead the pure heavenly drops of a mother's tears continually fell; there are many of you here who were trained up by one whose knee, whenever it was bent, was ever bent for you. She never rested in her bed at night till she had prayed for you, her first-born son. Your mother has gone to heaven, it may be, and all the prayers she ever prayed for you are as yet unanswered. Some-times you wept. You remember well how she grasped your hand, and said to you, "Ah! John, you will break my heart by this your sin, if you continue running on in those ways of iniquity: oh! if you did but know how your mother's heart yearns for your salvation, surely your soul would melt, and you would fly to Christ." Do you not remember that time? The hot sweat stood upon your brow, and you said—for you could not break her heart—"Mother, I will think of it;" and you did think of it; but you met your companion outside, and it was all gone: your mother's expostulation was brushed away, like the thin cobwebs of the gossamer, blown by the swift north wind, not a trace of it was left. Since then you have often stepped in to hear the minister. Not long ago you heard a powerful sermon; the minister spoke as though he were a man just started from his grave, with as much earnestness as if he had been a sheeted ghost come back from the realms of despair, to tell you his own awful fate, and warn you of it. You remember how the tears rolled down your cheeks, while he told you of sin, of righteousness, and of judgment to come; you remember how he preached to you Jesus and salvation by the cross, and you rose up from your seat in that chapel, and you said, "Please God I am spared another day, I will turn to him with full purpose of heart." And there you are, still unchanged—perhaps worse than you were; and you have spent your Sunday afternoon the angel knows where: and your mother's spirit knows where you have spent it too, and could she weep, she would weep over you who have this day despised God's Sabbath, and trampled on his Holy Word. But dost thou feel in thine heart to-night the tender motions of the Holy Spirit? Dost thou feel something say, "Sinner! come to Christ now?" Dost thou hear conscience whispering to thee, telling thee of thy past trans-gression? And is there some sweet angel voice, saying, "Come to Jesus, come to Jesus; he will save you yet?" I tell you, sinner, you may have rejected Christ to the very uttermost; but he is still able to save you. There are a thousand prayers on which you have trampled, there are a hundred sermons all wasted on you, there are thousands of Sabbaths which you have thrown away; you have rejected Christ, you have despised his Spirit; but still he ceases not to cry, "Return, return!" He is "able to save thee to the uttermost," if thou comest unto God by him.

3. There is another case which demands my particular attention to-night. It is that of the man who

_____

has gone *to the uttermost of despair*. There are some poor creatures in this world, who from a course of crime have become hardened, and when at last aroused by remorse and the prickings of conscience, there is an evil spirit which broods over them, telling them it is hopeless for such as they are to seek salvation. We have met with some who have gone so far that they have thought that even devils might be saved rather than they could. They have given themselves up for lost, and signed their own death-warrant, and in such a state of mind have positively taken the halter in their hand, to end their unhappy lives. Despair has brought many a man to a premature death; it hath sharpened many a knife, and mingled many a cup of poison. Have I a despairing person here? I know him by his sombre face and downcast looks. He wishes he were dead, for he thinks that hell itself could be scarce worse torment than to be here expecting it. Let me whisper to him words of consolation. Despairing soul! hope yet, for Christ "is able to save to the uttermost;" and though thou art put in the lowest dungeon of the castle of despair, though key after key hath been turned upon thee, and the iron grating of thy window forbids all filing, and the height of thy prison-wall is so awful that thou couldst not expect to escape, yet let me tell thee, there is one at the gate who can break every bolt, and undo every lock; there is one who can lead thee out to God's free air and save thee yet, for though the worst may come to the worst, he "is able to save thee to the uttermost."

4. And now a word to the saint, to comfort him: for this text is his also. Beloved brother in the gospel! Christ is able to save thee to the uttermost. Art thou brought very low by *distress*? hast thou lost house and home, friend and property? Remember, thou hast not come "to the uttermost" yet. Badly off as thou art, thou mightest be worse. He is able to save thee; and suppose it should come to this, that thou hadst not a rag left, nor a crust, nor a drop of water, still he would be able to save thee, for "he is able to save to the uttermost." So with temptation. If thou shouldst have the sharpest *temptation* with which mortal was ever tried, he is able to save thee. If thou shouldst be brought into such a predicament that the foot of the devil should be upon thy neck, and the fiend should say, "Now I will make an end of thee," God would be able to save thee then. Ay, and in the uttermost *infirmity* shouldst thou live for many a year, till thou art leaning on thy staff, and tottering along thy weary life, if thou shouldst outlive Methusaleh, thou couldst not live beyond the uttermost, and he would save thee then. Yea, and when thy little bark is launched by *death* upon the unknown sea of eternity, he will be with thee; and though thick vapours of gloomy darkness gather round thee, and thou canst not see into the dim future, though thy thoughts tell thee that thou wilt be destroyed, yet God will be "able to save thee to the uttermost."

Then, my friends, if Christ is able to save a Christian to the uttermost, do you suppose he will ever let a Christian perish? Wherever I go, I hope always to bear my hearty protest against the most accursed doctrine of a saint's falling away and perishing. There are some ministers who preach that a man may be a child of God (now, angels! do not hear what I am about to say, listen to me, ye who are down below in hell, for it may suit you) that a man may be a child of God to-day, and a child of the devil to-morrow; that God may acquit a man, and yet condemn him—save him by grace, and then let him perish—suffer a man to be taken out of Christ's hands, though he has said such a thing shall never take place. How will you explain this? It certainly is no lack of power. You must accuse him of a want to love, and will you dare to do that? He is full of love; and since he has also the power, he will never suffer one of his people to perish. It is true, and ever shall be true, that he will save them to the very uttermost.

III. Now, in the last place, WHY IS IT THAT JESUS CHRIST IS "ABLE TO SAVE TO THE UTTERMOST?" The answer is, that he "ever liveth to make intercession for them." This implies that *he died*, which is indeed the great source of his saving power. Oh! how sweet it is to reflect upon the great and wonderous works which Christ hath done, whereby he hath become "the high priest of our profession," able to save us! It is pleasant to look back to Calvary's hill, and to behold that bleeding form expiring on the tree; it is sweet, amazingly sweet, to pry with eyes of love between those thick olives, and hear the groanings of the Man who sweat great drops of blood. Sinner, if thou askest me how Christ can save thee, I tell thee this—he can save thee, because he did not save himself; he can save thee, because he took thy guilt and endured thy punishment. There is no way of salvation apart from the satisfaction of divine justice. Either the sinner must die, or else some one must die for him. Sinner, Christ can save thee, because, if thou comest to God by him, then he died for thee. God has a debt against us, and he never remits that debt; he will have it paid. Christ pays it, and then the poor sinner goes free.

And we are told another reason why he is able to save: not only because he died, but *because he lives to make intercession for us.* That Man who once died on the cross, is alive; that Jesus who was buried in the tomb is alive. If you ask me what he is doing, I bid you listen. Listen, if you have ears! Did you not hear him, poor penitent sinner? Did you not hear his voice, sweeter than harpers playing on their harps? Did you not hear a charming voice? Listen! what did it say? "O my Father! forgive—!" Why, he mentioned your own name! "Oh my Father, forgive him; he knew not what he did. It is true he sinned against light, and knowledge, and warnings; sinned wilfully and woefully; but, Father, forgive him!" Penitent, if thou canst listen, thou wilt hear him praying for thee. And that is why he is able to save.

A warning and a question, and I have done. First, a warning. Remember, *there is a limit to God's mercy.* I have told you from the Scriptures, that "he is *able* to save to the uttermost;" but there is a limit to his purpose to save. If I read the Bible rightly, there is one sin which can never be forgiven. It is the sin against the Holy Ghost. Tremble, unpardoned sinners, lest ye should commit that. If I may tell you what I think the sin against the Holy Ghost is, I must say that I believe it to be different in different people; but in many persons, the sin against the Holy Ghost consists in stifling their convictions. Tremble, my hearers, lest to-night's sermon should be the last you hear. Go away and scorn the preacher, if you like; but do not neglect his warning. Perhaps the very next time thou laughest over a sermon, or mockest at a prayer, or despisest a text, the very next oath thou swearest, God may say, "He is given to idols, let him alone; my Spirit shall no more strive with that man; I will never speak to him again." That is the warning.

And now, lastly, the question. *Christ has done so much for you: what have you ever done for him?* Ah! poor sinner, if thou knewest that Christ died for thee—and I know that he did, if thou repentest—if thou knewest that one day thou wilt be his, wouldst thou spit upon him now? wouldst thou scoff at God's day, if thou knewest that one day it will be thy day? wouldst thou despise Christ, if thou knewest that he loves thee now, and will display that love by-and-by? Oh! there are some of you that will loathe yourselves when you know Christ because you did not treat him better. He will come to you one of these bright mornings, and he will say, "Poor sinner, I forgive you;" and you will look up in his face, and say, "What! Lord, forgive me? I used to curse thee, I laughed at thy people, I despised everything that had to do with religion. Forgive me?" "Yes," says Christ, "give me thy hand; I loved thee when thou hatedst me: come here!" And sure there is nothing will break a heart half so much as thinking of the way in which you sinned against one who loved you so much.

Oh! beloved, hear again the text,—"He is able also to save to the uttermost them that come unto God by him." I am no orator, I have no eloquence; but if I were the one, and had the other, I would preach to you with all my soul. As it is, I only talk right on, and tell you what I do know; I can only say again,

> "He is able;
> He is willing: doubt no more.
>
> Come, ye thirsty, come and welcome,
>   God's free bounty glorify:
> True belief and true repentance,
>   Every grace that brings us nigh—
> Without money,
> Come to Jesus Christ, and buy."

For "he is able also to save to the uttermost them that come unto God by him." O Lord! make sinners come! Spirit of God! make them come! Compel them to come to Christ by sweet constraint, and let not our words be in vain, or our labour lost; for Jesus Christ's sake! Amen.

NEDERHOOD
(1930 -   )

Joel Nederhood is currently the radio and television minister for the "Back to God Hour," a denominational broadcast of the Christian Reformed Church. Dr. Nederhood has held this position since 1965, when he took over the preaching responsibilities for the "Back to God Hour" at the death of its founder, Peter Eldersvelde.

Nederhood had worked with Eldersvelde for some years and had already filled in for him during summer vacations and various other times. The two men had developed a style of preaching so well adapted to the medium that it won national awards for religious broadcasting. I mention both men because Nederhood succeeded Eldersvelde in as smooth a transition as there has ever been in the history of broadcasting. It was as though he stepped into the footprints that were being made by his predecessor at the time of his death, and, without a moment's hesitation, measured and matched his stride. They even sounded alike.

Nederhood's sermons are a model of Christian broadcasting in terms of all the technical factors that make an exceptional program. They could be studied from the broadcasting perspective as well as that of the sermons themselves.

Of course, being largely evangelistic in nature, there is not as much exposition as one would find in a sermon preached to a congregation. Nederhood cautions readers of his sermons to understand that he has adapted his preaching to the medium and to the target listening audience. Just so! It is superbly adapted—that is the point.

But what was this style that Eldersvelde developed and which Nederhood has continued and improved over the years? There are many aspects to it that shall not be discussed such as the modulation of the voice, pause, rate, et cetera. But there are four that we shall consider. These four elements are found in the sermons reprinted in this textbook by permission of Dr. Nederhood. They are:

1. An oral style of English.
2. References to interesting contemporary facts, events and occasions that involve the listener. Note, in particular, the masterful way in which he uses these in his introductions.
3. Relevancy to the times in which we live.
4. Clarity of the gospel.

Anyone needing help in one or more of these four areas could not do better than to engage in an intensive study of the sermons of the "Back to God Hour" preacher.

No one is taught to write oral English in school. Rather we are all taught to write in quite a different style. That is one of the reasons why preachers have so much difficulty developing skill in reproducing good oral English when preaching. When writing, even when writing outlines, we tend to fall back into the practices drilled into us over long years by our English teachers. They were more effective than we may think. Here, in these sermons is a rare phenomenon: self-taught, good oral English written out. There are so few examples of this in the history of preaching that you should take advantage of it through a careful analysis of all of its components (the use of contractions, incomplete sentences, et cetera).

Nederhood knows his audience; he knows that unless he grabs them at the outset and holds them, they will turn him off. Look at the introductions to his sermons, the interest value they contain, the occasional references and the relevancy of what he has to say to the times in which we live. Look, study and learn. And don't miss the clarity of the gospel in what he has to say.

Recently, since he has had a serious illness, Nederhood's preaching has deepened. His penetration into the thoughts, fears and inner concerns of men in trouble has been incisive. This newness of emphasis in the sermons of the eighties, especially in those sermons that have to do with illness, also constitutes a remarkable source for sermon analysis. Don't miss Nederhood's powerful use of the second person at points. Could he have used it more frequently?

The sermons in this textbook could not exhibit all of the qualities that I have mentioned, so I urge the reader who finds them helpful to obtain and study others which the "Back to God Hour" so graciously makes available. Their address is 6555 West College Drive, Palos Heights, Illinois, 60463.

GOOD NEWS FOR THE SICK

"This sickness... is for God's glory...." (John 11:4)

I know you have had it happen to you just as I have had it happen to me: someone comes up to you and tells you that one of your dear friends has suddenly become seriously ill.

"Did you hear about John?"

You look at the questioner and you know that something shocking is coming. You wait for the briefest of seconds before the answer comes, and in that millisecond, you know that your life will be changed by the answer.

"John has cancer." Or the answer might be: "John had a heart attack this morning." Or it could be: "John had an accident."

"Oh, no," you say. And then you ask for details. What kind of cancer is it? A heart attack—how is he doing? How bad was the accident? Is John going to live?

Oh, those are horrible moments. Depending on how close the person is to you, you experience different degrees of shock, dismay, and despair. "I hope he makes it through—I hope he lives"—this is what you think, or you say it to your friend who is telling you the bad news. You shake your head. Possibly you feel tears forming. You look away and wonder where you can go to pray for his recovery.

Now, it's happening to John. But sometimes it happens to us. Maybe you've experienced this.

"Well, what do the tests say, doctor?" you ask. It's three right on the dot, Thursday afternoon—he had told you, "Call me around three on Thursday, and I'll know more." You try to keep your voice calm, as if you are asking the time, but your stomach is in knots and you are tense because you know that if the news is bad, your life will never be the same.

The doctor hesitates on the other end of the line, and then the words come: "It's malignant; pathology says it looks like a . . ."—he says one of those obscure words that refer to one of the tumors we human beings get. "I'm sorry. But it could be worse. We've had some success in treating this. We'll have to see and run some more tests. I'll be in to talk with you tomorrow."

And that is that. That is everything. That changes everything. Nothing is as it was five minutes ago. The message has come to you: You are sick, and you have a disease that could kill you; in fact, it might kill you.

If you have ever had that experience, you know how hard it is to receive news like that. Over the years, our brains develop hundreds of little mechanisms we automatically use to deny that this could happen to us, hundreds of little mechanisms that assure us that we are indestructible. But now just a few sentences spoken over that innocent-looking telephone by your bed have destroyed in 48 seconds what you spent a lifetime building up. *You are sick, and you are going to die.*

Those first few moments after you hang up are like nothing else you have ever experienced. Frustration, anger, disbelief, and fear all fill your head and heart. For several minutes your imagination runs wild: you see yourself withering away beneath the merciless attacks of this disease—whatever it was the doctor called it—and you envision the way it will be at the very end . . . the very end. But you could survive, so in your mind you start to wish that the next few months, years even, of treatment would hurry by so you could be well again. In those first moments of panic, you do not think very rationally; you are not quite sane.

Maybe this has happened to you. Right at this very moment, perhaps, you are going through the discomfort of treatment. You are experiencing the downward pull of horrible anxiety.

I'm wondering: do you know about the 11th chapter of the book of John in the New Testament part of the Bible? I must tell you about it because it can help. It's about what Jesus said and did when His friend Lazarus became sick and died.

John 11 begins this way:

Now a man named Lazarus was sick. He was from Bethany, the village of Mary and her sister Martha. This Mary, whose brother Lazarus now lay sick, was the same one who poured perfume on the Lord and wiped his feet with her hair. So the sisters sent word to Jesus, "Lord, the one you love is sick."

When he heard this, Jesus said, "This sickness will not end in death. No, it is for God's glory so that God's Son may be glorified through it."

Lazarus was sick unto death—he did die within a few days, and Jesus knew he was going to die. Even so, Jesus told those who were with Him that Lazarus' sickness was not going to end in death; instead it was going to bring glory to God and to the Son of God.

One of the reasons John 11 is in the Bible is that God wants us to know that when friends of Jesus Christ become sick, even with diseases that could and may in fact cause their deaths, their sicknesses will not end in death but will bring glory to God. Lazarus was Jesus' friend. I hope you are.

A friend of Jesus is a person who believes that Jesus is the only begotten Son of God and who trusts Jesus for salvation. A friend of Jesus knows that Jesus alone can pay for his sins. A friend of Jesus tries to live as Jesus lived and he believes what Jesus has revealed about God. In the 15th chapter of the book of John, Jesus talks about people who are His friends:

You are my friends if you do what I command. I no longer call you servants, because a servant does not know his master's business. Instead, I have called you friends, for everything that I learned from my Father I have made known to you.

Eric Hoffer, the longshoreman philosopher, described human life as a brief bus trip that is taking everyone to the place of execution. With all of our fretting and fussing, according to Hoffer, all we succeed in doing is changing our seats on the bus. But we never get off the bus. He was right. Hoffer himself is dead now. Lazarus was on that bus, and you and I are on that bus, too. But for those who are friends of Jesus, the bus ride is not going to end in death.

Bad news, say, of a life-threatening illness, drives some people to Jesus Christ, the Son of God. If you are very sick and very frightened and you have never asked Jesus to be your friend, to be your Savior, you should do that. You should pray to Jesus Christ. You should confess your sins to Him, and you should ask Him to be your Savior. Tell Jesus that you want Him to be your friend, and that you want Him to help you now that you are terribly afraid. If you are a friend of Jesus, you can be sure that your sickness will not end in death. Even if your sickness does kill you someday, it will not end in death. If Jesus is your friend, you can be sure that Jesus will use your sickness to bring glory to Himself. And when you are a friend of Jesus, Jesus' glory becomes your glory, too.

But I must tell you more about John 11.

After Jesus announced that Lazarus's sickness was not going to end in death, He continued what He was doing for two more days. He was in a region east of the Jordan River, and Bethany, where Lazarus lived, was about two days' journey to the west of the river. But finally He told His disciples that He was going to go to Bethany. They tried to dissuade Him because Jesus had many enemies in Bethany. Jesus insisted, and then He said to His followers, "Our friend Lazarus has fallen asleep; but I am going there to wake him up."

Notice the way Jesus spoke about His friend's death. Even the men who had been living with Him for many months did not understand what He was saying. Jesus said that Lazarus had *fallen asleep*. That terminology confused the disciples, so Jesus told them plainly, "Lazarus is dead."

When believers in Jesus Christ die, when His friends die, what really happens is that they fall asleep. In the book of Acts, we read of the death of the first martyr, Stephen: "When (Stephen) had said this, he fell asleep." The phrase *to fall asleep* emphasizes two very important things about the death of Jesus' friends: first, there is a gentleness about it; and second, the time will come when the friend who has fallen asleep will be awakened.

If you are terrified because you have received terrifying news about your own physical condition and you are terribly afraid of dying, you need Jesus, don't you see? You need this friend. If you believe in Jesus, you can be sure that your death—when it comes next week, next month, next year, whenever—will not really be death, but it will be *falling asleep* in Jesus.

Have you ever tried to get a restless baby to fall asleep? The little one has been crying and finally you pat his back very gently, and you hum a little tune, or you say a few soothing words, and you pat and you hum, and finally the rhythm of his breathing changes, and there's a little snicker, and another one, and then the infant child is sleeping. That's the way it is when a friend of Jesus dies. He falls asleep. She falls asleep.

But back to John 11. This is what happened when Jesus and His disciples arrived at Bethany:

On his arrival, Jesus found that Lazarus had already been in the tomb for four days . . . . When Martha heard that Jesus was coming, she went out to meet him, but Mary stayed at home.

"Lord," Martha said to Jesus, "if you had been here, my brother would not have died. But I know that even now God will give you whatever you ask."

Jesus said to her, "Your brother will rise again."

Martha answered, "I know he will rise again in the resurrection at the last day."

Jesus said to her, "I am the resurrection and the life. He who believes in me will live, even though he dies; and whoever lives and believes in me will never die. Do you believe this?"

After this magnificent statement by Jesus, *I am the resurrection and the life*, John 11 continues, reporting how Jesus went to Lazarus's tomb and called him to come out. We learn how Martha protested when Jesus asked that the stone be rolled away from the tomb; she was afraid of the odor of death. But instead of the odor of death, Lazarus, wrapped in grave clothes, came out of the tomb. Jesus, who is the resurrection and the life, raised him to life anew.

When Jesus came to Bethany and raised His friend Lazarus from the dead, He was actually on His way to His own death, to His own tomb. Within days, He would experience the agony that frequently accompanies death. Oh, we can talk about death as falling asleep, but anyone who knows anything about dying knows that before the final sleep comes, there can be times of horrible suffering and pain.

If the doctors have told you that you are seriously ill, I am sure that one of the thoughts on your mind involves what you may have to go through before you die. Will there be much suffering? Will there be much pain? Will I need so many drugs to kill the agony that I will not be able to think straight anymore? Well, Jesus was headed into suffering more intense than that experienced by any human being before or since. Not long after He raised Lazarus, He knelt in anguish before His Father in heaven and asked Him if there was any way the cup of suffering could be taken away from Him.

The Jesus who invites you to believe in Him and be His friend is not an ordinary person by any means. Another book of the New Testament says that "he suffered death, so that by the grace of God he might *taste* death for everyone." Jesus *tasted* death. He did not die like that butterfly that hit my windshield the other day; one moment it was flying blithely through the air and the next instant—oblivion! Jesus approached death fully conscious of what it was going to mean. He plunged voluntarily into the depths of death's degradation. As He talked with Martha and as He stood by the tomb of His friend Lazarus, He knew that He would soon die.

Even so, He knew that He would win the battle over death and would rise victorious. This is why He said, "I am the resurrection and the life." With this statement,

He established the great fact that gives sick people hope today: *Jesus is resurrection; Jesus is life.*

As He talked with Martha, He also told her that His victory over death was not a benefit for Himself alone, but also a benefit for Lazarus, her brother, who at that moment was decaying in the grave. Jesus said, "He who believes in me will live, even though he dies; and whoever lives and believes in me will never die." Notice this very carefully: belief, faith, is the important factor. Lazarus believed in Jesus. His faith was the same as his sister's faith; Martha said, "I believe that you are the Christ, the Son of God . . . . "

Everything Jesus did as He prepared to go to Bethany and everything He did when there was designed to show sick people that when they believe in Jesus they will overcome death. Because Lazarus believed in Jesus, he was as safe as a baby in his mother's arms, even when that fatal disease struck him. His sisters thought he was in great danger—and from a human point of view he was—but Jesus knew that Lazarus was going to glorify God's Son in being raised in the power of Jesus. For this reason Jesus didn't drop everything He was doing when the message of Lazarus's illness came to Him.

If you have never heard this message before, I'm so glad I can tell you that faith in Jesus Christ guarantees that believers will not be conquered by death. This is why I must stress again that you must believe in Jesus. It's so important that you do. If you don't, death will conquer you. If you believe, you are safe.

Isn't it true that when bad news comes and you are stunned by it, you feel totally unsafe? Here you are, you had been living along from day to day and feeling fairly well. Then things started to go wrong, and you went to the doctor. And then there were some tests. And finally there was the operation, which has left you rather weak. And now the results of the tests have come back, telling you what you were most afraid to hear. You are sick. What you have could kill you. It kills a certain percentage of the people who have it. You know the figures; you know what your chances are. And now, sometimes you weep and even wail like a baby because you are so afraid. You feel so unsafe.

And maybe things are going pretty well for you, and the doctors have congratulated you because you are recovering so nicely. Fine. You're happy with that; but you watch the calendar. Sometimes, little things go wrong, and you think that your illness has come back. One day you are happy that you are recovering so well, and the next your life is shattered.

But if you believe in Jesus, there is one thing you can know for sure: your illness is not going to kill you. You are not going to die because of it. I know that what I am saying seems strange; it even seemed strange when Jesus talked about it. If you believe in Jesus, He says to you, "Your sickness is not going to end in death, but it will end in my glory. I am going to perform a great miracle in your life when death finally comes for you. I will be right there when it happens. I will make sure that you don't really die—that instead you fall asleep." And then Jesus adds, "If you die believing in me, you won't really die at all. If you die believing in me, you will live again."

When a person believes in the Lord Jesus Christ, he is safe; death cannot touch him. Jesus went to the cross of Calvary to conquer Satan, who was the great prince of death. Jesus rose again on the third day and He's alive right now. Those who believe in Him will be raised to new life through Jesus' great power.

We are talking about the 11th chapter of John. Many more books and chapters and sentences in the New Testament assure us that what Jesus said is the truth. Romans 8:11 says:

If the Spirit of him who raised Jesus from the dead is living in you, he who raised Christ from the dead will also give life to your mortal bodies through his Spirit, who lives in you.

In 2 Corinthians 5:1 we read:

We know that if the earthly tent we live in is destroyed, we have a building from God, an eternal house in heaven, not built by human hands.

And in 1 Corinthians 15:51-52 we read:

Listen, I tell you a mystery: We will not all sleep, but we will all be changed—in a flash, in the twinkling of an eye, at the last trumpet. For the trumpet will sound, the dead will be raised imperishable, and we will be changed.

One of the major themes of the Bible is eternal life through faith in the Lord Jesus Christ. Some people criticize believers for believing in Jesus only because they are afraid of death. All right. I'll admit it. Fear of death can drive a person to look at Jesus in a way he has never looked at Him before. Maybe last week you were not afraid of death because you were healthy, but this week you are very much afraid. Don't be ashamed to run to Jesus and ask Him to save you.

Here is good news for sick people. If you are sick and you are afraid of dying, I can do nothing better for you than what I have just done. I have told you about Jesus, the resurrection and the life. Believe in this Jesus. Confess your sins. Believe that this Jesus, who is the Son of God, is your Savior. Believe that He is alive. And believe that someday you will experience the fullness of life in Jesus Christ.

If you believe in Jesus, and you are sick right now, you can be sure that your God will use your sickness to bring glory to Himself and to His Son, Jesus. And you can be sure that you are safe. At worst, you will fall asleep. And when that happens, Jesus will wake you up.

INSTEAD OF DARKNESS

"If we walk in the light, as he is in the light, we have fellowship with one another, and the blood of Jesus, his Son, purifies us from every sin." (I John 1:7)

When grade school children wonder if they will have time to commit suicide before the bombs hit, you know you are in trouble. I'm told there's a new generation of nuclear kids—very young children who know enough about nuclear war to conclude that they don't really have a chance. And one of them told a psychiatrist he was worried there wouldn't be enough time to destroy himself between hearing that a nuclear attack was underway and the time the first bombs began to fall.

Back in the late fifties and early sixties there was a war scare also, and children were taught to hide under their desks and, if possible, to escape to a shelter somewhere. Back then, people really believed that with a shelter they could get away from the destruction. But now, it's different. Children don't feel there's much use doing anything to get away from the bomb. Even the young ones are talking about doing something to end their lives once the bombs are on their way.

Oh, we surely live in an ugly world, don't we? Those of us who are adults now know we cannot keep this fact secret from our children anymore. It really is a world full of darkness in so many ways. We look ahead and what do we see? What do you see? Well, may I tell you what I see? I see light, and it's not the light of devastating nuclear holocaust. I see another light, the light of God, and it's beautiful; and it's for you and it's for me.

I want to talk about that light . . . to walk in it is good; to walk in darkness is unspeakably bad. We all know this by instinct. We get up in the middle of the night for some reason and stumble through the living room, looking for the light switch, and we feel a helpless frustration, especially as we stumble over a chair we had forgotten was there. Sometimes our lives seem like this: we are stumbling along looking for the light switch. Where is it? Where in the world is it? We furtively put one set of toes before the other while we grope along the wall . . . until our fingers touch it.

Well, use your fingers now to open the Bible, you who are looking for the light switch. Turn the pages, turn the pages, there, there, now, nearly at the end of the Bible is this short book called 1 John. And in its opening sentences we discover the light we need in order to make our lives sensible and beautiful.

Notice how the apostle John begins this little book; he is talking about Jesus and about God. John, who was especially close to Jesus on the night of Jesus' betrayal, speaks from the experience of nearness to the Savior:

> That which was from the beginning, which we have heard, which we have seen with our eyes, which we have looked at and our hands have

_____
_____
_____
_____
_____
_____
_____
_____
_____
_____
_____
_____
_____
_____
_____
_____
_____
_____
_____
_____
_____
_____
_____
_____
_____
_____
_____
_____
_____
_____
_____
_____

touched—this we proclaim concerning the Word of life.

With these words John introduces us to Jesus Christ, the Person he had seen and touched, the Person he knew as the "Word of life."

He continues and tells of the way he learned about eternal life when in Jesus' presence:

The life appeared; we have seen it and testify to it, and we proclaim to you the eternal life, which was with the Father and has appeared to us. We proclaim to you what we have seen and heard, so that you also may have fellowship with us. And our fellowship is with the Father and with his Son, Jesus Christ.

When Jesus appeared, _life_ appeared. And when Jesus appeared, _light_ appeared. John goes on to tell us how, when he was with Jesus Christ, he learned that God is Light:

This is the message we have heard from him and declare to you: God is light; in him there is no darkness at all. If we claim to have fellowship with him yet walk in the darkness, we lie and do not live by the truth.

This is getting extremely interesting, isn't it—for people like us who so often feel we are walking in darkness? It most certainly is. And it is especially so because the apostle concludes by announcing that you and I can walk in the light of God—we can walk in the light with God; we can walk in the light together.

I'm not talking about a figure of speech now; I'm talking about reality. Even for people like us who feel the darkness closing in, there is a chance really to live a life bathed in God's holy light. Ah, let me tell you more about this.

Notice what the apostle says further:

If we claim to have fellowship with God yet walk in the darkness, we lie and do not live by the truth. But if we walk in the light, as he is in the light, we have fellowship with one another, and the blood of Jesus, his Son, purifies us from every sin.

There are a few things here, about walking in the light, that we should notice very carefully. The first is certainly this: _walking in the light is not automatic;_ it does not merely go along with being a human being. No. There is another possibility for people like us. It's possible for a human being to walk in darkness.

The apostle John talks about that, and we should take a minute to do so. What is this _walking in darkness?_ Does this refer simply to picking your way through a world that is full of danger? No, not really. It means choosing a life-style that is rebellion against God. And this life-style, unfortunately, is very widespread these days.

There are many activities that could illustrate this _way-of-darkness_ life-style. I'll just mention the word _playboy_. It's a word that stands for many things we all have heard about: sexual liberation, freedom, free love . . . all that. This is a way of life that emphasizes satisfactions, enjoyment, fun, hedonism. For men there are women, for women there are men, and for people who like their own sex best, there is that too. There's whatever you want, whenever you want it.

Now this way of life is a fantasy, purely a fantasy, but

it's a crippling, corrupting fantasy that millions have fallen for. And sometimes when I talk with people who have tumbled into this trap, I have to tell them that the only way they will be able to have some good and truly wholesome experiences in their lives is to extricate themselves from the way of life they are tangled in. You cannot live in the light as long as you are living in the darkness. This means that you cannot expect to get away with giving part time to darkness and part time to light and have this work. People who have convinced themselves that it's fun to live in darkness might as well know there isn't any chance they will benefit from the light we've been talking about.

For the light we are talking about is, in reality, living with God, that is, living with God as your Friend, being able to trust Him and to talk to Him and to know He is genuinely interested in you and will most certainly take your life experience all the way through to perfection and glory. You cannot live with God when you are walking in the darkness, because God isn't there in the darkness where you are living. The apostle John reminds us that God is light and in Him there is no darkness at all.

Right here you may have a great deal of thinking to do. Do you wonder why it is your life is so hopeless, so full of despair and distress? Why is it so dark? Maybe the answer is simple. Your life is so dark because that's where you have chosen to live it . . . right there in darkness. So what can you expect? You have to get hold of yourself. You have to change. You have to cut yourself off from some of the friends you have made, out there in the darkness. Maybe once you get in the light yourself, you will be able to help them get into the light too. But for now, you have to get as far away from them as you can.

One of the Old Testament prophets, Isaiah, speaks clearly on this very subject—he's talking to people who want to get close to the light of God, and he says, "Let the wicked forsake his way and the evil man his thoughts." Now, there you have it. Very simple. Those who want to walk in the light have to turn away from the darkness.

No, walking in the light is not automatic; it never was and it most certainly is not today. But, and this is the second matter I want to stress, *it is possible*. The apostle John says, "If we walk in the light, as (God) is in the light . . . ." Isn't this astonishing language? How is it possible to walk in the light as God is in the light?

Well, right here we learn a great fact about ourselves: we are something like God. Really. The Bible is about the glory of God and it's about the glory of man. God created man in the image of God. We must never forget that. This is why it's so ugly when a human being, created in the image of God, lives impurely, selfishly, dishonestly, murderously, or however darkly. We were not created to live in darkness; we were created to be like God and to live in the light.

How can you live in the light?

First of all, you must believe in Jesus Christ, the Son of God. This is the Person the apostle John talks about in the material we are looking at. He is the One who has revealed that God is light. We believe in Jesus Christ when we confess our sins and ask God to forgive us our sins for Jesus' sake. We can ask God to do this because Jesus has paid for human sin through His death on Calvary's cross. When you believe in Jesus Christ, Jesus Christ will give you His Holy Spirit to equip you to live according to the will of God. This means turning away from darkness and doing what God wants you to do.

Walking in the light, then, means believing in Jesus and living in a God-fearing way. Anything else is not worthy of a human being who has been created in the image of God. God is righteous, God is pure, God is holy, God is loving, and He wants us to be like this too. Now I know we cannot do this perfectly, and if you would continue to read the book of 1 John, you would learn how God continuously forgives those who keep coming to Him and asking Him for forgiveness.

Everything I am talking to you about today is a possibility; I am talking to you about reality. There are some people right now who are walking in darkness. There are other people who right now are walking in the light. Where are you? If we were talking together and I asked you that, would you have to say, "I'm walking in darkness, and I'm not having much fun doing it"? Do you realize that if you believe in the Lord Jesus Christ, your life can be changed? *It can be changed,* and this is the reason I am telling you about all this: it's possible for people who would otherwise be walking in darkness to turn away from darkness and come to the light. Ask God to send His Holy Spirit into your life so that you can experience the joy—the benefits—that goes along with living in the light.

Number 1: we will have fellowship with one another. Fellowship—I find that millions of people these days are desperately longing for fellowship. I know that many of you who are reading this right now are lonely. And some of you have caused your own loneliness—you've disregarded others, you've hurt others, and now there you sit in your own little room; your wife is gone and your children are gone and you feel alone. Oh, how terrible! Just to feel there are other people whom you can reach out and touch, people who are concerned about you, people who love you—wouldn't that be wonderful?

Listen, the Bible tells us that believers have fellowship on the grandest scale. When we walk in the light, we are friends of those people who lived in the first century; why we are friends with the apostle John who wrote the book that helps us so much today. And we are friends with Christians throughout the entire world. We can feel ourselves part of an innumerable host of people who have lived throughout the years and who are living now; and there are many of our good friends who must yet be born—those who will be Christians later. But all of us together are bound in a common tie of love and life and light.

And this fellowship which binds those who walk in the light with one another is expressed right in the local church where people are able to live together as brothers and sisters in the Lord Jesus Christ. Does this sound mysterious and strange to you? Have you been believing all the false reports some people like to circulate about the church? The church isn't perfect, but it's the best thing we have when it comes to fellowship and friendship. I know; I'm part of a local church in which the members are concerned for each other. They pray for each other when they are sick and when they have other problems.

People walking in the light together are bound together by a tie of concern that is very, very real. That very fellowship is part of the light they walk in together. And if you are looking for fellowship, there's the place to find it. You won't find it in the darkness. Lots of lies come from that dark world, trying to get us to believe that when we live in the darkness we will have fun, fun fun; but that just isn't true. Only when we believe in the Lord Jesus Christ, only when we are living the way God wants us to live, only then, will we experience the fellowship we need.

Benefits—incentives. God gives us great incentives to walk in the light; if we do it, we will find fellowship, and, *number 2,* we will find purity. Once again, notice the sentence we are talking about today: "If we walk in the light, as he is in the light, we have fellowship with one another, and the blood of Jesus, his Son, purifies us from every sin."

The blood of Jesus purifies us. Think about that strange statement: the *blood* purifies us. The apostle John was present when the blood of Jesus Christ was shed. I can talk with you about Jesus' blood, but when I do, I am talking about something I heard about from someone else. Not so, John; when Jesus was crucified, John was standing right by the cross with Jesus' mother. He saw Jesus' wounds: His head wounds where the thorns had torn His scalp, His wounded hands and feet; and John saw the blood. He saw it flow and form a brief pool on the earth before it was absorbed into the soil, just as Abel's blood had soaked into the earth centuries before. For John, there was nothing secondhand about experience with Jesus' blood. That blood, John wrote, will purify you.

Can you figure out what that means? This is the way it seems to me, as I think about this idea in the light of the rest of the Bible. When Jesus died on Calvary's cross, He did two things: He paid the price of sin, thus taking away the guilt of those who believe in Him; and He earned the right to send His Holy Spirit into the lives of believers so that they could live righteously.

And so, says the apostle, when you walk in the light as God is in the light, you have fellowship and you have this purification process starting to work itself out in your life. Your sins are paid for and your guilt is gone; and along with this, you receive special strength from God, which enables you to keep away from darkness and to stay in the light.

I wonder if you are able to see what I see here? I see a circle. There is circular reasoning here, and oftentimes we don't like circular reasoning. Look at the circle with me for a moment. The Bible says we have to walk in the light, and then we will have fellowship and then we will be purified. In other words, the Bible says we have to walk in the light in order to be enabled to walk in the light—that's really what being purified means. We are told to do something we cannot do fully except through the special power that comes to believers because of Jesus' shed blood. And so the question comes, How can a person ever leave darkness and walk in the light since one cannot leave darkness and walk in the light unless one is in the light already?

Good question. And I don't know the answer. But I do know that God assures you that if you believe in Jesus, it will all work out for you. If you believe in Jesus, Jesus will give you the power to turn away from darkness and live in the light. And when you live in the light, you will find that your life will be much, much more satisfactory than it was when you existed in darkness.

There are many of us who, looking ahead, see the light of life. We see it because we have Jesus as our Savior, and we know that as we walk with Him, we will advance into a circle of splendid illumination where we will enjoy fellowship and where we will be purified by the continuous work of Jesus. If you are living in darkness, you can be sure that God wants you to believe in His Son, Jesus Christ, so that you can join those who live in God's light-filled world.